Volunteers with
Children Everywhere

by
Florence Koenderink

First Published in 2017 by Orphanage Projects
www.orphanageprojects.org

ISBN 978-0-9935023-1-6

Copyright © Florence Koenderink
All rights are reserved

Photos by Florence Koenderink, except for p73, 94, second photo 97, 108, 123, 177, 181 Lily Lu, p48, 49 Ajit Sivaram, second photo p64 Milind Kulkarni, p65 Suresh Kumar, p141, 208, 251 U&I

Lay-out and cover design by Bert Koenderink

Icon design by Claartje van der Meer

Editing by Willow Editing

Volunteers with Children Everywhere

How to Provide Good Institutional Care

Book 3:
Manual for Volunteers in Children's Homes

by
Florence Koenderink

Orphanage Projects

Contents

	Acknowledgements	8
	Introduction	10
Part 1:	**Getting There**	
	Introduction	16
	Chapter 1: Gathering Information and Deciding	18
	• How Long and When to go	18
	• Is This Kind of Childcare for You?	20
	• What Country to Go to	23
	○ Language	25
	○ Visas	26
	○ Safety	29
	• Volunteering Through an Organisation	30
	• What Type of Children's Home	32
	• Ethical Considerations	34
	• Religious Background	37
	• Making Arrangements	38
	○ Accessibility	39
	• Conclusion	40
	Chapter 2: Practical Preparations	41
	• What to Bring	41
	• Bring What You Cannot Do Without	42
	• Vaccinations and Medication	46
	• Having an Emergency Plan	49
	Chapter 3: Cultural Preparations	52
	• Do I Have to?	53
	• Find out About the Culture You Visit	56
	• Learn Some of the Language	59
	• Choose Appropriate Clothes	64
	Chapter 4: Mental Preparations	67
	• First Time Away from Home	67
	• Initial Loneliness	69
	• Culture Shock	70
	• Being Different	71
	• Conditions in the Children's Home	74
	• Leaving Things Behind	78
	Chapter 5: Arriving	83
	• Communicate About Transport Before You Leave	83
	• Jetlag	85

- Strange Food — 86
- Being Overwhelmed — 88
- Getting to Know People — 89

Part 2: Getting to Work

Introduction — 94

Chapter 1: Working Together — 96
- Discuss Your Role with Management — 96
- Accept Any Training Offered — 100
- Respect the Seniority of Caregivers — 100

Chapter 2: Work Ethic — 103
- Be Reliable — 104
- Be Responsible — 105
- 'Not in Front of the Children' — 110
  - Role Model — 110
  - Exclusion — 112
  - Discussing Circumstances — 114
- Respect the Rules — 115

Chapter 3: Donations and Treats — 118
- Discuss Donations with Management Before Giving — 120
- Think Carefully About Treats and Donations — 123
- Careless Use of Gifts — 126
- Conclusion — 127

Chapter 4: Interaction with Children — 128
- Only Make Promises You Know You Can Keep — 128
- Why Talking to Children Is Important — 131
- Lying to Children — 132

Chapter 5: Special Needs — 138
- Introduction — 138
- Mental Retardation — 138
- HIV/AIDS — 145
  - What Is the Difference Between HIV and AIDS? — 146
  - How Does it Spread? — 146
  - What Is the Effect of the Stigma? — 148
- Seizure Disorders — 150
  - What Should Be Done? — 153

Part 3: Basic Childcare and Child Psychology

Introduction — 158

Chapter 1: Hygiene — 160

- **General Hygiene** — 160
  - Washing Hands — 160
- **Nappy Hygiene** — 162
  - Cleaning Bottoms — 162
- **Bathing** — 164
- **Grooming** — 166
- **Dental Hygiene** — 166
- **Food Hygiene** — 167

Chapter 2: Safety — 169
- **Safe Surroundings** — 169
- **Supervision** — 170
- **Precautions** — 172

Chapter 3: Essential Psychological Needs — 175
- **The Difference Between Care in a Family and Care in an Institution** — 175
- **The Impact of the Difference Between Family and Institution** — 179
  - Physical Contact — 180
  - Attachment — 181
  - Giving Attention — 184
  - Showing an Interest in the Child — 185
  - Balancing Praise and Reprimand — 186
  - Stimulation — 186

Chapter 4: Global Developmental Stages of Childhood — 189
- **Birth to Eighteen Months** — 189
- **Eighteen Months to Three Years** — 191
- **Three to Six Years** — 194
- **Six to Twelve Years** — 196
- **Twelve to Eighteen Years** — 198

Chapter 5: Discipline — 203
- **Setting Limits** — 203
- **Breaking the Cycle of Negative Attention Seeking** — 206
- **The Purpose of Rules** — 210
- **Not the Purpose of Rules** — 211
- **Imposing and Enforcing Rules** — 213
- **Discipline Strategies** — 215
- **Physical Punishment** — 218

Chapter 6: Fevers and Hypothermia — 220
- **Fever** — 220
- **Interpreting Temperatures** — 221
- **Fever Suppressants** — 225
  - Paracetamol — 225
  - Ibuprofen — 226

- **Causes of Fevers**   229
- **Hypothermia**   230

Chapter 7: Dehydration and Malnutrition   235
- **Diarrhoea and Vomiting**   235
- **Dehydration**   237
  - Signs of Dehydration   239
  - Causes of Dehydration   239
  - Preventing Dehydration   241
  - Treating Dehydration   242
  - Weighing Babies   248
  - Acidosis   248
  - Send to Hospital   249
- **Malnutrition**   249
  - What Children Need   249
  - How to Recognise Malnutrition in Children   252
  - Refeeding Starved Children   253
  - Problems with Refeeding   255

Afterword   258

Appendix   260

Word List   261

References   265

Index   270

Acknowledgements

Accumulating the knowledge that eventually led to the writing of this manual has been a process of many years. I have by no means finished finding better ways to do things. Learning, to me, is a lifelong process that I thoroughly enjoy. There are so many people that I am immensely grateful to. People who have helped me, supported me, and taught me, helping me grow in skill and understanding. It would take a separate book to name them all. Not doing so does nothing to diminish my gratitude to them at all.

My family are still my first and foremost beacon of support, without whom I would never be able to do what I do. Where many people feel pressured to 'go and get a real job', I have always had my family's understanding and encouragement through the many years of essentially being a poor but happy fulltime volunteer. Many of my family members have volunteered right along with me, helping Orphanage Projects in one way or another, putting in many hours. Bert Koenderink first and foremost. He has done the lay-out and cover design for all the manuals without asking for a single cent. Claartje van der Meer, who has designed the icons for all the manuals. Tijl Koenderink, who organised the storage and distribution of *Sick Children Everywhere*. Elze Koenderink, who gave me feedback on early drafts of this manual as a volunteer, as well as editing the manual as a professional. And Yolanda Koenderink, who helped out as a hand model on several occasions.

I have worked alongside, provided guidance to, and benefited from the work of dozens of volunteers over the years. In different ways, they have all taught me things and given me insights into the rewards and the challenges of volunteering. In this book, I would like to take the opportunity to especially thank some volunteers who have kindly supported Orphanage Projects by sharing their expert opinions and skills with me. In no particular order: Melanie Labindao, Elizabeth Rafferty, Yvonne Risi, Katherine Reak, and Dr Ann Coxon. All together you make me look smart by providing me with answers when I do not have any. I also want to thank the many volunteers who were kind enough to share their experiences with me. They helped me get a clearer insight into what information is most needed to prepare well for volunteering in a children's home.
I thank Miranda Hudson and Nick Cox for the useful discussions and their valued input and suggestions.
I am very grateful to Paul Albada Jelgersma for sponsoring the cost of the editing of this manual. A very generous contribution.

Every effort has been made to obtain permission for the use of materials. If by unintended oversight something has been used without your approval, please contact me so I can rectify the situation. Finally, as always, my eternal gratitude goes out to the hundreds of children that I have worked with over the years. No one has taught and shown me more than they have. It will always continue to be a privilege to be awarded the trust and love of a child, especially one in a difficult situation. I will continue to try to be worthy of the trust and to improve their world bit by bit.

Introduction

Volunteering abroad is an amazing experience. For many people, it is their first real chance of getting to know another culture upclose. By immersing themselves, they get to know very different living circumstances from what they are used to at home. In many cases, the experience broadens the mind, and it can even lead to different ways of thinking and problem solving, which can be of use throughout their entire life. However, it can also be a shock. At times, volunteering can be quite overwhelming and people sometimes feel they were not as well prepared for it, as they would have liked. This manual aims to help you feel a little more prepared, so that your volunteering experience is likely to be a positive one, and to make sure your visit is useful to the children's home that you are visiting.

You are holding the third book in the series of manuals called 'Children Everywhere'. This book stands out, because it is addressed

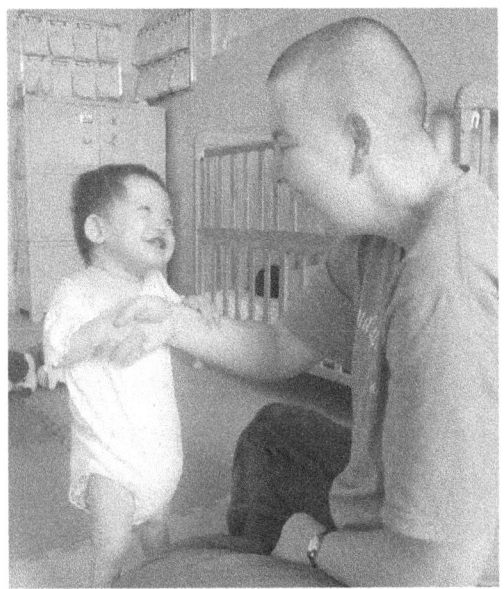

to a different audience than the other manuals, which are written for people who run and work in children's homes. This manual is written especially for people who decide to do volunteer work in children's homes. I decided to write this manual for two reasons, with the bottom line always being the aim to improve the lives of children in institutional childcare. The first reason is that over the years I have seen that volunteers can be a huge help and blessing, but they can also be a huge inconvenience and drain on scarce **resources**. No one intends to go into a children's home and complicate things by being there, but it does happen. So I want to give prospective volunteers some information, to improve their chances of being of real help. The second reason is that, in practice, the majority of people who volunteer to work with children in children's homes have no education or work experience relevant to childcare at all. While they mean very well, their best intentions may not always end up being in the child's best interest. So this manual, particularly Part 3: 'Basic Childcare & Child Psychology', gives a kind of mini-course in some important aspects of childcare.

Another reason to write this manual for volunteers is that I have noticed that many volunteers feel they did not quite know what they were getting into when they started. I have often heard volunteers say: 'If only someone had told me about this in advance.' This does not necessarily mean that if they had known they would not have gone, just that they might have been better prepared. So, based on my own experiences and those of other volunteers, I give information here on things that are useful to prepare for and on what you can, generally speaking, expect when you arrive. All in the hope to not only make your volunteering experience more useful, but also to make it more enjoyable. I distributed a questionnaire among people who have volunteered in children's homes, and their answers have given me a clearer understanding of their experiences. The quotes that you will come across throughout this book are mostly taken from the responses to the questionnaire.

This manual was not written to 'sell' volunteering in children's homes. It will not paint a pretty picture and show everything from its best side. The aim of this book is to show things in a more realistic light than they are usually presented in. That includes mentioning – sometimes somewhat bluntly perhaps – the more challenging aspects of volunteering, as well as the ways in which volunteers can make a situation worse rather than better. The purpose of this is not to accuse or blame anyone, just to help you make informed decisions and to avoid pitfalls.

It is important to keep in mind that, however much experience I personally have with volunteering in various countries, in various children's homes and under various circumstances, I do not know everything. I can only give you the kind of advice that I think I would have found useful. I am not you, I am unlikely to have visited the precise children's home that you will be volunteering at, and I may not have encountered circumstances quite like the ones waiting for you. In other words, the advice and information given in this manual should never be taken to be complete, or as a failsafe way of dealing with volunteering. You always need to use your own judgement to deal with the situations you end up in, and use your common sense. If you do that, and show sensitivity and respect to people who might have a different way of doing things, you will generally be okay.

As you may have noticed, I make a point to refer to the childcare institution where you may end up volunteering as a 'children's home' rather than using the more popular word 'orphanage'. This is a conscious decision. First of all, there is a certain amount of **stigma** attached to the label 'orphan', which I prefer to avoid. Secondly, in practice, not that many children in children's homes are full orphans – meaning that both their parents have passed away. Some have lost one parent and the remaining parent is unable to care for them without the other parent. Some children have been abandoned. Some have been removed from their home by the state in order to protect them. Some children have been 'recruited' to live in a children's home, for a variety of reasons. This is why I think that 'children's home' is a more accurate label. It states exactly what it is: a home for children.

This manual is not a standard reference book. My aim is to make the suggestions and solutions offered as widely accessible as possible. To illustrate why I came to certain conclusions, there will be a lot of case studies of why things do or do not work. Especially with possibly dangerous situations that might be taken for granted by some, I use examples to illustrate why I choose to emphasise these particular situations. Cases studies are divided into several categories that are indicated by the use of an icon. The icons and their meaning are:

 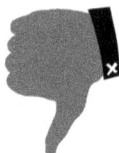 

A situation well handled   A situation poorly handled   An example to give a more concrete idea of an abstract concept that was just introduced

Something that is essential to keep in mind   A quote from a volunteer about their experience*   General information

---

* These are represented unaltered, apart from making sure they can be understood and to respect the privacy of the children's homes.

I have chosen not to complicate the text in this book with footnotes or other referencing tools to indicate which information came from where paragraph by paragraph. For each of the three parts of the manual, the books, the articles and the websites used to gather this information are all listed in the reference section at the end of this book.

Because many of my readers will be non-native English speakers, there is also a word list at the back of the book, to explain the more complicated words used in the text. Words that appear in the word list will be bold the first time they appear in the text.

Throughout the book, I have chosen to address the reader directly, as if the reader is the person who will actually take care of the situation that is being discussed. On the subject of personal pronouns, I have chosen to refer to all adults involved in the running of insti-

Introduction

tutions and to caregivers as 'she' and 'her', because in my experience the vast majority of people working at childcare institutions are women. If any adults outside the institution – including volunteers, although I know that many of you are women – are referred to, I will refer to them as male, simply in the interest of clarity and distinction. In examples when a specific individual is mentioned, the pronouns will vary. I will alternately refer to the children as 'he' and 'she' in different parts, while sticking to one of the two throughout a section.

It is my hope that this manual will help you make a real difference in the children's home that you will be volunteering in.

My motto, and that of Orphanage Projects, is:

I cannot change the world, but I can change the world for one child. And then another. And another... And so can you!

PART 1:
Getting There

Introduction

Deciding to volunteer in a children's home can be both exciting and scary at the same time. There are decisions to be made about what country to go to, what organisation to volunteer with and what kind of children's home to spend your time in. There is so much to prepare that it can be hard to keep track of what exactly is needed. So, in Part 1 of this manual, 'Getting There', a description is given of some of the things to think about when making your decisions and your preparations. Some things, like getting the right vaccinations, are extremely practical, while other things, like ethical issues around volunteering in children's homes, might be almost philosophical. Hopefully, this part will help you to think about these things before diving in head first.

As mentioned in the general introduction, while volunteers can be helpful and useful, they can also cause a lot of work, drain resources, and may even cause unintentional harm to the children they are trying to help. So it is very important to spend some time thinking about exactly what it is you would like to do as a volunteer and what kind of impact you want to make.

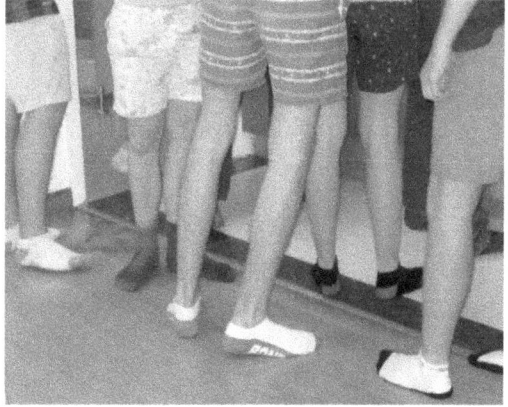

Imagine being a small child, looking up at the legs of this many strange-looking people you do not know: it is daunting.

Short term volunteering in a children's home – that is to say anything less than two months – is almost never to the advantage of the children. In the minds of the children it will mostly be like having a stranger barging into their lives, only to be 'abandoned' by their new friend by the time they are starting to get to know him and depend on him. This is emotionally scarring for children. If this is something that happens regularly, what they learn from it is that people cannot be depended on to stay and that relationships do not last. So, it will harm their **ability** to form relationships and to keep relationships going as they grow up. Part 3, Chapter 3: 'Essential Psychological Needs' will give more information about this.

What volunteers may not realise – because after all they are going over to help – is that it takes time and effort from the people running the children's home to have a volunteer visit. At least it does if the children's home handles the situation with the children's best interest and safety in mind. They will need to provide a new volunteer with someone who shows him the way things are done, who keeps an eye on how well the interaction between the volunteer and the children is going, and who assesses whether the volunteer has what it takes to do certain things unsupervised. This usually takes, at the very least, a week or two. During this time, the person who provides you with guidance has to take time away from her other duties to help you get settled. So, if after the two or three weeks you are gone again, there are no two ways about it: it will have cost more work than they could have possibly gotten out of you in that time. So, essentially, they are worse off than if you had not come. The only exception is if you are an 'expert volunteer'. This means, for example, a doctor or a therapist of some kind, who spends his limited time training staff in necessary skills, rather than interacting with children.

In the end, it's about what is best for children like her.

A lot of people are not aware of what I am about to say, and nothing will change if no one says anything about it. So let me be blunt for a moment: if you are thinking about volunteering in a children's home to fill up a short holiday, to fill a few days here and there in between traveling through the country, or just so you can tell people at home what a great thing you have done, taking care of 'the poor orphans'... please don't! There are a lot of other **worthy** kinds of volunteer work that you could be doing – such as building projects, saving rainforests, protecting endangered animals – that may benefit from short term volunteers. There, you can help make a difference without psychologically scarring children, who are living under difficult circumstances to begin with. Please consider this carefully.

If, after careful consideration, you still feel that you should volunteer in a children's home and that you will be able to leave a greater positive impact than damage, I wish you the best of luck and hope you will enjoy your experience. Hopefully, the following chapters will help you prepare.

> "Learning through experiences with actual human interactions with people who are less fortunate or children who have special needs will hopefully help adults to become more humble, empathetic and caring towards those in need. Many adults live in "bubbles" with no experiences of different food and cultures outside their own race in their communities. If volunteers are willing, hopefully they will gain a humble understanding of culture differences and learn at the same to become more culturally sensitive interacting with people from other ethnicities."

Chapter 1: Gathering Information and Deciding

The very first step in the process of going to another country to volunteer, is deciding what you want to do and where you want to go. In this chapter, some of the things that are useful to think about when you are making your decision will be discussed. Many of these things are quite straightforward, and you might feel that they go without saying. However, the fact is that not everyone is aware of all of these things, and if you do not take all of them into account, it could lead to disappointment or frustration later on.

How Long and When to Go

How long you are willing and able to volunteer is usually determined to a great extent by **external** circumstances. For example, you might want to do volunteer work during your holidays, which will be a set amount of time between your work or study obligations. Or you might use a gap year or a sabbatical as an opportunity to go abroad to volunteer. You might be limited by the time your family – be it the one who raised you, or the one you are raising – is able and willing to do without you. Money can also be a limiting factor: for how long are you able to take care of your expenses with the money that you have saved for volunteering? And last, but by no means least, visas can dictate how long it is possible for you to stay in a certain country.

If the timing is flexible, being there for an important festival, or avoiding it, can be a factor in your decision-making.

Because these external factors are often clear from the beginning, most prospective volunteers start out with the thought: 'I have this much time available to volunteer, now where shall I go?' The decision of what to do when volunteering is influenced by how much time you have. As mentioned in the Introduction to Part 1, if you are unable to commit to two months at the very least – though at least three months would be better –, spending that time in a children's home might be enjoyable for you, but it is not likely to be useful to the people working there, nor is it in the best interest of the children. So please, only volunteer in a children's home if you are going to spend at least two months there, and that means spending most of that time with the children.

Two girls arrived at a children's home in Kenya to volunteer, during their summer holidays. When they were asked how long they would be there they said 'two months', but in the course of the conversation it became clear that they also wanted to see a little of Kenya during that time. In fact, in the end, it became clear that between the trips to the coast, to the interior and to Zanzibar, they would really only be at the children's home for four to five days at a time, in between 'holidays' that would take one to two weeks each. In other words, the children never really got the chance to get to know them and saw them as new strangers every time they returned, and the volunteers never got familiar with the children.

It's important to make up your mind about whether you are going for this...   *... or for this.*

How long you are able and willing to go, may also influence where you are able to go. Some children's homes have rules or guidelines for volunteers and will only accept volunteers for a minimum amount of time, or, in some cases, for no longer than a maximum amount of time.

Something to keep in mind when you are deciding the *when* of you volunteer period, are the **precautions** you need to take. For example, how long in advance you need to start your vaccinations and possibly anti-malaria tablets to make sure that you are safe while you are abroad. When you are planning to volunteer in a country that does not require you to add or update any vaccinations, you are of course free to leave tomorrow – if you can afford to buy the tickets at such a late **stage**. However, for most destinations in Asia, Africa and Latin America you will need vaccinations, and often anti-malaria medication. It is often necessary to start vaccinations six weeks before you travel, to make sure that you have time for all the vaccinations needed and that they have taken effect before you arrive. So, generally speaking, you will need some advance planning. More information on vaccinations and other precautions is given in Part 1, Chapter 2: 'Practical Preparations'.

When you are going, is often also determined by outside factors. Again, things like when your holidays are and when you can have a certain amount of money saved, may leave you with little to say over the timing. However, within the limits of being free from your regular duties and financial restraints, you do have some influence over your exact travel dates.

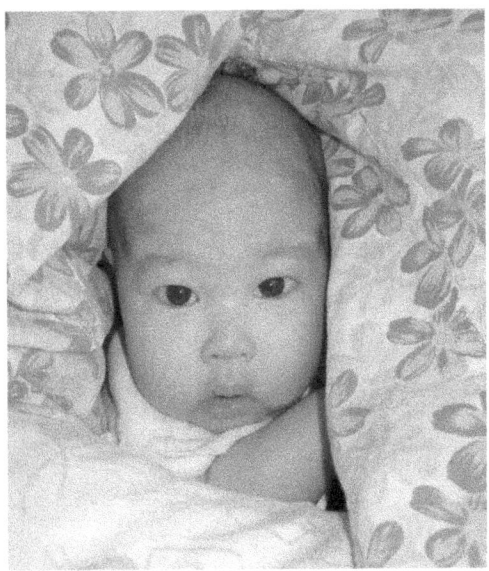

Who would not want to go help this little guy? Cuteness is powerful.

With regards to these exact travel dates, it is a good idea to give some thought to the return journey. With time being limited and the adventure being great, the temptation is to stretch the journey out for as long as you possibly can. However, while it *is* going to be a big adventure, and it *is* going to be exciting, it will also be overwhelming at times. Particularly if it is your first time doing something like this, when you get home, you are almost certainly going to need some time to process everything that you have been through and what it means to you. You will likely feel very sad about having left behind the children, whom you have gotten very close to. Not to mention needing some time to readjust to your own country, culture and time zone. In other words, you need some time to get used to everything. This means that arranging your flights so that you arrive home during the weekend, to then have to start university or a new job on Monday, might not be the smartest way to go. Be kind to yourself and give yourself at least a few days to rest, process and readjust once you return, before duty calls again. This is one of the things that catch a lot of volunteers by surprise when they get home. Several of them have said that they wished they would have known what was waiting for them. Part 1, Chapter 4: 'Mental Preparations' under 'Having to Leave It Behind' will go into this in more detail.

 Is This Kind of Childcare for You?

Presumably – since you are reading this manual – you are interested in volunteering in children's home. If, after reading the Introduction to Part 1, you still feel that this is what you want to do and that you can do it in a way that will be of use to the children, you should know a few other things about volunteering in children's homes, to make sure you have a realistic idea of what you are getting into. This will help you make a definite, informed decision.

The problem is that children have a huge 'cuteness-factor'. All those pictures of beautiful children with huge eyes and torn clothes, which you see all over Facebook and on campaign posters raising money for various charities, just make your heart melt. You want to wrap your arms around the child and protect her from all the harm in the world. You feel determined to make a difference. You will go over there, you will raise some money and make sure the children get nicer clothes. You will take a little girl onto your lap and love her, and she will feel loved and her troubles will melt away, like snow before the sun. These feelings can be very strong. That is why campaigns use these photos, because they work. They make you pull out your wallet. However, this is not the reality of volunteering in a children's home.

Yes, in most cases when you arrive at the children's home, the children will be running out to meet you. They will be hugging you and fighting each other to touch you and sit on your lap – those are signs of indiscriminate **attachment**, a problem that will be explained in Part 3, Chapter 3: 'Essential Psychological Needs'. However, your arrival will not be the end of all their troubles. You will be confronted with children whose troubled past still haunts them, and you will find that other than holding their hand and listening to them, there is nothing you can do – believe me, doing that is already a huge thing, which has a big positive **impact**, but it will not feel that way. There may be very few caregivers for many children – either because there is no money to hire more, or because there is no **awareness** of the importance of having people there to provide attention and supervision (this will also be discussed in Part 3, Chapters 2 and 3) –, which leads to children desperately seeking attention, even through negative behaviour. Sometimes, it leads to a 'survival of the fittest' among the children, with the weaker ones being bullied by the stronger ones, and again, you are powerless to change this.

A tiny scratch that turned into a major infection, because of hygiene conditions. For me: still worth it. But not for everyone.

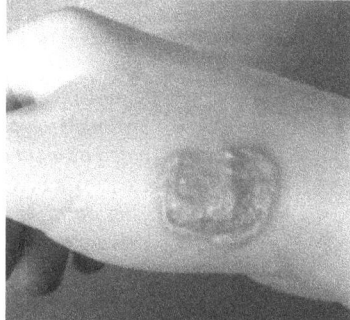

The sheer crowdedness that is the reality in most children's homes can be very overwhelming. **Hygiene** may be an issue, because of a **lack** of (safe) water, or because of a lack of caregivers. Crowded living conditions will almost always bring lice with them, which you are likely to get if the children have them.

"You were right. This is like Lord of the Flies!"

You may think that I am exaggerating, but I am not. In fact, I have not even scratched the surface of the things that I have seen and experienced in children's homes. My point is not to make you think it is like hell. My point is that the images and stories that you usually hear, which are designed to persuade you to donate or to go volunteer, paint a rosy, unrealistic picture. Because the reality is that the truth would repel too many people, and that volunteering is a business for some organisations. They want to sell it. This does not mean that no one should do it, just that it is not for everyone. And that both the volunteers and the children are better off if people who are discouraged by the reality do not go.

I was explaining the effects of certain elements of the care system in a children's home on the children to a long-term volunteer when she told me: 'Stop talking, it's too depressing!' I pointed out that I had only pointed out one or two issues. That while she found that too depressing to contemplate, there was much more going on that had very serious long-term consequences to the children and that I was walking around there, seeing all of it day in, day out, fully aware.

Some of the accommodations that were arranged for me. Bunk bed in staff dorm, a bed by night and a physiotherapy treatment table by day, and a bed in the girls' dorm with the bags on chairs to prevent rats nibbling on them.

There is a beautiful side to volunteering in children's homes too, but you do not get to choose one or the other. The choice you have to make is whether you are willing to take both the good and the bad.

To me personally, it is more than worth it. Even though I go around with no hair, to **prevent** getting lice, I feel it is worth it. When I spent several weeks not getting enough to eat, just like the children, I felt it was worth it. When I got several hundred new bedbug bites every night for over three weeks, sharing a **dorm** with the children, I felt it was worth it. I would not trade what I do for anything in the world. To me it is the most wonderful and satisfying work imaginable. But that does not mean that is the case for everyone. You need to think about whether it is worth it for you, and whether you are suited for this kind of work.

"Be prepared to go out of your comfort zone."

You also need to ask yourself whether you are the kind of person who is able to witness sometimes quite terrible situations, and just get on with it and be there for the children. The people who burst out in tears when they see a photo of a severely malnourished child are usually not the people who are able to be of practical use as volunteers in childcare. If you are going to be reduced to tears when you see a child who is dressed in rags, you are not going to make the child feel better about herself. She might actually feel worse. However you can provide excellent help by making donations or spreading awareness.

*"At times it is best not to show emotion!!
These are people's everyday lives, fit in."*

Finally, for your own sake, you need to look closely at yourself and decide if you are going to be able to leave. This may sound strange, but it is always hard to go away, having to leave the children behind. Some people find it harder than others. If you are able to predict that you will completely go to pieces when you have to leave the children after you have been with them for several months, are you sure that you want to put yourself through that? You are the only one who can answer that question.

*"I had been fascinated with China since I was 15.
So, when in my late 20s I decided I would take a year away,
it was immediately 'I'm going to China for a year'.
Next came the question of what I would go do there."*

What Country to Go to

For some people, the country where they are going to volunteer is never a question at all. Their decision to go volunteer starts with an

In some places, air pollution is a serious problem; also something to take into consideration.

old fascination with, or connection to a particular country. In their mind, going anywhere else is not even an option. However, there are also a lot of people who first decide that they want to go to volunteer in a children's home and then start thinking about where they will go to do it. If you are not sure about where you want to go, this section will bring a few things to your attention that are useful to keep in mind while you figure it out. If you are reasonably sure where you want to go, it might still be a good idea to have a quick look over this section, to see if there are any issues that you have not thought of that may cause serious obstacles.

"Several years ago I went to Brazil to volunteer in a specific children's home, but that did not work out. So, after a few weeks I left there and started looking for another place to volunteer. This is when I found out that officially Brazil had a law that said volunteering was only allowed for four hours a week. Several places I went to wanted my help, but they did not want to take the risk of breaking that law. This complicated things a lot. Because for me it didn't make sense to volunteer less than full time."

Some general things you might want to take into consideration when deciding where to go, in order to make your stay as enjoyable as possible:

If the thought of having a gecko - or several - as your roommate freaks you out, the tropics are probably not your best option.

- **Climate**
    o How do you deal with heat/cold?
    o How do you deal with extreme drought/humidity?
    o Is the place you are considering accessible during the season you intend to go?
- **Food**
    o Are you allergic/intolerant to their staple food?
    o Do you have trouble dealing with spicy food?
    o Are you a vegetarian/vegan and do they have vegetarian/vegan options available where you want to go?
    o Are you a meat-eater who finds it hard to do without meat?

Chapter 1: Gathering Information and Deciding

A guy in his mid-twenties was volunteering in a remotely located children's home where the diet was strictly vegetarian, for religious reasons. This man was really struggling with not being able to eat meat, he said he felt weak and he was craving meat. One day I asked him if he had seen that the water buffalo had given birth to her calf. He answered: 'Yeah, it looks delicious!'

Language

Language is an important thing to think about. It is going to be the tool you need to communicate with everyone around you while you are volunteering. If you are unable to communicate at all because you do not share any language, this is likely to lead to problems and frustrations. It may even put the children in danger, because you may be unable to understand important instructions given about their needs.

"I got by but would have been useful to know a little Marathi."

This is not to say that you should only go to a place where everyone speaks your mother tongue. Just that you need to give the issue some thought:

- What languages do you speak?
- What languages are spoken in the country where you are going to volunteer?
- What languages are spoken in the children's home where you will work by
    o The management?
    o The caregivers?
    o The children?
- Are you willing and able to spend time learning another language?
- Are you willing to fumble around, speaking in loose words and broken sentences – even if it means making a fool of yourself with your mistakes – to get your meaning across?

This last question sounds like it deserves the answer 'no'. But being willing to make mistakes will really help your language learning. Even though you probably do not want to make a fool of yourself, a willingness to ignore that is a big asset, which will get you a long way. Not to mention the fact that you gain an enormous amount of goodwill from both the staff and the children if you make an attempt to speak their language, no matter how many foolish mistakes you make. It is usually a sure way of making contact and slowly making

Children this age are not likely to speak English yet, they are starting to communicate through language, but only their own.

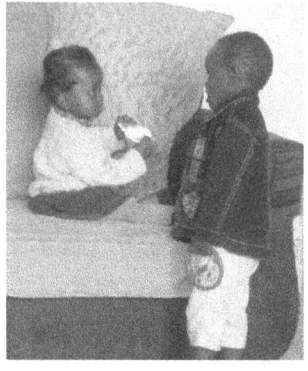

the move from being an outsider to becoming 'one of us' in the children's home.

There is a reason I mention 'management', 'caregivers' and 'children' separately when asking what language is spoken in the children's home. While people in management may speak languages other than their mother tongue, this is often not the case with caregivers and children. In Part 1, Chapter 3: 'Cultural Preparations', you will find more information about this in the section 'Learning some of the Language'.

"Most of the children were able to speak a little English, it would have been nice to have learnt a little more of the language though, to be able to interact with some of the younger children more."

You should not be too afraid of different languages. You will pick up things much more quickly than you would think, if you are willing to put in a little effort. When you are in a country, surrounded by people who speak the other language and with no choice but to try to say things in it, you will probably find you become able to bring your meaning across pretty quickly, even if it is not done in the most elegant way.

"Before I went to China, to volunteer there, I spent six months learning Chinese using a self-teaching course with a book and a CD. Towards the end of the six months, I was starting to become quite confident and impressed with myself in my own living room. However, when I arrived in China, I was unable to understand anything and I suddenly could not remember more than 'hello' and 'thank you'. Still, I kept trying in daily life. Through pointing at things, I started 'collecting' nouns and verbs to do with baby care (which were not included in the language course, anyway) and then I started building on that. After three months I was able to have very basic conversations, in which I used incomplete – and doubtlessly badly pronounced – sentences, but communication was taking place. And once you have gotten that far, progress keeps going faster."

Visas

The vast majority of countries where people go to volunteer in children's homes require a visa before you are allowed to enter the country. In some countries, getting a visa is as straightforward as automatically getting a stamp in your passport when you go through immigration after landing. There may or may not be a fee attached to this. However, many places require you to have a visa in your passport before you board an airplane to go to that country. In this case, you will need to visit the local embassy or consulate of the country you are traveling to and find out what kind of visa you need and what documentation you have to gather to be able to apply for that specific visa. This information can often also be found online. When looking up what you need for a visa on the internet, you should visit the official website of the embassy/consulate, rather than general travel pages where fellow travellers give advice. This is because on the official website, all the information relevant to the combination of the country

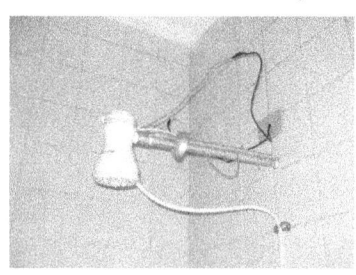

In hot countries, IF there is running hot water, this is often how it is done: an electric wire to the shower head, a luxury compared to many other situations.

you are resident in and the country you are traveling to should be included (there can be different **requirements** for people traveling from France or the USA, even though they are traveling to the same country, for example), and this should be the most recently updated information. Some countries change their rules quite regularly, and advice from a traveller who went through the process you want to go through may already be incorrect.

Some countries will have special requirements or even special visas for people who wish to volunteer there. Traveling on a regular tourist visa is not allowed in these countries when the purpose of your visit is to volunteer. Sometimes you need a letter of invitation from the children's home where you will be volunteering, and the consulate or embassy may also ask you for copies of the documents that prove that the children's home you will be volunteering in is officially registered. These are all things to look into.

"I went to visit the consulate of a country I was planning to go to, to find out what I needed for a visa. I asked if there were any special requirements for volunteering in that country. The answer was 'Yes.' Since nothing more followed, I asked what the requirements were. 'A permit.' Again, that was it. So I asked what I needed to get this permit and where I could apply for it. 'The organisation you volunteer with will know.' That was all the information I was going to get. Sometimes it is not easy or straightforward to find out these things."

The amount of time you will be able to get a visa for is dependent on the country that you are going to – and its relationship with the country where you are from. The same goes for how complicated the visa application process is and how likely you are to actually get a visa. When you start the visa application process, you are not guaranteed to be granted the visa. In some cases, you are required to have a return ticket (or a reservation for one) to prove when you are planning to travel. If this is not the case, it is usually a good idea to wait to book the flight until after you have your visa and you are sure you will actually be traveling. It can cost you a lot of money if you have already booked your flight and you end up not getting the visa.

When I previously made a visa application to this particular country, I had been required to show that I had bought plane tickets. So, when I applied for a visa to the same country a few years later, I booked my flights and included the proof of this with the other documents. When I submitted everything, I was told off for already booking my flight; they said that it was not necessary for the application process and I was told that I was not guaranteed a visa. On the website, it said that I could expect the processing of the visa application to take ten working days, so I had taken a three-week window (fifteen working days) from the start of the application process to the time of my flight. The day before my flight, I still had not received news that I could pick up my passport. So I knew that I had lost my flight, which was due to leave in the morning the next day. The question remained whether I would be given the visa or whether it would be declined. The afternoon of the day when my flight had left in the morning, I got a message saying that I could come and pick up my passport the next day. I had a visa. Now I just needed to book a new flight. Unfortunately, not receiving a visa was not seen as a valid reason to use the cancellation refund of my travel insurance.

When the visa becomes valid is also something that varies from country to country. In many cases, a visa is valid for 90 days, to start within 90 days of being put in the passport. This means that from the date it says on the visa that it was given – which is almost always a few days before they actually hand it back to you – you have 90 days to enter the country. After these 90 days, the visa is no longer valid. Once you enter the country, the duration of your visa starts counting – whether this is 28 days, 90 days, 180 days, or whatever the duration is. So, this means you will be able to stay in that country for the entire duration of the visa. This is not true in for all countries, however. For some countries, the duration of the visa will start from the moment of the visa being put in the passport – which, again, is generally several days before you get your passport back. This means that a 90-day visa can never cover a 90-day stay. This is something that you need to check before you start planning your trip and that you need to take into account. If this is the case, you should not arrange the visa a long time in advance, because that will leave you little time to actually stay in the country.

For this country the 90-day visa starts on the date of issue. So when the passport with the visa in it is picked up – immediately after being notified that it is ready for collection – on 24 April it says on the visa that it was issued on 19 April. This means it is valid from 19 April to 18 July. Knowing on 24 April that you definitely have a visa, you can start booking your flight. This is usually going to be at least a week in the future, if not more, because of flights that are fully booked and prices that are hiked up sky high at the last moment. Say you find something affordable for leaving on 2 May and arriving on 3 May, that means you will have a maximum of 76 days left on your visa for your stay.

Make sure you are properly prepared.

As soon as you have a general idea of the country that you would be interested in visiting, it is a good idea to get information about their visa application process and to find out how complicated and expensive it is. Then you can make a decision on whether you are willing and able to go through that process, or whether you would prefer to look at other countries instead.

When applying for a visa, one thing is extremely important to keep in mind: people at the visa application desk of an embassy or consulate – of any country at all – do not mess around. Please, do not go in there thinking that it will probably be all right even though you do not have EXACTLY what was indicated on the website. They will turn you away to get all of the completed documents, and it will make absolutely no difference if that takes so much time that you cannot make the flight you already booked anymore. When you arrive to make your application, it serves no purpose to try to debate things or get them to make an exception, even if you discover new rules that are not on the website yet. The people helping you are generally friendly, but immovable. Their job is simply to make sure that people who want to travel to their country do so according to the rules. They do not have the power to change those rules. However, if you are properly prepared, friendly and respectful, things usually go smoothly.

Safety

The political and health situation in a country are important to take into account when deciding where you want to volunteer. In theory, it might sound very heroic to be able to say that you went into a war zone to help out orphaned children there. However, the practice is not likely to be either idyllic or heroic. First of all, there is a very real

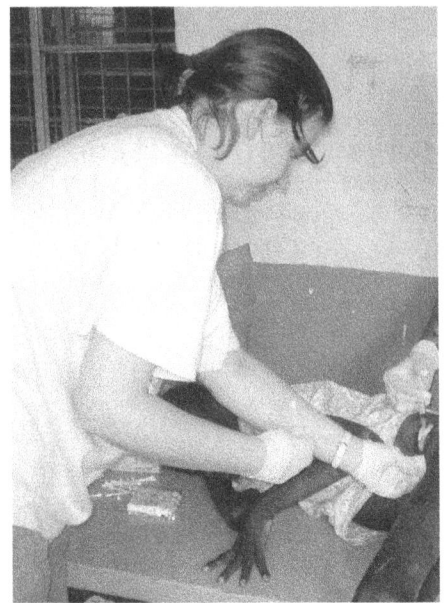

No need to put yourself at risk to find people who need your help; in too many places, anyone who knows basic first aid can almost find themselves elevated to doctor-status.

danger that you will not come out of the experience in one piece or even alive. Secondly, unless you are a qualified expert in a field that has been indicated by the country itself to be something they want help with, you are quite frankly not only going to be of little use, but you are going to be a nuisance to many people. You will just be in the way, if you are lucky, or in the cross-fire if you are not.

In other words, neither the children nor yourself will benefit from you going to a country that is in political turmoil, in civil or international war, or that is experiencing a major health crisis – such as an outbreak of the Plague or Ebola – or a natural disaster. There is plenty of work to be done and help to be given in countries that are not experiencing these circumstances. Once the situation has **improved** and stabilised in these countries, you may be able to safely go and help out there. The website of the Foreign Affairs Ministry of your country will usually have warnings for people wishing to travel to countries that are not considered safe. It is worth checking these warnings.

For more general information about the countries that you might be considering as a destination for your volunteering, the latest edition of travel guides from Lonely Planet, Backpackers Guide, Insight Guide and Rough Guide generally give very accurate, up-to-date and reliable information.

Volunteering Through an Organisation

Another choice to make is whether you want to volunteer independently or through an international volunteer organisation. Both options have advantages and disadvantages, and you really are the only one who can decide what is most suitable for you. Here are some things to keep in mind:

	Independent	Through Organisation
Finding a children's home	It can take a long time to find a suitable one, but you have the freedom to make your own choice.	Presented with a few set possibilities.
Logistics	You often need to arrange your own transport once you arrive, as well as a place to stay.	Transport from the airport to accommodation and the accommodation itself are usually part of the package.

	Independent	**Through Organisation**
Back-up	The only back-up or help in trouble you have, is what you arrange for yourself.	A local representative will often be available to help you if you have problems.
Fellow Volunteers	It will depend on the children's home that you volunteer in whether you will meet other volunteers at all, but you may feel more free in your choice of whom you associate with.	Often several volunteers are placed in the same children's home or guest family, and you might know these people from earlier information gatherings, giving you an instant circle of acquaintances. On the other hand, there may be social pressure, making it harder for you to break out of this circle if you want to.
Costs	You only have to pay for your travel and accommodation expenses.	The fees for having everything arranged for you can be quite high – often several hundred dollars a week. Some people are under the impression that some of the money they are paying will go to the children's home in which they volunteer, but this is often not the case. You should check this with any organisation you are considering.
Requirements	You only need to take into consideration the requirements of the children's home itself, and possibly those of the country you will be visiting for visa application.	On top of visa requirements and possible demands from the children's home, many volunteer organisations have their own requirements with regards to qualifications, experience and length of commitment to volunteering.

These are all things to take into account when you make your decision. For example, the costs involved in using an organisation to arrange things for you may be too high for you, or you may prefer to donate the money you have left – after you have covered your expenses – directly to the children's home. Then again, it could be

If this is what you are looking for, an organisation that arranges placements in South America is not going to be of much use to you.

that the idea of having to make your own arrangements, in a country that you do not know at all, is so scary so you that you would gladly pay to feel secure that the children's home, the accommodation and the transport on arrival will be arranged for you.

The requirements of some organisations can be encouraging to some and discouraging to others. For example, one major volunteer organisation only offers volunteering positions – for which you can get some pocket money – with a duration of no shorter than two years, and they require professional qualifications in the relevant field.

If you have already set your heart on volunteering in a particular country or in a particular kind of children's home (this will be discussed in the next section) and you want to use a volunteering organisation to help you arrange everything, you will need to make sure that the organisation you choose actually has programmes for the country and the type of children's home that you prefer. Most volunteering organisations have contacts with particular children's homes in a select few countries, and they will not be able to organise anything for you in other places.

What Type of Children's Home

When asked the question 'What kind of children's home are you going to volunteer at?', most prospective volunteers will probably look at you blankly or answer with 'Well, you know, it's an orphanage.' Most people do not realise that there *are* differences between children's homes and that this *is* a relevant question. It makes a big difference whether the children's home you volunteer at is an adoption centre that houses babies aged newborn to about one year old, caring for them until they are **adopted**, or whether it is a long term care facility caring for **mentally** retarded people aged twelve years and older.

It would be impossible to name all the different kinds of set-up that exist. But it is useful to give some thought to broad categories and their implications.

- How many children are cared for at the children's home? I have been to places caring for anything between 6 and 300 children, and it makes a big difference on what end of the scale you are.
- Are the children living as a large group, sleeping in big dorms and eating in a dining hall, or are they living in group homes – artificial family-like situations?
- Children from what age to what age are cared for at the children's home? Around what age are the majority of children? Some people are great with teenagers but scared to hold a baby, and the other way around. It will do no one any good if you do not take this into account.
- Are the children mostly present at the children's home or mostly away at school? It depends on what you are looking for whether having several hours a day with no children present is a relief or a disappointment.
- Do the children have special needs? One person will be excited by the prospect of helping out children who have handicaps or who are ill, while another shudders at the thought and would be of much more use in a place where all children are mostly healthy. You certainly do not want to end up in a **hospice** type children's home without knowing what you are getting into.

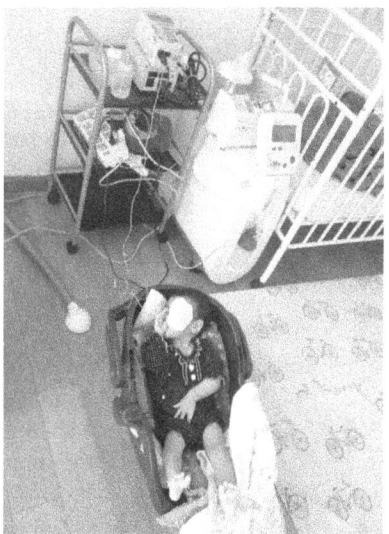

Not everyone is ready for this, and that is okay. Just make sure you know what you get into.

Try to think what your personal preference would be in each of these categories and then see if you can find a good fit. You can find a good fit by actually asking the children's home contact person – or the organisation that is arranging things for you – about these things and making a decision based on the answers you receive. It is all right to have a 'wish list', as long as you stay realistic and realise that you will not necessarily get everything you hoped for. The purpose of the 'wish list' should be to become aware of things that you think you could not handle well and should therefore stay away from, rather than listing the ingredients for 'the ideal volunteering experience'. You can make a list for that too, but it is not very likely that you will get exactly what is on it.

Ethical Considerations

At first glance, you are likely to think: 'What ethical problems can possibly be attached to volunteering in children's homes?' While this is understandable, there *are* ethical considerations to think about.

It is painful to think that, even with the best intentions, going to volunteer in children's homes could have more children end up living in them.

There is a surprisingly large number of so-called 'orphanages' around the world where the children are not really orphans at all, they have living relatives, or sometimes even parents. While the people in many children's homes around the world genuinely care for children who have no one else to take care of them and nowhere else to go, in some places the children do have other people who would most likely take better care of them.

As the popularity of volunteering in children's homes and sponsoring children in children's homes **increases**, some people have discovered a market in the running of 'orphanages'. It has become a source of income. The result of this market is nothing more than the **exploitation** of the children, their families, and the emotions that the idea of orphans stirs up. This does not have to mean getting a lot of money out of foreigners' pockets. The thing to understand is that creating a situation where you can share the housing and the food for the children, paid for by foreign donations, is a way for people to make a comfortable living. Comfortable enough that they may be motivated to put children in a children's home who do not need to be there. And if they inflate the monthly cost by a dollar or two they have some spending money too. This is a form of exploitation. Some of these places are run out of a certain sense of idealism: to give children an education or a more thorough religious upbringing. However, even though the people running these 'orphanages' want to help the children that are in their care, it is not in the children's best interest to be taken away from their family to be raised in a children's home. Even if they come from a very poor background, in the end the children will be worse off living away from their family. Part 3, Chapter 3: 'Essential Psychological Needs' will explain more about why this is.

It was explained to me that while the children from this children's home had living relatives, they came from the poorest area of the country, where there was hardly any education or healthcare available and in many places not even electricity. So, the children were taken into a children's home in the big city to provide them with an education. The reality, however, is that the school age children live in a house in the city

with the person who set up the 'orphanage' (and sometimes some of his extended family). They are removed from the family, the environment and the life they know and put into the completely different surroundings of the city. They receive food, clothes, schooling and tuition and when they are not in school, they are expected to behave well and take care of chores like cleaning, cooking and generally serving the person who set up the 'orphanage' and his guests. Attention, affection, and concern for the children's emotional well-being are rarely seen.

When asking whether these children ever get to visit their families, the answer was 'no' in all cases. When asking whether these children are in contact with their family at all, the answer was only 'yes' in some cases. They said that it was too difficult, because of the great distance, the great cost and the difficulty of reaching the remote villages that these children come from. I was told that if they were allowed to visit their family, they might not want to come back again. As long as they were in school, they would live in the children's homes, and when they have finished their studies – in four, eight, or twelve years' time – they are free to go back if they wish. But after so much time without any contact with their family, having lived in a city and not being used to rural life anymore, what reason will they have to go back?

The majority of children in these places have families, who sent the children to these places in good faith, believing they were doing a good thing for the children. The problem is that many people still think that living in a children's home can be a good solution. But it is never a good solution for a child. Even if the highest standard of care is available in the children's home, it does not make up for the long lasting negative effects of being separated from your family and a loving environment that meets your essential basic needs. (What these needs are is explained in the first three chapters of Part 3.) When we are not talking about the highest standards of care – which is the case in the majority of children's homes around the world – the negative **consequences** are even greater: they can include **physical** and mental handicaps, and in some cases even death. Institutional care should only be the very last option, if there are absolutely no other possibilities. When this is the case, the stay at the children's home should be as short as possible, putting every effort into reuniting a child with his or her family, or having the child **fostered** or adopted as soon as possible. No child will benefit from living in a children's home for years. The gap between the care that is received in a family and the care that is offered in a children's home is quite simply too big to meet all of a child's essential needs. It is an illusion that institutional childcare is preferable to living in poverty, to not having access to formal education, or to having a less

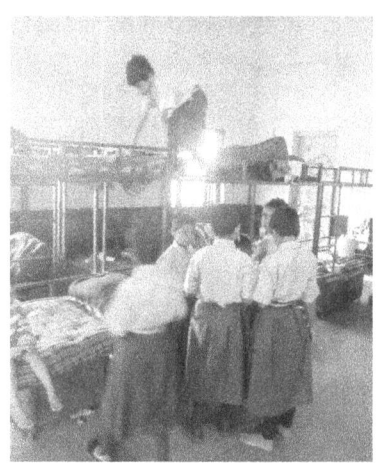

Even with a better chance of education in a children's home, children still are better off not living there.

thoroughly religious upbringing. In short, institutional childcare is preferable to almost nothing, except when the child has absolutely no one care for her, or is in a life-endangering situation within the family. Research has shown that children living in extreme poverty in a family situation have better chances in life than those growing up in a children's home. Despite receiving an education in a children's home, many children raised there will end up in the streets, because of their essential needs were not properly met as they grew up, which negatively affected their brain development.

While these places may have the intention of helping children, and while the poor quality of the care may be mostly due to lack of awareness, the fact cannot be ignored that these places are a valuable source of income for their owners. Most of these children's homes are sponsored by foreigners. These are visitors who are struck by the poor living conditions of the children and the heartfelt story of the owner. Visitors who really want to help make a difference. Unfortunately, what they unintentionally do is make the owning of an 'orphanage' an appealing way to make money. This means that more and more children's homes appear all over the world.

So, what can you do about this situation? To start with, gather information about a children's home before you decide to give a donation to it or to volunteer there. Particularly, look for information about whether or not the children have families that can be found and whether the children's home works towards returning the children to a family situation as soon as possible. This can be by reuniting them with their family, having them fostered or having them adopted. By not donating to children's homes that should not exist, you help avoid their existence. Secondly, supporting community projects such as respite care homes – which give care several hours a day, but allow the child to live with his family – or health and education centres is a great way to help more children grow up in their own families.

Another ethical issue is 'voluntourism'. This means day trips to children's homes, a form of what I tend to call 'monkey watching': having a look at 'the poor little orphans', handing out some treats, feeling good about yourself and leaving. The situation is often demeaning to the children, even if that is not the intention of the visitors. In Cambodia, Friends-International, with the backing of UNICEF, has started a campaign to discourage voluntourism called 'Think Child Safe: "Children Are Not Tourist Attractions"'. The unintended effects and harm caused by daytrips can be caused by short-term volunteering too.

The people on the left came for a tour of the children's home and are filming the children as they sing their national anthem, showing no respect for the children.

Together with the caregiver I was working to cool down a girl with a high fever, and make her as comfortable as possible. She was stripped down to her underwear, and we were using damp cloths to cool her down. Then, a group of more than ten people appeared in the doorway of the dorm. They were being given a tour of the children's home. I positioned myself so that I mostly blocked their view of the girl, with my back to the door. After a minute or two, two of the people actually came into the dorm to get a better look at the girl. I turned around and pointed out that we do not usually enter the dorm with shoes on. Then I told them that I would be happy to come outside the room to talk to them, but that this girl was feeling miserable enough without an audience. There were nods, but no one moved. I got up and left the room, and the group reluctantly followed to ask me questions.

For some people, the work done by many international volunteering organisations that place volunteers in children's homes for a fee, also belongs on the list of ethically questionable practices. Because these organisations almost all work for a profit, it can be seen as a form of exploitation: making money using children who live in very poor circumstances. Whether you feel this issue will stop you using volunteer organisations to set you up with a placement is up to you.

These are all ethical issues that you might not have been aware of, and that deserve some thought while you decide where you want to volunteer.

If you are very religious, but not Hindu, you may not feel comfortable working here.

Religious Background

Unless you are very religious yourself, you may not have considered that religion might be a factor to take into consideration, but it is. The majority of children's homes that are not run by the state, are founded by religious people as a way to help God help the most **vulnerable**. These can be people from all different religions, be it Muslim, Christian, Jewish, Hindu or any other. Religious people founding a children's home do not necessarily run it in a clearly religious way. Some founders just want to open the doors to provide shelter for all children who need it, and welcome the help of staff and volunteers from different (religious) backgrounds.

However, there are also people who run a children's home with the specific purpose to raise the children in it within the teachings and traditions of their particular religion. These homes usually only welcome staff and volunteers who are actively practising the same religion, incorporating it in every aspect of their lives so they can be a suitable role model to the children. If religion is important in your life, you may want to look specifically for a children's home like this, where you are able to share your religion with the people and children you will be working with, even if they are from a different country. If you are not at all religious, or if you prefer religion as a private thing rather than something that shows in your everyday actions, you may want to make sure whether or not religion (and which particular one) is a big part of life at the children's home you are considering going to.

Making Arrangements

If you have decided to volunteer through a volunteering organisation, there will generally be systems in place to arrange everything that needs to be arranged, and to make sure everyone is kept up to date. If you follow the organisation's instructions, things should be taken care of properly.

If you have decided to arrange things yourself, it is your own responsibility to make sure that you gather and receive all the information you need to make your decision, and to make sure that clear agreements are made with the children's home about your arrival. That you have contacted a children's home for information, does not necessarily mean that you will decide to go there. If you decide not to go there, please let the person who provided you with the information know, so that there will be no confusion or expectations. Similarly, if you do decide to go there, ask for explicit confirmation that you are welcome to come, and for how long and on what specific dates. As your travel arrangements progress, keep the children's home updated. For example, let them know when you have received your visa – or if the visa application has been declined and you can therefore not travel – and that you have booked your flights.

Make sure that you know and ask for confirmation about whether someone will come and pick you up at the airport or whether you will have to make your own way to your accommodation. And whether you will be staying at the children's home or whether you have to arrange a place to stay somewhere else – and how to get to the children's home from there. In other words, every detail needs to be communicated and confirmed.

Take into account that communication, even through e-mail, can be very slow. Usually the person who is communicating with you does not only have the job of keeping in contact with volunteers. They are doing this on top of a mountain of other responsibilities. Also, something to remember is that while people in rich countries have come to take constant internet access for granted, the reality is different in many places outside of Europe, Australia and North America. People may not have internet at the children's home, or at their own home. Their internet access may consist of visits to an internet café, for which they may need to travel. So if you are getting frustrated with slow communication, ask what the situation is concerning this matter, so that you can understand the circumstances and will have a realistic idea of what you can expect – also with regards to your own internet access once you arrive.

"There was no internet at the children's home where I stayed. I was shown an internet café a ten to fifteen minute walk from the home, where I could go. The computers in the internet café were very old and the internet connection was so slow that the loading of pages kept timing out regularly. Occasionally I managed to read an email, but I was almost never able to successfully answer one. To start with, I went to the internet café once a week, but in the end I got so frustrated that I just gave up."

Accessibility

If you have a physical handicap, it is a good idea to ask for detailed information about the situation, both about the children's home itself and about the environment in which the children's home is placed, to get an idea of how accessible it is to you. In many places, there are no smoothly paved streets, but rather rough dirt roads with many holes and rocks

The thought is nice, but a ramp this steep is not going to help anyone get inside.

in them. In the children's home itself, living areas and dorms may be located on higher floors, only accessible by stairs. When you have more information about what you can expect, you can assess for yourself whether you will need to bring additional or adjusted equipment to be able to deal with the practical challenges that are waiting for you.

Having to make sure the information about accessibility is detailed is not an exaggeration. In some cases, the people at the children's home will make an effort to make certain rooms or buildings accessible, but other – crucial – areas may be forgotten. So ask specifically about all kinds of areas that you can think of that you expect to need to be able to access.

A volunteer in a wheelchair arrived at the children's home. The guest accommodation was accessible by a ramp, and the furniture in the bedroom had been arranged so that he could move around in his wheelchair. The terrain of the compound was very rough, with hills in places, but with the deeply grooved wheels and some force, the volunteer was able to get across it. However, when he went to have breakfast on the first morning, he discovered that to get into the dining hall, he had to go up three steps, and there was no other way in.

Conclusion

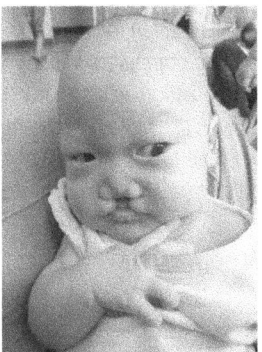

Plenty to think about.

Hopefully the information in this chapter has given you an idea of the thought process that will help you make an informed decision about where exactly you want to go to volunteer. No matter how well prepared you are, it is still possible that things do not work out for some reason, or that you will end up disappointed. Unfortunately, no one can guarantee against that. However, if you spend some time really considering the issues that were brought up here, it should help **decrease** the chance of disappointment. In the end, the aim is to make sure you have an enjoyable volunteering experience and that the children will be able to benefit from it.

"It may not be to everyone's liking to volunteer in a place out of their comfort zone, but if anyone has an inclination I'd say try it, but make sure you can be of service to the organisation. Whatever skills you have it will be greatly appreciated and go a long way. It's amazing what you learn."

Chapter 2: Practical Preparation

What to Bring

You will probably have an idea of what you need to pack in general by way of clothes and basic necessities, but there are a couple of things to take into consideration. Because you will be volunteering amongst lots of dirty children's hands, in places that might be very dusty or dirty, and because you may find yourself having

Near the equator, forgetting your sunscreen even just once, like here, has serious results.

to hand wash your clothes (something that is quite hard on them), you may want to consider leaving your spotless white clothes, your favourite shirt and your delicate materials at home. In other words, please only bring clothes that you will not get upset about if it turns out that you are no longer able to wear them after your trip.

Using the travel guides mentioned before (see 'Appendix' at the end of the manual for a list) or by looking it up online, you can find out what kind of climate to expect in the country you are traveling to and, more specifically, what kind of weather you can expect in the period that you will be there. This will help you make a decision on what to bring and what to leave at home. These guides will generally also give you some information about what kind of clothing is suitable in order to avoid giving offence or getting into trouble. More information about this can be found in the next chapter: Part 1, Chapter 3: 'Cultural Preparations'.

In places where it is very hot and sunny – particularly in places close to the equator where the sun is very intense – it is important to protect yourself against very serious sunburn (particularly if you are light-skinned) and heat exhaustion. To do this, you need to bring a lot of high factor sunscreen and something to cover your head with when you are in the full sun.

> "I ran out of sunscreen and had to buy more. There was no problem finding sunscreen in the supermarket, but almost all sunscreen that I could find contained skin-whitener. For someone like me, with skin so white and unable to tan that it is more of a handicap than a skin-tone, skin-whitener was the last thing I needed."

At temperatures above 32°C, you generally get more protection and coolness from wearing loose fitting clothes of natural fibres that cover you completely than from short, tight fitting clothes. Particularly, clothes made of synthetic materials can become intolerably sweaty very quickly.

Cold conditions require their own kind of protection, especially because heating may not always be reliable.

If you are volunteering in a place where it can get very cold, on the other hand, you need to make sure you have suitable clothes with you to stay warm enough, especially during the cold time of the year. Combining various layers of clothing is usually an effective way of keeping warm. It gives the possibility to **regulate** your temperature by adding or taking away layers. This is also effective in situations where the temperature varies a lot. In some places, particularly in dry desert places with clear skies, temperatures can fluctuate enormously within the space of 24 hours. It might be very hot in the afternoon, while at night the temperature may drop to freezing.

In places where malaria and dengue fever frequently occur, you will need to bring mosquito repellent that contains DEET to minimize the chance of getting bitten. At the moment, vaccinations for dengue fever and malaria do not exist yet. To prevent malaria, there are tablets you can take to reduce the chance of getting infected. This will be discussed later in this chapter, under 'Vaccinations and Medication'.

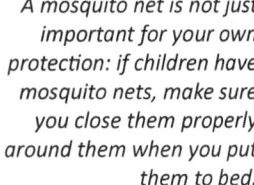

A mosquito net is not just important for your own protection: if children have mosquito nets, make sure you close them properly around them when you put them to bed.

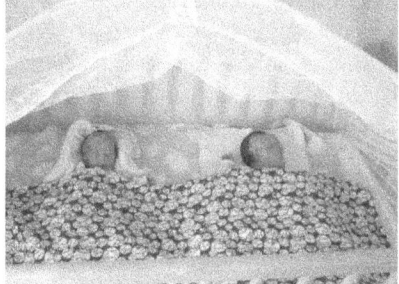

There is no shame – and indeed a lot of wisdom – in asking your contact person at the children's home or at the volunteer organisation if there are any things that they would advise you to bring, because it might be hard to get them where you are going. However, be aware that people from another country will give you advice based on what they would need when going abroad; they may not be aware of everything you are used to having around in your daily life and that you might struggle to do without.

Bring What You Cannot Do Without

So, aside from asking people who know more about what you can and cannot expect to be available where you are going, you need to ask yourself: 'What do I really need?'. This question should be looked at from two sides:

1. You need to identify what you cannot do without, because you should bring it, so that you do not get caught without the essentials.
2. When you have identified what you cannot do without, you will realise that although you are used to the comfort of having a lot of other things in your home life, you should not bring things that you do not absolutely need. You will find out soon enough that even if you only pack essentials, it will be a struggle to stay within the limits for baggage weight and size.

> A young woman went to rural Indonesia for several months. Half her suitcase was filled with what she considered to be essential electrical devices, such as a hair dryer, hair straightener and eyelash curler. On arrival she found little use, and indeed little electricity, for these items.

Things to think of when determining what you cannot do without:

- Medication: if you are on any medication, you should talk to your doctor about getting a prescription for the entire time you are going to be away and you should take the medication to make sure you will have what you need. For some medication, it is not possible or safe to buy it in large quantities or to keep it for a long time. You should discuss this with your doctor and see if a solution can be found. It can also be a good idea to bring a back-up prescription with you, in case anything should happen to your medication while you are there. **Oral** contraceptives should be on the list of medications; you do not want to get stuck without these. Other contraceptives, such as condoms, should also be considered. Even though you may not be planning on having any adventures, it is better to be safe than sorry. When you travel, make sure that you carry medication for at least a couple of days in your hand luggage, in case your checked baggage does not arrive on time.

It is amazing how quickly things start to add up. And I travel a lot lighter than most!

- Foods: Some people really struggle to do without certain kinds of foods and drinks. Of course, it depends on what it is whether you can take it with you or not. Rib eyed steaks do not travel or keep well, but things like peanut butter, sweets or coffee might fit in your baggage and may help you at moments when you really long for a reminder of home.
- Electrical Aids: In many countries it is a good idea to have a surge protector to place between the electrical socket and any equipment you plug in. This is because with frequent power cuts generally come power surges too, which can destroy any electrical product directly connected to the grid. The surge protec-

Surge protector and plug convertors.

tor will cut off the power in your cable, before it reaches your equipment in the event of a power surge. Often, you will need converter plugs to be able to plug your leads into the local power sockets. It is also a good idea to check what the normal voltage is in the country where you are going. Plugging an electrical device made for 110V into a 240V grid will destroy it. In this case, you will need a current converter to prevent problems. Make sure you bring a charger for everything that needs one (phones, laptops, cameras etc.).

- Electrical Devices: While in the first instance you might think that the list of electrical devices you cannot do without is very long, if you are honest, there is quite a lot you *can* do without. Particularly when it comes to things like hair straighteners, hair curlers, hair blowers, trouser presses, etc. There are few people who would not survive without these items. In practice, you will usually be using them a lot less than you normally would at home, anyway. This is because the people around you are unlikely to be using devices like that, because power might not be available, or because your equipment might be too demanding on the power grid and might blow the fuse every time you plug it in, to name a couple of reasons.

- Toiletries: just like with the electrical devices, you can usually do with a lot less than you think you can. The things you do really need you should bring along, because you might not be able to get them where you are going – sanitary products for example. When you realise the weight of what you have accumulated, you might start to find it easier to eliminate some things. Something to keep in mind: if you go to a very hot climate, you are going to sweat. There is no way around it, and all the deodorant in the world is not going to change that (and if it did really stop you sweating completely, you would end up in hospital pretty quickly, because the sweating serves an important regulating function). You can still bring deodorant, but just know that you will need to accept that sweating will happen and that people around you will not judge you for it, because it happens to everyone when you are in a place like that.

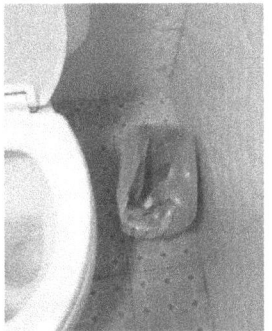

Toilet paper goes in the bin, not in the toilet.

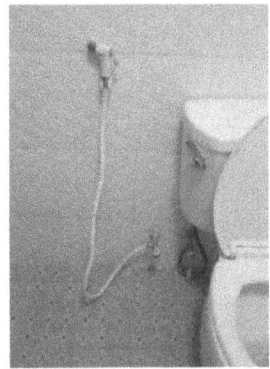

In some countries, water is used to clean yourself up instead of toilet paper.

Chapter 2: Practical Preparation

It is usually a good idea to bring a good supply of tissues with you. In most countries, most public toilets do not provide toilet paper. So, if you do not want to be caught short, you need to bring your own supply. Another bit of toilet information that somehow rarely gets mentioned, but which is very important, is that pretty much anywhere outside of the very richest countries the plumbing systems are not able to cope with toilet paper. So, please, DO NOT throw toilet paper into the toilet, it will lead to clogging up the system. In most places a basket or bin will be placed near the toilet where you can drop your toilet paper.

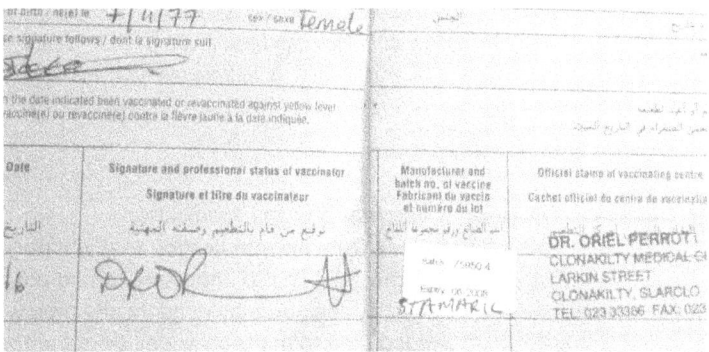

For some countries, even proof of yellow fever vaccination is needed in order to get a visa.

- Documents: Of course you will need your passport, with a visa if needed, and your plane tickets. It is a good idea to keep a sheet with the booking confirmation of your flight with you for the flight back, as it is not always possible to check in online, to print out a boarding pass or to check in by just handing over your passport. In fact, in some countries you will only be allowed into the airport after you have shown your flight reservations. It is also a good idea to have a few copies of the picture page and of the relevant visa page of your passport. You can carry these around with you instead of your passport in situations where you think the risk of losing your passport is high. You sometimes also need to be able to hand copies over when you get caught up in bureaucratic issues of some sort. If you have been vaccinated, it is often a good idea to bring the booklet in which the information about the vaccinations (dates and so on) have been registered. Some countries want to see proof of a yellow fever vaccination before they let you into the country. If you have to get your visa at the airport on arrival, you may also be required to hand over certain documents. You need to check what these are online, before you travel. You can ask your volunteer organisation or your contact person at the children's home if there are other documents that you should have with you in certain situations. If you are a student, bringing your student card can get you discounts in certain touristic places . It is generally a good idea to bring a copy of

45

the details of your travel insurance, in case you need the information.

"Armed with my passport and the reservation code for my flight home I arrived at the airport. There was a queue to get to the door into the airport. When I got the front of the queue I was asked for my passport and flight reservation. The reservation number was not accepted and I was told I would have to go get a print out from the airline, at one of the windows. I spent about half an hour walking around – with my 20kg hiker on my back – looking for a window with the logo of my airline, without luck. I asked somewhere and was sent back and forth a few times, until someone was finally able to give me a slip and I could join the back of the queue again. I sweated hard, during those 45 minutes, both from the heat and from fear that I might not make my flight."

Vaccinations and Medication

Aside from any medication that you normally take and should have with you, it is also important to find out about any vaccinations and medication you may need for the area where you are going. It is a good idea to make an appointment with your doctor or at a specialised travel clinic at least six weeks before you plan to travel, to get advice on what you need. The reason that this needs to be done at least six weeks in advance is that some vaccinations need to be repeated before you go to make sure they will be effective, and some vaccinations need time to really become effective in your body.

Whether or not you need vaccinations and what kind of vaccinations you will need depend entirely on where you are going and what kind of vaccinations you have already had in your life. Even if you have already had certain vaccinations, if it has been a long time since the last vaccination, you may need a booster to make sure the **antibodies** are still active in your body. The diseases you commonly need to be vaccinated for are:

- Hepatitis A
- Hepatitis B
- Yellow fever (some countries want to see proof of yellow fever vaccination before they let you into the country after you've visited a country where yellow fever is endemic)
- Typhus
- Diphtheria
- Tetanus
- Polio
- Cholera
- Rabies
- Abdominal typhoid

Chapter 2: Practical Preparation

Some of the vaccinations I've accumulated over the years.

If you were not vaccinated for measles and chickenpox when you were a child and you have not had these illnesses yet, it might be worth considering getting vaccinated for these too. In many children's homes, the children have not been vaccinated against these illnesses, which means that there is always a possibility that an outbreak will take place while you are there. Adults tend to get much more seriously ill with these diseases than children do. Also, particularly if you plan on spending time in more than one children's home, being vaccinated eliminates the risk of you spreading these illnesses between different locations. Even if you only go to one children's home, but you also spend time out in the community or with children of friends, you might communicate these illnesses in either direction if one of the children on either end gets the illness and you are not immune to it yet.

"Before the first time I went volunteering I had to get a total for nine shots over four weeks to get me up to date. After that is has only been the occasional booster."

In some countries you will also need to take malaria prophylaxis You can buy these at a travel clinic or from your doctor. These are pills that help prevent you from getting malaria even if you are bitten by a mosquito carrying malaria. Malaria is an illness that is very serious. There is no cure for it. While the fever episodes can be controlled by medication, the illness stays in your blood for life and at times when your **immune system** is weakened – for example by exhaustion or stress – you will get sick with it again. It is a disease that can kill if you do not have access to the correct medication to control the high fever it causes. So protecting yourself from getting malaria is very important. Not all tropical countries have malaria going around, and sometimes if you only stay in high areas within a country where malaria does occur, the risk is not very high, but this is something that

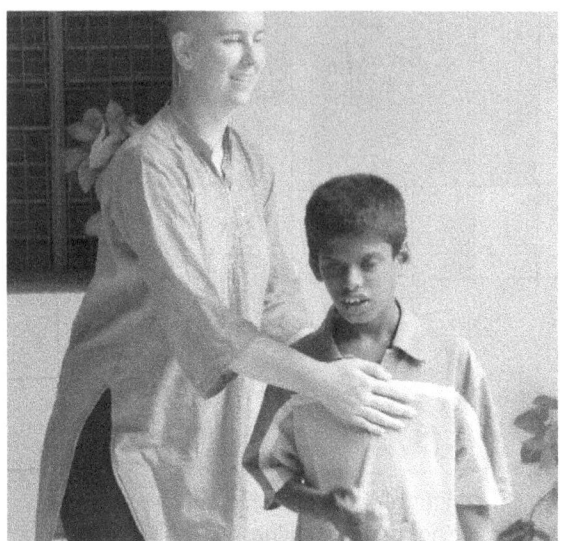

Loose fitting long clothing is pretty effective against being bitten.

you need to check with an expert. You need to check this every time you travel, because sometimes there are changes or new outbreaks, meaning that for an area where previously the risk was low, now you do need prophylaxis. It is also possible for malaria in a certain region to become resistant to a particular malaria medication, so you may need to take a different kind of prophylaxis from the one you used before. In some cases, especially if you are going for six months or more, a doctor may feel it is safer to give you medication to take at the first symptoms of malaria, rather than having you take the medication preventively for so long.

If you are infected with malaria, it can be many, many years before you get sick with it for the first time. It can stay alive, dormant in your body, for a long time. Dengue fever on the other hand, has an incubation time of only four days. So if you have not gotten sick by day five after you left the area, you know that you got away without dengue fever. Dengue fever is also a very serious illness that can in some cases be fatal. Like malaria, there is no cure for dengue fever, you can only treat the symptoms. And unlike malaria, there is no medication that can protect you from getting dengue fever.

Even when you are taking malaria prophylaxis, it is important to take every precaution against getting bitten by mosquitoes. The two main reasons for this are that 1) while malaria prophylaxis are very effective, there is no 100% guarantee that you will not get malaria, even when you take it and 2) in almost all regions where mosquitoes carry malaria, there are also mosquitoes carrying dengue fever.

You can protect yourself from mosquito bites, which in the best case are annoying and itchy and in the worst case can land you with serious illnesses like malaria and dengue fever, by covering yourself with loose clothing – when you wear tight clothing, they may bite right through the fabric. Your chance of being bitten is smaller if you cover more of your skin. Using mosquito repellent that contains DEET is also a good idea. DEET is a very strong chemical that is very effective in repelling mosquitoes. However, if you are pregnant or breastfeeding or if you are looking for an insect repellent to use on a child, you need to get information on whether or not it is safe to use a repellent containing DEET. Generally speaking, it is recommended to use a repellent with a lower percentage of DEET in these cases. When you use mosquito repellent and you happen to be wearing a skirt – even if the skirt goes all the way down to the floor – you need to cover your entire legs with repellent, otherwise you might still get bitten. You should also check with your doctor whether insect repellent containing DEET might interact with any medication you regularly need to take.

There are other things you can bring to prevent mosquito bites. A mosquito net, preferably one that has been treated with insecticide – something that kills insects –, is one of them. Sleeping under a mosquito net – one that is properly tucked in under your bedding and does not have mosquitoes trapped on the inside – provides good protection against bites and may also help you sleep more peacefully. Mosquitoes do not only bite at night; in fact the ones causing diseases often bite during the daytime. So choice of clothing is relevant here too. In other words, wearing long loose sleeves and trousers can help prevent mosquito bites.

Having an Emergency Plan

The hope is, of course, that your trip will go smoothly, without any accidents, and that you will stay healthy and happy. While this is often the case, unfortunately it is not something that can be guaranteed. Just like when you are at home, it is always possible for you to fall ill, for an accident to happen or for someone to steal your valuables. Because you will be in a very different part of the world, your chances of falling ill are higher than at home because you have no defence against the bacteria and viruses that go around – simply through lack of previous exposure to them – and because you are unfamiliar with the food and your digestive system needs to adjust to it, which may make you feel unwell for a few days.

Crazy traffic is one of those things that may get you into trouble, no matter how hard you try to be safe.

One important preparation is to make sure you have travel insurance to cover your costs if anything happens. Things you should have with you at all times are: copies of all your important documents, contact details for your insurance, for your local embassy and for your contact person at the children's home – if you work through a volunteer organisation, for your local contact person of that organisation too. Do not keep this information just in your wallet or in your phone, because if you do, it will be gone if those get stolen – in other words, when you most need it. Make sure you store the documents in different places. Having this information on you at all times will also be helpful in the unlikely case of you getting into an accident and being unable to tell people who you are. They will be able to call the local numbers, and someone you know will be informed of what has happened.

In some places, you will be more of a target for theft than you would be at home, because, coming from a 'rich country', you are designated 'rich' by default. And in a way, that assessment is not wrong. Even if you are only a student who at home is struggling to get by, when you convert your money into the local currency, you can be considered wealthy. The MP3 player, laptop and mobile phone that you consider to be old and outdated are out of reach for many of the local people around you. The quality of your clothes, though possibly looked down on at home, represents wealth here. So the 'rich' label is simply a relative thing. Because of that, especially when you are moving around in busy places in big cities, you should not carry anything of value that you do not absolutely need, and only the amount of cash that you expect to spend, because you are likely to be targeted by thieves.

> In China, an American college student from New York City was volunteering in a children's home. She had travelled into the centre of Beijing and came back saying that she had been very nervous using the metro system, constantly afraid that she would be robbed. I was quite surprised by this. The Beijing metro system is one of the safest I've travelled on, and then this fear from someone who is used to travelling on the metro in New York City, where there are lots of pickpockets?

It is a good idea to put some thought into the risks you may encounter, and what you can do to minimize them, without getting yourself more worried or panicked than there is a reason to be.

It is also important to let your contact person at the children's home know whom they should contact for you at home in case anything should happen to you. And people at home should not only be given your local telephone number to be able to contact you directly, but also a way to contact the children's home or your host family, in case they urgently need to contact you but are unable to get hold of you.

Making sure you bring any medication you need has already been mentioned. However, what is often overlooked is letting someone at the children's home know if you have a serious medical condition. If there is a chance that you will become seriously unwell and may need urgent medical attention, it is essential that someone has this information. If there is a chance that you may lose consciousness and will not be able to give doctors the necessary information, you need to make sure that someone has this information to pass on for you. If you do not do this, you could be putting your health and even your life at serious risk.

Within a week of arriving, a volunteer got diarrhoea and started vomiting. She was unable to keep anything in her stomach, even water came back out. After three rounds of vomiting she asked to be taken to the hospital. Another volunteer went with her. In the taxi the girl who was sick handed the volunteer who went with her a vial of medicine and a syringe and told her: 'If I lose consciousness, make sure they give me this'. That was the first anyone had heard about her needing to have a certain kind of medication in her system at all times.

This is also relevant when you have severe allergies and carry an Epipen. You need to make people around you aware of your allergy and of the fact that you have the pen, so that they can help you in case of trouble. Using your common sense is always the most important part of staying safe.

Chapter 3: Cultural Preparations

When you go to another country, no matter whether it borders on the country you are from or whether it is on the other side of the world, you will discover that people have different ways of

doing things, different beliefs and different social rules. These are cultural differences. Culture is the foundation of how someone feels the world and the people in it should exist and interact. Culture is something that is very important in all of our lives, but that is almost invisible. For the most part, people are not aware of their own culture until they are confronted with people who have a different culture and a different way of doing things. Until that moment, your own culture seems to you to be the only logical, reasonable way to do things

Life here is different from the one you know; it's up to you whether you want to make adjustments to fit in.

and to think about them. However, culture and cultural rules are not universal, and people are not born with them. They are rules and ways of thinking that have developed by a general agreement over time and that keep on developing to adapt, as well as possible, to the living circumstances that a group of people is confronted with. These rules and ways of thinking are taught to children as they grow up within a specific culture.

"For example, the different working style, sense of time, communication and importance of honouring guests. I was shocked by the social system of hierarchy and castes, the unbelievable amount of religious festivals and the rancidity around me in the streets. I think that I can conclude that the longer I stayed in India, the less I understood of the culture because it has so many different sides..."

Especially if it is your first time visiting another country, it can come as quite a shock to discover that people have very different ways of doing things and different expectations of how people should act. This is appropriately named 'culture shock'. Some people react to this shock by becoming very determined that their own way of doing things is the only right way, and that what is happening around them is primitive. Unfortunately, if this is your response, you are not likely to make much contact with the people around you. It will make you feel very isolated. So, making an effort to learn a little bit about the rules of the culture you are visiting and doing your best to adapt to them may really help you connect to the people around you, and maybe make new friends in the process.

"You can't prepare for visiting a country like India, it's all about embracing it when you get there as nothing is ever how you imagine it."

 Do I Have to?

The choice is up to you, of course. But as mentioned just now, if you choose not to adapt to local customs at all, you are likely to isolate yourself very much. This will make working together with your colleagues at the children's home much harder. You are more likely to be excluded, less likely to receive the guidance that you need to become part of the whole, and will feel lonely. If the caregivers are distant or hostile toward you, their example will be noticed by the children. So your relationship with the children may also be more difficult than it might be if you open up to their culture.

"Don't be insulted by how different the culture is."

Volunteers enjoy learning to make 'jaozi', a dish traditionally eaten at Chinese New Year.

Of course, no one expects you to fully assimilate everything that is expected locally. People are going to go easy on you because you are a foreigner. Most people will realise that you have no way of knowing all the cultural rules they take for granted in daily life. The way you transgress social rules may at times be a source of amusement to them. Please do not take offense when this happens. If they laugh at a mistake you have made, it is usually done in a friendly way, and not in an attempt to embarrass you. Remember that it is always better that they have a laugh at a foreigner making a mistake, than for them to become seriously offended, which would probably be the case if, for example, their neighbour would have done the same thing. Generally, just seeing that you are making attempts at following the rules that you are aware of, people will appreciate your efforts and forgive your mistakes.

"I would say that the vast majority of people positively appreciated that we dressed and looked different, but there were a few negative looks when some of us were flashing our cameras and phones about."

You can also look at it from the other side. If you do not feel it worth learning how to behave correctly so that the people around you will accept you more easily, it might still be worth looking into how you can expect other people to behave towards you. When you do not know anything about the culture of the people you are visiting, you may be surprised or even shocked by the way people act, even though they are only trying to welcome you warmly, in the way their traditions demand. Not knowing anything about the correct way to interact with other people in the country you are volunteering in can also lead to very serious miscommunication, which can lead to annoying problems.

Another reason to do your best to learn about the local rules of **propriety** is to make sure you are seen in a positive way. There are certain things in certain cultures that are considered so offensive or disgusting that it is very hard not to awaken an image that the person doing them is in some way disgusting or bad. This is an image you certainly want to avoid.

Eating with just your right hand.

For example, in most countries where people eat with their 'hands', they actually only eat with one hand. In these cultures it is only acceptable to eat with your right hand, because the left hand is supposed to be used to clean yourself in the toilet. So, bringing food to your mouth with your left hand is really stomach-turning to watch for them, and you can imagine what it would make people think of you.

Even when the people around you are willing to make allowances for your ignorance, you can see how something like this is hard to ignore in your mind. Imagine a foreigner visiting your country, and naively, but **consistently**, greeting you by sticking out his middle finger at you. Even when you keep in mind that the person does not know that this if offensive to you, it would make you feel very uncomfortable.

"I would also strongly educate young adults, especially women, if they want to volunteer in third world countries to be fully aware and become educated of the possible dangers of volunteering in countries with different attitudes and treatment of women."

Certain **transgressions** of social and cultural rules are not just embarrassing or potentially offensive. If you are not in any way aware of the cultural rules, or you choose not to adjust your behaviour to them, you may be giving out signals that can be misinterpreted and can even put you in danger. This is particularly true with regards to rules about interactions between the sexes, and the danger is greatest if you are a woman. You may not agree with the way women are treated in a certain country, or find the strict separation between men and women there ridiculous or offensive. However, if this is the case, I would advise you not to go to the country rather than to go there and disregard the rules, or to 'make them see how it should be done'. Because that will cause great offense and might end up with you being kicked out of the children's home you are volunteering in. It can even put you at extreme risk of sexual assault or rape. I personally do not think there is any situation in which anyone has the right to sexually assault or rape another person. However, I do want to point out that in some countries the only women who would *ever* make any kind of physical contact with a man who is not a close relative or a husband (or even sit next to him on a sofa), are prostitutes. So in these situations, as a woman, even shaking a man's hand can give an unintended message. And while women certainly bear a greater risk when it comes to crossing the boundaries between the sexes, men should be mindful of those boundaries too. Because, as a man, touching or moving to shake hands with a woman may not only make her recoil from you, but in some places you may be faced with her angry, and possibly aggressive, male relatives over a transgression like this.

"I didn't receive many looks for dressing differently, but I think the girls did, a lot of Indians also took pictures of us, which I wasn't too happy about."

Another example of possible serious dangers lying ahead if you are not informed about a certain culture's views and do not take some precautions to adjust, is the subject of homosexuality. In quite a lot of countries, it is outright dangerous to be open about the fact that you are gay. In some places, there are laws that can lead to imprisonment and in rare cases even execution. But in some places, where there is no law against homosexuality, the prejudice against it among the population is so strong that you might risk being violently attacked or stoned in the street if it becomes known that you are gay. It is not uncommon for homosexuality to be seen as being the same as paedophilia (people who have sex with children) in places where there is not much education on the subject. If it becomes known you are gay, in many places you can expect to be kicked out of the children's home you are volunteering in at the very, very least. So while of course you have every right to be open about your sexuality, you may want to consider whether it is worth, quite literally, risking your life for.

Something that is important to take into account when deciding whether or not you want to go through the trouble of learning about the culture that you will be visiting, is that you are not just planning to go on a holiday, stay in a hotel and remain separated from the local population. You are traveling to do volunteer work. And not volunteer work with trees or bricks, but with children.

Working in a children's home, you do not only have to take into account a good working relationship with the caregivers and management, you have to be aware that you are also there as a role model for the children. In Part 2, Chapter 2: 'Work Ethic', I will give some more information about how big the impact of any adult working with children is, in a general sense. However, here I want to point out that this impact is important in a cultural sense too. The children in the children's home you will be volunteering in have their own cultural background and they need to learn to act **appropriately** in their own culture. There is usually enough of a stigma on being an orphan or abandoned child, without adding more negative perceptions because the child does not behave appropriately according to cultural and social norms. So, if not for yourself or your colleagues, please consider making the effort for the children.

Find out About the Culture You Visit

If you have decided to make the effort to learn more about the culture you are about to visit and the social rules that are used there, how do you get the information?

The first and most readily available source of information is once again travel guides, a list of which can be found on the 'Appendix' page at the end of the manual. The better quality travel guides usually include some information about local customs, particularly the ones that you are likely to come across in daily life and that are most different from the way things are done in rich countries. The internet can also provide valuable information, but make sure that you always check how reliable the sources you are using are.

As a volunteer, you have a different role than you do as a tourist.

If you decide to do a language course – either in the form of classes or by yourself using books and audio media – this is likely to include some cultural aspects too. Things pointing towards correct cultural behaviour that are automatically included in language courses, are things like the proper way to greet other people, how to apologize or draw someone's attention, and ways to indicate respect for the person you are speaking to. A language course may also point out topics of conversation that are taboo, either in general or between people of different genders or of different generations.

Chapter 3: Cultural Preparations

Some cultural rules explained at the start of a language course:

'Every culture has its set of conventional signs and gestures that show respect or cause offense. Things to remember in Burma:

- *Treat older people and Buddhist monks with respect. Also Buddha images and other religious objects.*
- *Don't tower over people senior to yourself: lower your head a little if you have to pass close in front of them.*
- *Don't point your feet towards a senior person.*
- *Don't touch people on the head.*
- *Behave modestly: don't wear revealing clothing, and avoid hugging and kissing in public.*
- *Use both hands to hand something to a person senior to yourself, and to receive something from them.*
- *Take off shoes and socks before entering a house or the grounds of a monastery or pagoda.*
- *Keep calm and courteous in all situations.'*

What is expected and what is appropriate may not be the same thing. In some countries the expectation may be that a white woman will have sex with any man she comes across. The expectation has been created by incomplete information coming from media like Hollywood movies in combination with a different cultural idea about appropriate clothing and interaction between the sexes. The expectation that 'white women are all prostitutes' does not mean that appropriate behaviour is in line with that expectation. In fact, appropriate behaviour in countries where this is the case most likely will consist of dressing modestly and holding back in all interactions with the other sex.

It helps to know what is expected of you. Once you know that, you can still decide to adjust or not.

If you know people who are from, or who have lived in the country that you will be visiting, they may be happy to help you out by explaining things about the culture, what kind of behaviour will be expected from you and what is most appropriate.

When talking to people who know something about the country you are going to, it is important to keep in mind that not everything everyone tells you might be entirely true or relevant to your situation. Certain ideas may be based more on prejudices than on truths, or someone may be afraid to offend you by telling is the truth about the way things are. Generally speaking, someone who has grown up in the country, someone who sees the country's culture as their own, will have the most complete and truthful knowledge, though they may not always be able to explain it very clearly, if only because to them it is obvious that their way is *the* way to do things.

If only there was a simple manual you could use!

If you get your information from a foreigner who has lived in the country for a long period of time, this person may be more aware of the things that you need to know and are likely to do wrong, because they may have faced the same obstacles that you are heading for. However, here again it is important to find out a little bit about the person who is giving you the information. Just having been inside a specific country does not make them an expert. Even if they were in the country for many years, if they have spent most of that time for example living in an expat-community, working in an international company, they may not have come into contact with the local culture all that much, while a person who has lived among the local population, who has shared their houses, meals and friendships can be an invaluable source of advice and information.

You can also ask people at the children's home where you will be volunteering for information that they think is important for you to have before you travel, to help you prepare. And when you are there, you can encourage them to point out things that you do that might cause offense or confusion. Once you have arrived, it is also helpful to simply observe the way things are done and keep an open mind. Some things may seem strange or downright silly at first, but often if you adjust your behaviour to the way people around you do things, you will find that communication becomes a lot easier.

"It took me some time to figure out what the Indian sideways head-wiggle meant. At first, it seemed like no one would give me an answer. Then I realised that it was an affirmative or positive response that did serve as an answer. Having gotten this far, I was still nodding my head to indicate 'yes' myself, which often led to blank stares and the repeating of the question. When I eventually learned to do the head-wiggle myself, communication became much easier."

If you are volunteering through an international volunteer organisation, the organisation is likely to organise a kind of introduction course, which will hopefully provide some essential information about important differences in proper behaviour between what you are used to and what will be expected in the country that you will be visiting.

Learn Some of the Language

Generally speaking, a children's home that takes in foreign volunteers will have at least one staff member who has conversational English. More than likely, this is the person whom you will be communicating with if you make your own arrangements. In most countries that have at some point been colonised, most well-educated people will be proficient in the language of the former colonist – usually English, French or Spanish, and sometimes Portuguese or German – and in many countries across the world these days, university students and some secondary school students are learning a little English. This means that there is a decent chance that whatever the official national language of the country is, the head of the children's home may speak a reasonable amount of English (or one of the other languages mentioned). Having at least one person there you can communicate with is definitely helpful, but it is no guarantee that anyone else there speaks anything else than the local language. Knowing that there is someone who speaks English (or another language you share), it may not seem like a very high priority to learn the local language, because during the preparations you were getting by just fine.

There is a large range of language courses to choose from if you want to make an attempt at learning some of the language.

"I found it an obstacle that I couldn't connect that easily with some children or staff because we were not speaking the same language. For example, when there was a conflict [...] I was not always able to solve it because the children couldn't explain their feelings in English and I couldn't talk with them in Marathi."

However, it is important to remember that having *someone* there who speaks English (or French etc.) is not the same as having everyone – or most people – there speak those languages. In practice, caregivers in children's home are usually lower class or lower middle class women, who have had little or no education. They are very unlikely to speak anything other than their mother tongue, and if you want to communicate with them that is the language you will need to use. Even if you have taken the trouble to learn the official national language, you may find that caregivers do not speak much of that. They may mostly speak the local dialect. The same goes for the children. Though some of them may eventually learn foreign languages, in school or from a succession of foreign volunteers, they are generally still in the early stages of learning and if you wish to talk to children aged three and over, you will have more success using their language, even if only in a broken fashion, than in using your own. If you are only going to be dealing with babies, then you are of course not likely to have a lot of language issues with them.

In one children's home, I was asked to help a nine-year-old boy with his English, because he would be adopted by an American family soon. He already had quite a large vocabulary, taught to him by previous volunteers. However, I discovered that while he had a lot of English nouns, unconjugated verbs, colours and numbers, he was unable to put a sentence together. He had been given lots of 'bricks', but no 'mortar' to put them together with.

Even being able to use a few basic words or phrases, such as 'hello', 'thank you' and 'yes' and 'no' can help create an enormous amount of goodwill towards you. It is an indication that you are interested in sharing their life and that you are willing to make an effort to be able to communicate with them. The mistakes you will inevitably make can at times cause amusement, which in turn can serve as an effective way to break the ice and become closer, having shared a laugh about your attempts at speaking the language.

In India, in one of the children's homes I regularly visit, my limited ability to speak the local language was a major source of entertainment among the children. A group of older children would come over, giggling and pushing each other. In their own language they would whisper loudly: Ask her if she has eaten! After some shoving and retreating, one of them would come forward and ask 'Have you eaten?' and I would answer 'I have eaten' or 'I have not eaten' depending on the situation. This was met with a gale of laughter and kids repeating 'She said "I have eaten"!' After this ice-breaker they would ask me other questions, to get to know more about me, some of which I would understand and some of which I would not. In any case, the next time these particular children would see me, they were less shy about talking to me.

Chapter 3: Cultural Preparations

Learning a new language is always daunting. Particularly if you have never learned a language other than your mother tongue. It is intimidating to see all those words that seem to make no sense, even more so if the language uses a different script from the Latin alphabet you are used to. So when you start learning a new language, here are a few things to keep in mind, to help make the experience easier and more fun.

Tips for learning a new language:

If you refuse to try to use a completely foreign language until you are fluent, you may as well give up now.

- Do not aim for fluency: it is helpful to set yourself small, manageable goals. As you reach those goals, you can move the goal posts when you feel comfortable doing so. Your overall aim should be to become able to bring the meaning of what you want to say across to the people you work with and to understand the essence of what they are saying. That is much more important, useful and attainable than aiming for flawless grammar and elegant turn of phrase. You will be surprised how effectively you will be able to communicate having just a few commonly used words in combination with pointing and gestures. Suggestions for goals:
  o First goal: learn to say and recognise some of the most commonly used words and expressions such as 'yes', 'no', 'he', 'she', 'thank you', 'hello', 'how do you say xxx' and 'I do not understand'.
  o Second goal: learn some nouns and verbs that are most relevant to what you are doing, such as 'boy', 'girl', 'age', 'child', 'bed', 'food', 'milk', 'nappy', 'name', 'to eat', 'to sleep', 'to cry', 'to play', 'to sit' and counting up to 20.
  o Third goal: start to put the words you know in sentence-like structures, and continue to add new words to your **vocabulary.**
  o Fourth and further goals: continue to build on what you have, gradually making your use of the language more correct and nuanced.

If you are very lucky, you may find someone (a colleague or a child) who is somehow on the same wavelength as you and who seems to instinctively understand your meaning, no matter how badly you express yourself. This can be invaluable, because a person like this is usually an excellent teacher, and because they can serve as your interpreter. In my early days in China, I had a colleague like that. I would make a suggestion for making one of the children more comfortable in extremely awkward Chinese and she would then pass on the message in real Chinese to the other caregivers. It helped my communi-

cation to have it passed on like this, and also gave me the chance to hear how I should have formulated what I wanted to say.

- Do not be afraid to make mistakes: if you are afraid to embarrass yourself by making mistakes when you speak a new language, you will end up not saying anything and therefore not learning the language. The only way to learn is to use it and improve as you go. When you start using a new language, you are guaranteed to make mistakes. It is part of the learning process. But the people around you will know that too, and although they may sometimes laugh at the funny outcome of what you say, they are likely to be understanding and supportive, rather than making fun of you.

Someone who was learning to speak Danish wanted to ask someone he met if he had any children. He almost got the question right, only he added one letter and ended up asking his new friend if he had any bears.

- Do not put too much weight on learning the whole language before you go: studying with a book or taking a class to learn a language before your volunteering adventure starts can be helpful to start getting a feel for the language. It can help you understand some basic principles and you can memorize some important phrases.

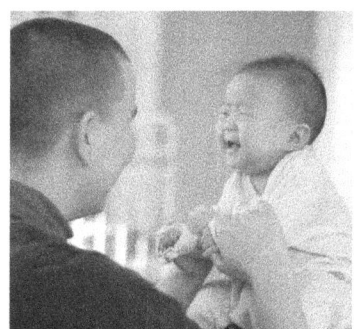

Even with broken language, you can still make intense contact.

However, in practice, the real language learning starts when you are in the country. It is much easier to learn a language when you hear it around you day and night and when you have no choice but to make attempts to use it, because you have no other way of communicating with people.

"I've found the kids take great delight in trying to teach me. This makes the roles reversed and not only empowers them when I get it right, but provides hours of mirth when I get it wrong."

- Remember that other people will almost always consider your language **skills** better than you consider them to be. It does not matter whether you are only able to say a few words or you are starting to approach fluency, you are almost certain to always feel that your grasp of the language still leaves a lot to desired, while other people continuously compliment you on your excellent use of the language. I believe that this discrepancy probably comes from the fact that the people you talk to are able to understand your meaning and therefore presume that you are communicating what you want to say, while in your head you are constantly rejecting topics of conversation or trying to find other ways to say things, because you cannot find the words to say what you would really like to say. This is a hidden process. It happens before you even open your mouth, so outsiders do not see this struggle and are just impressed with what comes out, without comparing it to what might have come out.

Having made a point of always learning as much of the local language of any place I work in as possible, I have now accumulated quite a list. Two languages in which I am fluent, six languages in which I am proficient (so able to have decent conversations, using whole sentences, but not very nuanced) and a further five or six that I only have basic knowledge of (meaning that I am often able to get my meaning across, but not to hold a real conversation and only using loose words and broken sentences). Yet with all of these languages I am often told that I am fluent or almost fluent by people that I work with.

A final little note on language, which is relevant to the children's well-being: There is absolutely nothing wrong with speaking to babies and children in a foreign language. However, for children up to six years old, it is quite important that one person does not switch between languages. So up to that age, you have to choose either to using your own language, or to use whatever you are able to of the children's language, but not go back and forth between the two. Up to age six, children generally do not have a very clear awareness of distinction between different languages. They are still gathering their vocabulary and to some extent listen more to your intention and tone than to the meaning of your words. To them it makes very little difference whether a new word or sentence comes in English, Kiswahili, French or Farsi, they will just add it to the store. If one person mixes languages however, this blurs the lines between different languages for them: it makes it seem to them like it is alright to mix up languages. While as long as the one-person-one-language rule is followed, this helps the child to discover the distinctions between the languages. So choose a language and stick to it when you are talking to the children.

Choose Appropriate Clothes

Clothing is something that is worth putting some thought into. How much thought is needed on this subject is very much dependent on the country you are going to and the cultural norms that they hold there. In some countries you can dress exactly as you are used to at home without anyone minding. Particularly in the large cities of many countries the style of clothes used in rich countries is in fashion. In some of the countries with a hot climate – particularly in South America – people may reveal a lot more of their bodies than you are used to seeing at home.

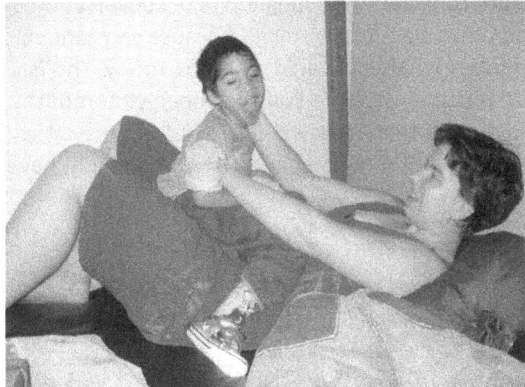

In Brazil, these clothes were perfectly acceptable...

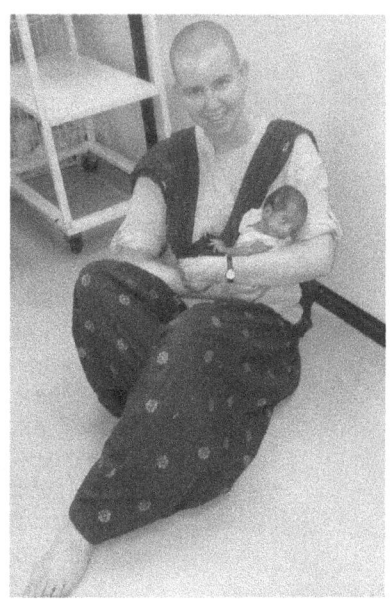

...while in many parts of India, dressing like this causes more acceptance, less disapproval and less risk.

Dressing 'too modestly' is not likely to cause any problems anywhere. Revealing 'too much' of your body, however, can cause very serious problems. Some countries – particularly in the Middle East – even have laws dictating what is appropriate dress and what parts of the body have to be kept covered. If you do not conform to those rules, you might get into trouble with the police. Generally speaking, these rules are mostly applicable to women.

> "I tried to dress simple in China and South Korea and blend in with the way locals dressed. I was usually mistaken as a local which I thought was a positive until they found I couldn't speak the language."

At what point you are revealing too much of your body is different everywhere. The limits are determined by cultural rules that tell people what is decent behaviour. In some places, it is considered obscene for a woman to wear trousers or anything that shows the clear outline of her legs. In some places, showing your knees is unacceptable, but wearing a skirt or trousers coming halfway down your calf is all right, while somewhere else, showing any skin above your ankles is considered 'walking around half-naked'. The same goes for whether you can show your bare shoulders, elbows or forearms. In some places, wearing formfitting clothes around your upper body and bottom is almost equalled to showing off your skin in those areas. Even within one country, there can be a big difference between what is acceptable in cities and what is acceptable in the countryside. Different parts of the same country may have different moral standards.

In India, when I am in Bangalore, I walk around in loose fitting trousers and a T-shirt. No one gives me any trouble or notice in these clothes. Many local women wear the same thing. However, when I am further north, in a more rural area, I would never wear a T-shirt. The stares I would get would make me feel naked. There, I wear a very loose fitting top, with a scarf (called a dupatta) draped over my chest to hide all of my body shape, and very wide, baggy bottoms or a loose, long skirt that covers me down to my feet. Wearing this, I find that I meet far greater respect and acceptance.

Not all ideas about how one should or should not dress are hung up on moral standards and decency. Some of the local rules are about what is suitable for people of different age categories to wear. Transgressing these rules will not make people think that you are morally reprehensible, but you may be treated with less respect, because the way they see it, you are dressing like a child or an old person. For example, if a foreign man were to wear shorts in certain countries, no one would think he was being obscene in showing off his legs. However, locally, no man above school age would even consider being seen in shorts under any circumstances: it is something only children wear.

I usually do not go around like this; I was dressed up by people who took me to a wedding.

There is no requirement saying that you have to dress exactly as the locals do when you go to another country. Though it is advisable to make sure to obey any dress code laid down by the law, to avoid potentially very nasty problems. Allowances will certainly be made for the fact that you are a foreigner. In other words, you will not be judged as harshly as a local person if you breach the cultural rules for dressing a little. However, it does make sense to take some time to find out what is considered very offensive and to avoid dressing that way. In the first place, it is a simple mark of respect that you pay to the country, which is hosting you. Secondly, it is likely to earn you a lot more respect and acceptance. It will make it much easier for you to really become a part of the group of people that you are working with. In the third place, as mentioned before, you are a role model for the children that you are working with. If you are setting an example that is considered completely unacceptable locally, you may be kicked out of the children's home or, if not, you may give the children very confusing, conflicting ideas of how one should and should not dress. Ideas that may cause these children to get into serious problems as they grow older and start acting on them.

A group of volunteers was painting the dorms, so they came to the children's home in old clothes. One of the girls was wearing a loose sleeveless top, with a low-cut neck and armholes that went down to her waist, showing off her bra and quite a bit of skin. This outfit received a lot of double-takes and frowns from the adults at the children's home, even though no one said anything.

As with most things, the main thing is to use your common sense and if you are not sure, to ask the people whom you are working with for advice. You can also **experiment** with what is acceptable by trying out outfits and seeing what the reaction is. If you are comfortable with the reactions that you get, go ahead. If the reactions make you feel uncomfortable, it makes sense to adjust your appearance.

"Most of the time the local people were very curious about the way I thought about topics, the clothes I wore or the food I liked. However, sometimes they reacted negatively when I was wearing something that was too western or when my approach was too different from theirs."

Chapter 4: Mental Preparations

Over the years, I have heard many volunteers sigh and say that they wish they had known to expect the things that will be discussed in this chapter. They did not say this because they regretted going on their volunteer trip. What they meant was that if they had known to expect certain things, these issues would not have been such a shock to them and they might not have had to spend so much emotional energy on them, leaving less energy for the volunteering work.

"Definitely, I had such an amazing experience. It was truly eye-opening and I feel like I've gained so much from the trip – would definitely do it again and recommend volunteering to anyone who may be considering it."

First Time Away from Home

Many people who decide to spend a period of time volunteering abroad are still quite young. Popular moments to undertake something like this are:

- During the summer between secondary school and university or college
- During a gap year between secondary school and university or college
- During the summer at some point during university or college
- Immediately after graduating from university or college

At this point in life – in their late teens or early twenties – most people do not yet have a lot of experience undertaking major adventures without having their family nearby as back-up. Many people do not have a lot of experience with living in a foreign country. While some of these people have been on holidays to different countries, this was most likely with their family. The adults probably made all the arrangements and took care of any problems along the way. During the holidays, much time will have been spent in hotels, visiting

Heading out into the world on your own for the first time is both exciting and scary.

touristic sites and spending days on beaches, rather than being surrounded by and living together with local people.

The prospect of going to a different country, without your family, most likely excites you. If it scared you terribly, you would not be likely to want to go volunteer abroad for several weeks or months. However, even if you are excited about going out there on your own, you may still at times feel slightly overwhelmed by the distance between you and your family, and you may feel homesick – miss home or family and friends very much.

> "I think some young volunteers should be educated that they will start to feel homesick after 2 weeks."

It is helpful to discuss the circumstances – as much as you are aware of them – with your family before you go. To discuss ways of staying in touch, times that would be good for calls/Skype/FaceTime/WhatsApp, taking into account the time difference and people's schedules. Try to find out if you are likely to have internet access and how reliable the connection generally is. In places where there are a lot of power cuts, for example, the internet goes down too. Remote rural places may not have internet access at all. While regular internet access is still quite variable and dependent on conditions, particularly remoteness and poverty, coverage for mobile phones, including smartphones, is becoming increasingly widespread.

It can be a good idea to buy a local SIM card when you arrive – some people choose to buy a cheap new phone, so they do not lose their own one in case their phone is stolen. This will make local communication much more affordable. Calls to the home front are going to be very expensive no matter whether you use your own SIM card or a local one, but at least it will be possible to stay in touch. Maybe your family is be willing to sponsor your phone costs, in exchange for the peace of mind of knowing you can be contacted. Through a smartphone you may even have internet access in unlikely places. Be aware though, that there is also such a thing as 'black spots', where aside from no internet, you will not even have a signal on your phone. It is worth checking in advance whether the children's home where you are volunteering is in such a place.

In some countries, it is possible to keep using your own SIM card, though the price of calls is likely to be very high. But this is not true everywhere. Whether or not you will be able to use your own SIM card or not depends on whether your provider has a contract with providers in the country where you are going. This is something you should check before you go, because otherwise you can be left stranded somewhere without any way of contacting people.

"Because I really did not need my phone for any day-to-day things, I did not think it made any sense to buy a Brazilian SIM card. I figured that if there was some kind of emergency, I would just pay the outrageously high price and that would still work out cheaper or roughly the same price. Only, one day something went wrong with the agreed transport and I needed to call someone to come and pick me up. That was when I discovered that my SIM card did not have any connection at all. This meant a very long, very hot walk back to my accommodation. When I checked with my provider's customer service, later, I was told that they did not have contracts with Brazilian providers, because they all charged too much. They said they did it to protect their customers. I did not feel very protected at that moment"

Initial Loneliness

Even when you are received with much enthusiasm and kindness, when you arrive in the country and at the children's home where you will be volunteering, it is still possible that from time to time you will feel a bit lonely at first. It usually hits after the first few days, when the **initial** novelty is starting to wear off. This is because things are different from what you are used to and while people are often kind, they are also busy. Plus, starting out, the people around you will not really know you yet. So, unlike the people who surround you when you are home, they do not know about the little things that your loved ones say to make you feel better. They are unable to share in your memories of home, because they are unfamiliar with it and you have not yet built up shared experiences to bond over. This can make you feel very far from home at times. However, this is something that passes. You get to know people better and you do things together, laugh together about what the children do, and become closer this way.

When you see groups of children playing or staff interacting, it can make you feel very alone when you are not yet a part of things.

"I think it took a week to try to read the staff at the orphanages."

There is nothing anyone can do to prevent the feeling of loneliness that usually occurs at times in the initial stages of your stay in a new place. However, it can help to be aware that this is to be expected. To know that feeling like this does not mean that you made a terrible mistake. And to know that it will pass. Knowing that the feeling is normal and that it is temporary will not take it away, but it may make it a little easier to deal with.

> "You also have to consider who you travel with. Different personalities especially if one has a strong and bossy personality and dietary restrictions start to really clash after a few weeks. You could end up no longer being friends with the same person you travelled with after the two weeks."

Culture Shock

If it is your first time visiting a foreign country, in the sense of actually living among the local people, culture shock may hit you harder than it does people who have done this kind of thing before. In the first week or two, while you are still trying to get over your jetlag, when you do not really know anyone yet, when it seems like you are beyond hope of ever understanding the language, when you

Being away from home for the first time can feel quite lonely at times; staying in touch helps.

are trying to figure out what it is you are eating and when everything just seems strange and alien, the situation can hit you very hard. For a while, you may ask yourself how you could ever have thought that this would be a good idea, and it may seem like you will never get a grip on things. This is a very hard feeling to go through, but it passes. Slowly, and without you even noticing, you will start to become more familiar with people and with the way things are done. There is never a clear turning point, but generally speaking at a certain stage you will look back and think that you have actually felt quite at home these past few days. Hopefully the knowledge that this light is there at the end of the tunnel will help you at the very start, when everything temporarily seems dark.

How much you are affected by the cultural differences cannot really be predicted. It is different from person to person. One person may mostly relish the exotic appeal of the differentness, while on the whole mostly seeing the world around him as people getting on with their lives, as they do all over the world. In other words, this person experiences the differences as only being details. Another person, in exactly the same situation, may feel quite overwhelmed by the otherness of everything. He may feel like the world is standing on its head and not know exactly how to handle this feeling. Now that

he can no longer depend on the way he was taught to do things and to interact with people at home, he may be at a loss of how to deal with everyday life. And then there is another group who are generally able to cope with daily interactions – different or not – but who have a very hard time coming to terms with the different standard of living they see around them. Some people are quite overwhelmed and almost paralysed with emotion when they first come into contact with real poverty.

Some people are shocked by their first look at real poverty.

"Most definitely, India is one of the craziest countries I've ever been to and is totally different to Britain in many, many ways. I tried to embrace this culture difference, however, to ensure that I got the most out of my trip"

I know of no way to prevent culture shock or how to make it disappear. However, if you are strongly affected by it, it is important to give yourself some time to find your bearings and to get over the worst of the shock before making yourself dive into active day-to-day life. If you take some time to observe life around you and talk to locals about the way things are done and why – if they are able to give you an answer on that –, you will gradually feel a little more familiar with your new surroundings and learn how to hold your own in daily interactions.

It is probably also helpful to try to remind yourself that, however strange the things done by the people around you may seem, in the end they *are* just people. Try to look for the things you can recognise in their behaviour rather than focussing on the differences all the time. This can help make other people seem more human and less 'alien', bringing them closer to you. Interacting with the children can also be a help in this. First of all the children are not as likely to obey all the cultural and social rules yet, and it will be more apparent in them than in adults, perhaps, that children are children, anywhere in the world.

Being Different

Something you may not be quite prepared for, and which rarely gets mentioned, is the effect of being confronted with the reactions to the fact that you are visibly an outsider. You will be confronted with this most strongly if you are of a different ethnicity than the people of the country where you are volunteering. Or, to put it bluntly: if you skin colour stands out. So being white in Africa and Asia, being black in Asia and being Asian in Africa will often provoke reactions. The kind of reactions that you can expect differ from country to country and from culture to culture, and they can range from anything like friendly curiosity to vicious racism – while

Children exploring 'weird'-coloured skin.

white people certainly have a gruesome track record when it comes to racism, they are not the only ones who hold prejudices and discriminate against other races. One thing you can be reasonably sure of in most countries where you are likely to volunteer: if the colour of your skin is different from that of the local people, you are not likely to get the chance to forget it.

"China has become more used to foreigners now, at least in the cities, but in the first years of my going there, there was no escaping the pointing and the shouts of 'foreigner' whenever I set foot outside the door. There were periods when I had to really brace myself before I went out, because I found it so exhausting to be constantly noticed and pointed out. One day, I was walking down the street and I heard a car driving very, very slowly. I looked to the side to see what was going on and found that someone was hanging out of the car window with a camera, and as I turned they snapped a picture and drove off. That was the first time that something like that had ever happened to me."

In certain situations the staring and curiosity is very understandable and easier to accept. For example, if you travel to a particularly remote rural area, where most people have never travelled beyond the next village, you may well be the first person of your ethnicity that people there have ever seen. Be quite honest, and take a moment to think about it. You will realise that – without wanting to cause any offence or being racist – when you have only ever seen people with the same general build and facial features as your own your entire life, the features of someone from another ethnicity look strange. Mouth, nose, cheekbones, eyes, hair, all have a shape or texture or colour that does not seem to make any sense when you have never seen anything like it before. I have no problem recognising that I must look very strange in the eyes of people seeing a white person for the first time. In places where people are respectful about it, I have no problem allowing people to feel my hair (when I have any) or my skin, to try to make sense out of it.

"Dark-skinned children are usually very puzzled by the many birthmarks and freckles that dot my arms and the rest of my body. The smaller children will usually try to scratch 'the dirt' of my arm at some point and be very surprised that it does not come off."

What is often harder to accept – and stay calm under – is when people constantly shout and point at you whenever you set foot outside the door. Initially, you may be slightly annoyed or you may just be amused and shrug it off as 'one of those things'. However, if you are in the same place for several weeks or months and it never stops, it can really start to get on your nerves from time to time.

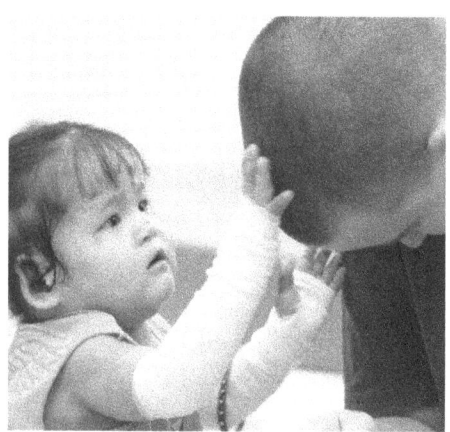

Like people in the street, the children may also be fascinated by your otherness - with an honest wonder - and may want to explore it.

There is, unfortunately, nothing you can do to change the situation. The only thing you can do is to realise that it is to be expected and to try not to let it get to you.

A white person walking through the slums of Nairobi is followed by a chorus of children shouting: 'Howareyou, howareyou, howareyou, howareyou.' It does not matter whether you give them an answer or not, the children do not really know what it means, only that it is something white people say, to them it is only a sound. I once answered them by saying the same thing in their own language, the children looked at me like I was mad: why would someone do something so idiotic! You can hear from a distance if a white person is approaching by the chorus, and you can tell what direction they are going. A colleague took to saying 'there is a "howareyou" on the way'.

When people get to know you better and you are among colleagues and friends, the fact that you look different will tend to become less and less of an issue. Surprisingly, people may become completely blind to the differences. When that happens, it can feel like a real victory.

"I visited the medieval city of Pingyao with a Chinese colleague during my first time in China. We had an enjoyable day, but my colleague was very indignant about the high entrance fees that were charged at all the different houses. Neither of us had much money, so we preferred to just wander around the streets instead. Then, we came across a rather large group of Chinese tourists who were taken around the city by a guide. My colleague suggested that we try to join the group and see if we could slip into some of the exhibitions that way. I laughed very hard at that. The fact that I had to explain to her that being more than a head taller than anyone in the group and very, very white might mean that they would notice my presence was very endearing. It made me feel like we were really equal."

In my work, I always do my best to give advice and solutions that are in line with local culture and religion, rather than give a one-size-fits-all answer. One day, the director of a children's home I was working in took me to visit another children's home nearby. As she introduced me, the director said: 'She is not like white people.' I took that as a great compliment.

Conditions in the Children's Home

It is not going to be possible to mentally prepare for the kind of conditions you will encounter in the children's home where you will volunteer, because you generally will have no way of knowing what the conditions are until you get there. However, what may help you in your mental preparations is to have an idea of what you *may* find when you arrive, as well as to think about the different ways you may react and the effect those reactions may have on other people.

All meals for more than 60 children are cooked here on the wood stove.

"In South Korea, the staff was very nice but I didn't feel much support when my friend and I were left alone with the children teaching English to them."

There are some children's homes where the staff will manage to find all the resources they need, and you may be astonished at the quality of care provided: the children look clean, well-fed, well-dressed and have plenty of caregivers looking after them. Unfortunately, this is only the case in very few children's homes across the world. Usually, due to a desperate lack of funds and sometimes an incomplete awareness of what children in institutional care need, you will probably be shocked by what you find when you first see it.

'There are three rooms, 12 cots in a room, side by side, with just enough room in between to stand sideways. Over the sides of the cots, wet children's clothes are hanging to dry. The overwhelming smell of urine, with lower undertones of mould and dirt is almost tangible. It wraps itself around you as soon as you set foot inside the door. Not even the weak human sense of smell, which so quickly phases odours to the background, is able to ignore this, not after an hour or more.
In most of the cots lie babies, or so they are called. The youngest is about a month old, but the oldest might well be two or three years old. It is very hard to say, growth and development are all stunted. Almost all are lying down, unable to sit or stand. Or perhaps they have learned that anything other than lying quietly is undesirable.'

There is running water for 1-2 hours a day, so it is stored in every possible container.

It is possible that there will be no running water, making it hard to keep the children, their clothes and their living space clean. There may not be enough to eat, causing children to be very skinny, possibly with bloated bellies, and there might be visible signs of illness or skin infections – caused by a weakened immune system due to **malnutrition** or due to lack of attention and physical contact given to the children. Clothes may be old, dirty and torn. In some places the building in which the children live may be made out of sheets of corrugated iron and wooden beams. There may be problems like rats, fleas, lice and bedbugs.
In some places, seeing the conditions in which the children live can feel like a punch in the stomach. It can come as a shock, and some people will have a hard time not to break down in tears on the spot. This is completely understandable, but there are a few things to keep in mind when this moment arrives:

- This is the life these children know: For you it may be heartbreaking to think about, but for them it is simply the way things are. To have people break down in tears and express pity for their terrible fate when they are proudly showing you around their home is not going to help them, and may even humiliate them. Instead of openly pitying them, try to **praise** whatever you can find to praise, and admire the way they make their daily life work with what little they have. This shows that you respect them. It allows them a sense of dignity, which everyone has a right to.

- Keep communication channels open: If someone walked into your house and showed open disapproval, disgust or pity for what they found there, would that make you want to listen to what this person has to say? For most people the answer is 'No.' When you do the best you know how to with what you have at your disposal, you do not appreciate being told that you are doing everything wrong. Least of all when it comes from someone who in your eyes has unlimited resources. Easy for them to talk! So if you want to be able to build and maintain a good working relationship with the people running the children's home and those who take care of the children, it is helpful not to start out criticizing everything or pitying everyone. A more diplomatic approach may allow you to accomplish more improvement in the end.

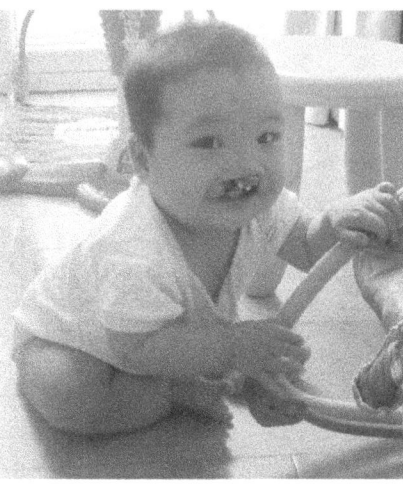

He is not looking for pity; he just wants you to play with him.

- Get familiar with the priorities first: It may break your heart seeing children walk around in clothes that have tears in them and stains that will never come out again, or in clothes that are too big or too small for them. In some places, you may notice that not a single child is wearing two matching socks, and you may see boys in pink clothes. Of course, clothes and appearance are important: they determine how the children are seen by the outside world. However, before you start making remarks about this, get to know more about the situation. If these torn clothes are the children's biggest problem, then by all means, something needs to be done to get them better ones or to mend the clothes they have. If the climate is very cold and the clothing is not warm enough, the clothes become a high priority. However, when you are in a warm country and the children's home does not have enough food to **adequately** feed the children, having nice looking, clean clothes with no tears in them moves way down on the list of priorities. As far as I am concerned, the situation in the children's home must be pretty amazing before I

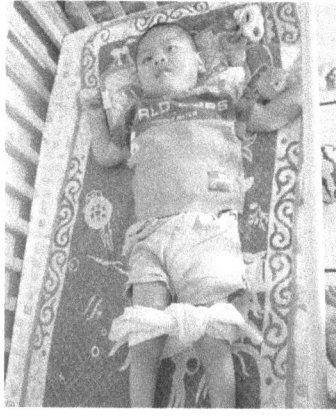

This looks like a cruel thing to do, while in fact it is done for a few hours a day as a gentle way to prevent his hips from growing in a deformed way: make sure you have all the facts before you judge!

can get myself worked up about mismatched socks. It is also a relative thing: if the children's home stands in a neighbourhood where everyone is well-dressed and well-groomed, the children will stand out like a sore thumb in their rags. However, the children's home may very well stand in the middle of a slum where most people are unable to dress better than these children. In this case, they fit right into the community where they are living. There is also a cultural aspect. While for a German boy, it may be humiliated to be dressed in pink trousers or in a top with frills and pink flowers, it is not a universal rule that only girls can wear pink or frills. When clothes have been donated from foreign countries, local people may not always have a clear idea which clothes were originally meant for girls and which for boys. The same rules do not apply in that country, and there is no shame for a Tanzanian boy in being seen in what a Canadian boy might call 'girly clothes'.

Taking into account all of these things, ask yourself whether you will be able to contain your shock, anger, pity and sadness over what you consider to be a situation people cannot live in. The fact is that these children *do* live in that situation, and if that idea is difficult for you to cope with, ask yourself once more whether volunteering in a children's home is the right choice for you.

"I wish that someone would have told me that there are certain things within the NGO that are maybe not as good as they seem to be. I expected a very honest/clear/open-minded organisation with only passionate and dedicated people. Unfortunately, this was not always the case and because I wasn't expecting that it was harder for me to cope with this."

The kind of conditions that you are going to find, and the way children are cared for are not the only things you need to prepare for. In many children's homes there will be children who have handicaps or medical conditions, and if you are not used to that, it may take some getting used to. Again, you may feel overwhelmed by various emotions, including pity, and you need to keep in mind that your pity will not benefit the child. Whether healthy or not, handicapped or not, children will tend to see their life as normal and valuable, just like yours and mine, as they should. It is the only life they know. Rather than pitying a child over what he is unable to do, take a moment to notice the child's qualities and potential. Help him reach his full potential, to become as independent as possible. That is your gift to give: a show of respect, and the preservation of the child's dignity.

Sometimes, when you are faced with so many children who lack so much in so many ways, it is hard to see how anything you might be able to do could have any meaning. A lot of people who for years were intensively involved in charitable work in one way or another, stopped because they just could not take it anymore. The reason why they were unable to continue, was that every time they accomplished something, they looked up, looked around and saw how much there was still to do, how much misery was still there. This inevitably turns what just a moment ago was a triumph into dust. Eventually, they felt crushed by this and could not go on. This is a great waste, because they were, in fact, accomplishing triumphs, even if they did not bring about the absolute end of war, hunger and poverty worldwide. Personally, I think it is not useful to take your accomplishment and hold it up against what still needs to be done before the world is perfect.

If I view the, say, 1000+ lives that I have touched in the course of the projects in relation to the several million children in institutional care around the world at this moment, I have done nothing. But if I look at it from the perspective of those individual 1000+ children, some of whom would literally not be alive today if not for something I did, plus a few hundred more who received better care after I left or survived because their caregivers have learned how to provide better care, I really did accomplish something.

Leaving Things Behind

It may sound crazy: preparing to go back home before you have even left to start your volunteering trip?! The fact is that most people do not really give much thought to what it will be like to leave the children's home to go home again. The focus of all preparations, and emotions, is on the arrival. This is why quite a lot of volunteers almost feel like they are ambushed by all of the emotions and feelings that overwhelm them when the time comes to say goodbye. It comes as a shock that what had always seemed like the easiest, most natural thing in the world, going home, turns out to be a huge challenge all of a sudden. This is why I mention it here, before you have even set off on your journey, as something to keep in mind while you make your preparations.

Just like with any other emotional response, it is not possible to

Chapter 4: Mental Preparations

A couple of hours before I have to leave again, even with a lot of practice, it is always hard.

predict exactly how you will react to an emotionally powerful, new experience. It certainly is not possible to give a one-size-fits-all description of 'this is what it will be like'. One person may feel like he is at risk of collapsing under the weight of the emotional turmoil, while another may take it in his stride. One person may feel mostly relief at the prospect of returning home, where there will be a reliable power supply and hot running water, while another may mostly feel saddened by having to leave behind the children and friends. Many people feel a mixture of all of these things at once.

"[leaving was] Extremely difficult, and I cried at one point. You can't help but get attached to some of the kids."

Whatever the exact emotional reaction that you will be having is, you can be pretty sure that it will not be easy to just walk away from the children's home and leave it behind. Having spent weeks or months sharing the lives of the children and working alongside the caregivers and management of the children's home, strong bonds are often formed. A lot of volunteers will have their favourites and to leave them behind not knowing if you will ever get to see them again is very hard. When you notice that you were making a real contribution in improving the lives of the children at some level with your presence and your friendship, taking this away from them is a hard thing to do. This can be said to be a price you have to pay for having had the privilege of being allowed into their lives in the first place.

The emotions that are whipped up during your goodbye are not always over in a matter of minutes or even hours. They slowly need to be processed. And the goodbye is not the only thing. For most volunteers, their period of volunteering teaches them a lot, not only about the country they visited and the people they met, but also about themselves and about the way they see the world. The experiences and the things you will witness may leave very deep marks on you. These are also things that will need time to be processed. Often, the processing does not get a chance to start until after you leave, because in the time before that, you are caught up in everything that is happening. You may grow quite a lot – in maturity – as a person as a result of your time volunteering, and when you return home to your old, familiar environment, you may suddenly look at it with very different eyes. You may need to find your new place among the familiar people and places. For some people, this takes time.

"I decided to return home on the Trans-Siberian Express rather than flying, after volunteering. This was to give myself time to process some things and organise my thoughts and feelings before being confronted with the family and friends who were eagerly awaiting my return on the other end. I was looking forward to seeing them again too, but I needed a bit of time on my own first. Several days on the train gave me that time."

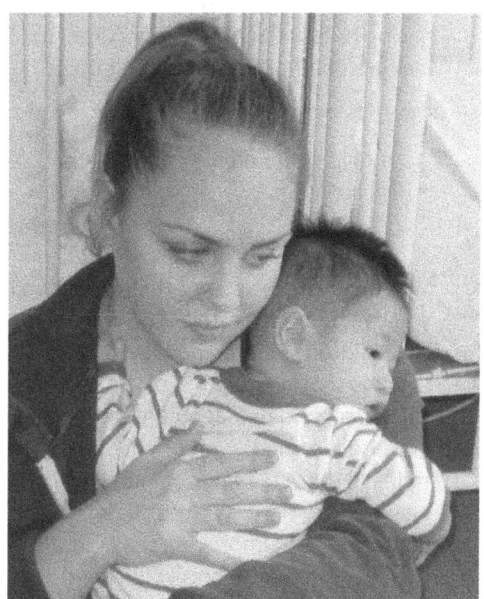

For some volunteers it can take weeks after returning home before they are able to process their volunteering experience and move on with their lives.

There are people who, when they return home to a rich country, after having become acquainted with real poverty, experience a kind of culture shock, even though they have known all the things around them their entire lives. They need some time to readjust. Walking into a supermarket stacked with aisle upon aisle of every kind of imaginable food after having lived on rice and beans for the best part of your time away can be a real shock and may feel overwhelming. Some people become quite angry when they see the overabundance of food and the way it gets wasted when they come home, even if this is no different from when they left. Having seen how other people are forced to live in poverty, the unfairness may strike them quite hard.

Chapter 4: Mental Preparations

"I struggled with my own taken for granted privileges [when I arrived back home]. About 2 months [ago I got back], am not sure if I have settled back!!"

It may also take some time to get out of the habits that you picked up while away, which can be anything from the urge to express yourself in the language of the other country with sudden remarks like 'sorry' and 'hello', to gestures that are seen as odd in your home country, but were an essential part of communication while you were volunteering.

Before leaving on their adventure, many volunteers start planning with friends for their return. They look forward to get-togethers with friends and family. Ways to catch up with as many people as possible in a short time after they return. For some people, this is the perfect homecoming. However, many people find that although they are happy to see their friends and family again after a long absence, they are not at all in the mood for constant socialising. They may find it hard to find the energy and to take the initiative to go out with friends or to listen to the stories of other people. Many volunteers remain preoccupied with everything they have been through and have seen while abroad for several weeks. They may find it hard to be really interested in other subjects. While in the initial week or two after arrival, people are keen to hear what you have been up to and the adventures that you have had, after some time this starts to wear off and friends may become fed up with just the single topic of conversation. If for no other reason than that they would also like you to show an interest in what they have been doing since you left. Some volunteers find that what they want more than anything else is to be allowed to be by themselves, to go over their memories and over the photos they have taken.

"I have never had any sense of culture shock when coming home. Quite the opposite, it always seems completely normal and matter-of-fact when I get back. As if I slip back into a slot that was there waiting for me, and I get on with things. This sounds perfect, but the first few times I got back from several months abroad, this was actually my problem. It feels so normal and so right to be home and to just get on with all the things that come with being home, that it almost seems like the great, awe-inspiring experience that I had just had never even happened. This really hurt me the first few times. It seemed like a denial of all the really important things that I had just been through. Over time, I have come to expect and accept it. I have learned other ways of remembering what has happened and affirming its importance to me."

So, before you commit to an endless string of parties and social engagements on your return, maybe give this some thought and allow yourself some freedom to decide after you have returned whether you feel like going out among people, or whether you would rather have some time to yourself to make sense of everything that has happened.

Chapter 5: Arriving

Communicate About Transport Before You Leave

In all of the excitement about the moment of the trip finally arriving, this is something that is easy to forget about, but it is essential. Make sure, well in advance of travelling, that there are clear arrangements about how you will make your way from the airport to the children's home where you will be volunteering or to the accommodation where you will be staying during your volunteering time. Do not take this as organised without checking, because that could leave you stranded at the airport, with no idea of where to go or how to get there. So ask explicitly if you will be picked up and if not, how you can best make your way by yourself and what this is likely to cost you. Even if you are being picked up, it is a good idea to check whether you will have to pay for this service and how much this will be, to prevent unpleasant surprises.

"As soon as it was agreed that I would volunteer at the children's home, I asked how I should make my way over there from the airport. I was assured that I did not need to worry about it. I would be picked up by the care manager. This happened and went very smoothly. Then, when we arrived at the children's home, the driver of the car was offered tea and the care manager said that I could pay the driver 3000 shilling. That was a shock. I did not have any local money yet, and this was not the kind of sum that I was expecting to have to pay during my stay at all. The manager paid the driver and when I had been to a bank, I had to pay her back."

Some children's homes and most volunteer organisations will send someone to the airport to pick you up. If this is the case and has been clearly agreed upon, make sure that you have a name of the person who will pick you up, so you can check that you are getting into the car with the right person. On arrival, it is also a good idea not to give your name but to ask the other person to say it, to indicate that they know who you are, as a little test.

When you go up to someone and say 'I'm Maria, are you from the Hope for Children Orphanage, to pick me up?' all the other person has to do is to say 'yes'. So instead, ask the person if their name is (fill in the name you were given) and then ask them to say your name.

In many countries at the airports, there will be a lot of people who will try to get you to come with them. They want to earn money as your driver or porter and some of them will not be above pretending to be someone they are not to make this happen. That is why it is important to be cautious and to make sure you know whom you are going with. Also make sure you have a phone number for a contact at the children's home, and if possible also a phone number for the person picking you up, so that you can call if there is a problem, or if you cannot find each other. It is also a good idea to give the phone number of the phone you will have on you on arrival to the contact person.

When making pickup arrangements, give your contact person the flight number of the last flight and the date and time of arrival. Giving flight numbers for earlier parts of the journey, or mentioning the date that you will be departing, which is not always the date that you will be landing, can cause unnecessary confusion. It will not always be possible for the children's home to arrange a pickup for you at the airport. This should not be taken as lack of hospitality, or lack of appreciation for your help. Many children's homes simply do not have a car or similar transportation at their disposal, nor the money to arrange it for you. It is also important to keep in mind that some children's homes are in rather remote places and it might take a full day's drive – or more – to get from the children's home to the airport and the same again to get back. There may not be enough staff to be able to afford for one person to be absent for two days or more.

In some places, transport may be different from what you were expecting.

If they cannot come to pick you up, ask for advice on how best to travel by yourself. The more details you can get – about for example names of bus companies, names of stops, bus numbers, train times and so on – the better, because while the journey may sound very straightforward when it is explained to you on the phone or in an email, often in the chaos of a bus station or a train station, there will be a lot of unexpected confusion.

> "I was told to take the night train to the town where the children's home was and that someone would pick me up at the train station, so I did. It was a good thing that I had been told when I could expect the train to arrive and that I had learned the local script, because it turned out that destinations were not called out on the train. So, when the train was slowing down about 10 minutes before I expected it to arrive, I peered out the window. I was able to spell out the name of the town that I was supposed to go to on the signs and rushed with my bags to the doors. Right by the station building, there was a name sign in Latin script, but not along the platform. I felt very relieved, when I had made it out onto the platform, with my bags, on time."

If you are to make your own way by taxi in a country that does not use Latin script, ask for the address of where you are going to be sent to you written in the local script (as well as a Latin transcription to allow you to pronounce it). Often taxi drivers have trouble understanding the foreign pronunciation of an address, and they are usually unable to read the Latin script version.

Finally, a little 'arrival tip' about clothing. On the flight to your destination you usually need to dress fairly warmly, because the airplane is air-conditioned and you are sitting still for hours. If your destination is one with a hot climate, please make sure that you are prepared for a quick change in the toilets – having thin clothing ready in your hand luggage – or a quick shedding of several layers. Especially if you still have a few hours of travel ahead of you before you reach your final destination, you will really regret not 'dressing down' and will likely arrive hot and irritated. Keep in mind that whatever kind of transportation you are using to get to where you need to go, the chance of it having air-conditioning is very small.

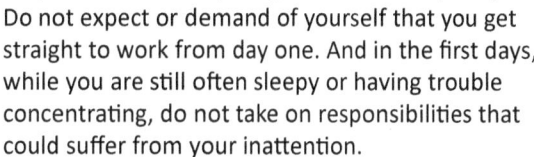

"... the journey to the charity before we had adapted to the heat. Going from British weather to Indian summer time where temperatures are up to 40 degrees was a bit of a shock."

Jetlag

The first few days, you are likely to be very tired, having trouble concentrating and needing time to adjust to another time zone. The long flight and the days of hectic preparations that came before it, will add to the tiredness. Prepare yourself mentally for the fact that you will most likely not be bursting with energy from the moment you arrive, and give yourself a few days to get used to everything.

Do not expect or demand of yourself that you get straight to work from day one. And in the first days, while you are still often sleepy or having trouble concentrating, do not take on responsibilities that could suffer from your inattention.

Adjusting to the time zone takes some people more time than others, and some people are more severely affected by not being adjusted than others. What works best to get adjusted as quickly as possible is different from person to person. However, generally speaking, it is helpful not to take afternoon naps in the first week after arrival – particularly if the afternoon locally falls within night-time at home – even though you may be very tired or sleepy. If you do take naps, you are likely to wake up feeling worse than before you went to sleep, and it will make it harder to get to sleep at a 'reasonable' hour in the local evening,

When you have just arrived, at times this is all you feel up to.

because you have already slept. But if you can manage to battle yourself through the sleepiness, which usually is at its worst over a one to two hour period, you tend to be extra tired at night and will probably find it easier to get to sleep.

I set myself a few rules for the first week whenever I arrive in a time zone several hours away from the one where I came from:

- *No sleeping before 7 p.m., no going to bed after midnight.*
- *No getting up before 6 a.m., no getting up later than 11 a.m.*
- *If awake during the night, stay lying down in the dark, do not worry about being awake, but do not create a habit of activity in the night either.*
- *No naps.*
- *Do something active in the afternoon, because if I just sit down somewhere trying to read or holding a baby, I will fall asleep within minutes.*

For me personally, this has been very effective in helping me hardly feel the effects of jetlag at all.

Strange Food

For some people, trying out different food and experiencing different ethnic **diets** is one of the biggest thrills they can think of, while for others, it is the biggest drawback to travelling. Something they suffer through with a lot of trouble. Whether or not you enjoy trying out new foods, your body may have a mind of its own on the subject, and may need some time to adjust to different spices, more or less fat than you are used to, and so on.

"There was this one dish I particularly liked: stir-fried garlic shoots. It was my favourite almost immediately. But after having eaten it a few times, I noticed that every time after I ate it, my stomach would be uncomfortable for several hours. So sadly, I had to decline my favourite dish from then on."

Some people, even those who enjoy the new tastes and textures, can get quite uncomfortable for several days while their body adjusts to a new menu. Together with lower energy due to jetlag, this is something to take into account and something to allow your body time for.

"I had to get used to the spicy food. I liked the taste, but my mouth burned and tears and snot were streaming down my face at every meal. Within a few days, the fluids stopped streaming down my face most of the time, and I didn't find most of the food all that spicy anymore. Then I was able to properly enjoy it."

Genuinely delicious, but not everyone can get past the visual.

Whether or not you decide to go all out in sharing any food put in front of you with the people around you, trying out all new things and immersing yourself into the culture, is up to you to decide. Some people literally are unable to eat certain things or are genuinely frightened of trying out a foreign diet. It is all right to express your own limits. If you have any allergies or religious food regulations, of course you need to observe those restrictions. On the other hand, it is also important to keep in mind that food is extremely important in many cultures and that sharing food or feeding a guest are an essential part of the rules of hospitality in many places. In other words, if the host is unable to offer you anything that you will eat, they will feel they have failed you and may feel humiliated. In some cases, they may even be offended and less inclined to let you into an 'inner circle' of acquaintances. Sharing food is often seen as a sign of acceptance and inclusion.

"At the children's home, I ate my lunch together with my colleagues, having the food that was cooked for us every day. I was complimented about this regularly, and they told me that a previous volunteer had stayed with them for almost a year, but had never shared a single meal with them. They said that she would always cook her own 'strange' food separately, instead of 'being one with them'."

So, while you need to be conscious of your own health and religious obligations, it may be a good idea to at give some thought to how you might be able to at least accept and eat *some* food, in order to create a positive relationship.

Readjusting to food can also be an issue when you return home, after your volunteering time. Particularly if you have been eating food lacking in **proteins** and **micronutrients** for a long time and you start eating good meals again, your digestive system is going to need a while to get used to this. This may mean that you will experience an upset stomach or for a few days. It can also happen if you have lived on a strictly vegetarian diet while away, and are going back to eating meat. Meat should be reintroduced slowly and gradually to avoid too much discomfort.

I stayed in a children's home that was struggling to feed its children, for several weeks. In that time, I almost exclusively ate rice or a cornflour-based substance with either beans or green leaved vegetables, eating

only two meals a day, just like the children. 36 hours after I had left the children's home – in which time I had taken four regular meals – I was overcome by very severe diarrhoea, which lasted a few days. My bowels were not sure what to do with so much rich food anymore.

Being Overwhelmed

Especially if it is your first time volunteering in a children's home, it is almost inevitable that you will feel overwhelmed at some point, usually within the first two weeks. Once the initial excitement has worn off and you are starting to really look around you at the circumstances in the children's home, and to think about what you have come to do,

However much you love the children, being constantly surrounded by the noise, the fighting and the number of them can be overwhelming at times.

it will almost certainly at some point – and for some people more than once – make you feel that it is all just too much. 'Why did I ever think that I would be able to do this?' This feeling tends to fade again, but at the moment when it hits, that is not much of a consolation. Being aware that this is almost certain to happen may help prevent you from being completely floored by it when it does.

"I felt overwhelmed and a little bit disorientated. When I prepared my stay as a volunteer back home, I had some abstract ideas of how I thought I could contribute, but when I arrived I found out that the whole situation is different when you are at the location itself. For me, it was needed to take 1.5 week to connect with the people around me, try to understand the current situation."

"The children at the orphanage were playful and friendly, but also impulsive and reckless. They were not used to following rules on safety and directions from adults. I understood how many teachers feel when they were with children with special needs who have ADHD or oppositional issues after the experience."

Some of the things that may play a central part in the feeling of being overwhelmed:

Chapter 5: Arriving

- The number of children
- The living conditions
- The hygiene conditions
- The quality/quantity of food
- Evidence of malnutrition
- Children who are ill or severely deformed
- Behavioural problems among children
- Lack of caregivers

"Unfortunately, a child died of HIV/AIDS while we were [there], this was a massive shock and quite upsetting, it actually makes it all sink [in,] the scale of the problem."

As mentioned various times, conditions in different children's homes vary enormously, and what affects an individual volunteer most is different from person to person. The main thing to keep in mind is that at some point, you are likely to feel overwhelmed. At the moment of being overwhelmed, try to focus on the fact that you have come to *help,* not to solve all the problems in these children's lives. No matter how much you are able to contribute, it will not put an end to all their problems. But on the other hand, no matter how little you feel you are able to contribute, it is likely to have a much bigger positive impact on the children than you are aware of. Very small things can have a very big impact, even if only emotionally.

One of the teenage girls came to sit on my bunk bed, in the dorm that I was sharing with six other girls in the children's home. We talked for a while and then she became quite emotional. 'You are really here with us,' she said. 'Other volunteers come to visit, but they don't want to live with us, you are here, just like us.' She had tears in her eyes. I had not done anything in particular with or for this girl, but just by sharing their dorm and eating the same food as them, I had apparently made her feel valued.

It is by focussing on what you *are* able to contribute, rather than on what you cannot change, that you are able to really add value to your visit. This is also discussed, in different ways, in the introduction and in Part 1, Chapter 4: 'Mental Preparations'.

 Getting to Know People
In the first days after arrival, you will be introduced to a great many people. The children in the children's home, the people who work there, people who come to visit, possibly other volunteers. You will be told everyone's name and most likely forget most of them again as soon as the introduction has passed. The combination of being introduced to many new people and not really knowing anyone yet

can also lead to a sense of being overwhelmed. Or even to feeling lonely. Again, it is all about giving yourself some time to get to know the people, to learn their names and to find out whom among the staff and the children you feel the strongest bond or connection with and you would like to get to know better.

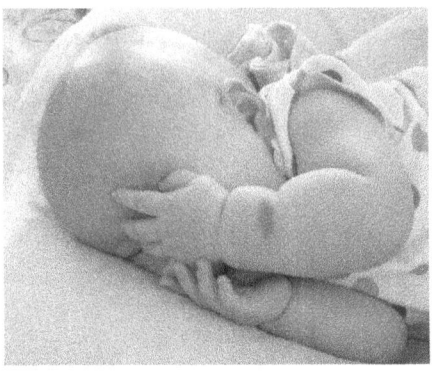

Sometimes you just feel like hiding away from it all, but it does get better.

This will happen if you give yourself the time and do not 'run away' in despair during the first weeks. Many people will at some point feel that they do not belong, that they do not know anyone, and why should they even be here? But when they have to leave for home, by far the majority of volunteers face the struggle of leaving behind good friends and children they have become very close to. This is not something that changes from one moment to the next on a certain day. It is something that slowly develops.

As said before, give yourself time, but also give the people around you time. To them, you are initially a stranger entering their domain. The children in many places will crowd around you and want your attention from the moment you arrive. This is cute, but not a good thing. Part 3, Chapter 3: 'Essential Psychological Needs' will explain what causes this behaviour and why it is a problem. The caregivers, however, are more likely to keep their distance and observe you for a while first, to try to from an impression of you. If you give them time, they usually will try to get to know you better after a while.

In my personal experience, in places where I am present full time, usually around the 10-14 day mark, caregivers start to try to address me – how successful these attempts are is mostly dependent on my grasp of their language – and despite having visited many different cultures, so far the opening to communication is almost universal. The first questions I get, almost anywhere I have been, are:

- *Where are you from?*
- *Are you married?*
- *How old are you?*
- *Sometimes 'do you have children?', but in many places, once I have said that I am not married, culturally having children becomes extremely unlikely, so they do not ask that question.*

Chapter 5: Arriving

Once this first obstacle has been overcome, I have shown myself willing to answer whatever questions they throw at me to the best of my ability. As they have seen for the past two weeks that I am willing and able to pull my weight, doing whatever work needs to be done, I slowly start to become accepted as one of them. From there on, I am included more in conversations and activities. Even if the language barrier is still high, we start to share the enjoyment of the little achievements of the children through pointing and smiles. Having seen this happen again and again, I am now more patient in the first two weeks. I know the connection will develop, if I give it time.

PART 2:
Getting to Work

Part 1: Getting There

Introduction

In Part 1, we have looked at ways to prepare yourself before you go and at what to expect in the first days after arrival. Hopefully this has helped you to make all the decisions and preparations needed for a successful trip. In Part 2, we will look at issues that you are likely to encounter when you dive in and start working at the children's home. Because circumstances in every children's home are different, there is no way of describing exactly what your work there will be like and what you should be doing, and when you should be doing it.

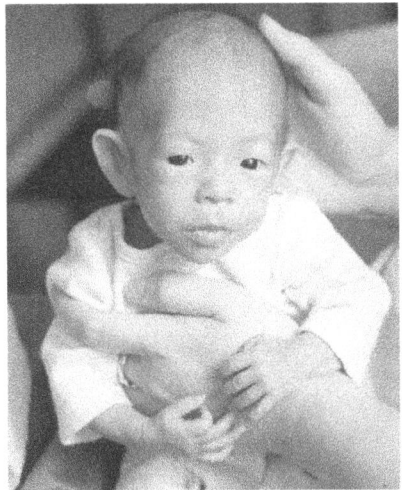

In the end it, is all about doing what you can for her.

It is possible, however, to provide you with some guidelines that are generally applicable in a lot of different situations. Just like in Part 1 of the manual, the impact of different behaviours and reactions that you might not be aware of will be pointed out in Part 2. The idea is to make you think about what you do and how you present yourself, and to allow you to decide for yourself what will be the best course of action in your situation. The aim is to help you to make a good impression, also with regards to things that you did not know are important, and to help you find a place among the staff and the children, to be accepted and included. In the boxes, there will be more examples of things that did not go so well than of how things should be done. This is because there are generally a lot of different ways to do things well, as long as you stay away from some of the pitfalls described. Plus, the best way to go about things is often very much dependent on the specific situation that you find yourself in. This manual is not written as a guide to be followed step by step. It is here to make you aware of things and help you use your own common sense in finding the best way to deal with situations.

We will look at how best to find a place among the regular staff at the children's home, at the responsibilities you may have and how seriously you need to take them, at how to handle the donations or treats that you would like to give to the children so that they do not cause more harm than good, and an understanding of the underlying effects of interacting with children. At the end of this part, in Chapter 5, a description will be given of certain medical conditions that are seen relatively commonly. The conditions that I have chosen to discuss in Chapter 5 are ones that may frighten people who are unfamiliar with them more than is necessary, and ones where some basic information on how to deal with them can greatly increase the safety and well-being of the child and those around her.

Again, in this part of the book, quotes about real life experiences from volunteers who have worked with children all over the world are included throughout the text, to give you a taste of the reality behind the theory.

Part 2: Getting to Work

Chapter 1: Working Together

Discuss Your Role with Management

Most volunteers expect that soon after they arrive, they will be given either a talk or a document explaining their role in the children's home and a schedule of what they will be doing and when. While this does not sound like an unreasonable expectation, the reality in most cases is somewhat different. It is possible that there are places where they have a clear idea of what they expect volunteers to do and where they communicate this to the volunteers, but I have not encountered a place like that yet.

This is, probably, in large part, because the managers of the children's home do not want to be too demanding and ask too much of you. Or they may not be sure what you are most suited to and most willing to do. Or they may simply feel that there is so much that needs to be done that no matter what a volunteer takes on, it will always improve the situation. What they are not aware of, is that if there is no specific plan for what a volunteer's duties are to be, the volunteer can end up feeling a little lost and may wonder if his presence is really of use.

> *"[I realise now] That we should have used our initiative earlier on to organise daily jobs"*

Although you should not put too much hope on getting a clear answer, it is a good idea to at least ask your contact person at the children's home what specific duties they would like you to take on and what kind of hours they expect you to work. If you do receive an answer, take a moment to consider what is being asked of you and whether you believe you will be able to properly handle the duties they have in mind for you. If you believe that you will not be able to handle them – for whatever reason – there is no shame in saying so. The real problem would be if you did not say anything, and then ended up unable to provide the children with what they depend on you to get. You go there to help the children, and the children should not become the victims of a sense of pride or competitiveness that does not allow for speaking up about limitations of skills or experience.

As mentioned, do not hold your breath on getting a clear description of duties and hours. If you do not get your answer, it is usually a good idea to look around for yourself and determine what *you* think you could contribute that would be of use to the children and/or the staff. Once you have decided what you think you would like to do

This can be just as important a contribution...   *...as this.*

– and it is fine to observe the situation for a few days to figure out what you think your role could be –, it is a good idea to talk to your contact person and ask if she agrees that what you propose would be a good use of your time and of benefit to the children's home. She may ask to make some adjustments to your initial proposal and this in itself will give you a clearer sense of the expectations, which is very helpful.

"Go out with an idea of what you want to do. Sometimes there is a lot of waiting around."

Do not go ahead with a plan before you have discussed it with someone from the children's home management. While on the face of it the plan might seem well thought out and useful, it may be something that has already been tried and that has failed in the past. Or it might be something that may involve more costs or other inconveniences to staff or children than you may be aware of. Or it might go against cultural or religious beliefs that you do not know about. In all of these cases, it would be a shame to go ahead with a plan when it is already known that it is not going to be of use.

If you do not decide on a role for yourself, and you are not assigned one by the management, it can leave you feeling very unfulfilled towards the end of your stay. Because in most cases, this will mean that you will end up spending a lot of time sitting around, interacting with whatever children happen to come to you. This in itself can already be a contribution, but it is not likely to make you feel very satisfied about what you have achieved. While, if you set yourself a certain responsibility or goal, meeting the demands you have placed on yourself, can give you a great sense of achievement and satisfaction.

So, if a meeting or talk is not suggested by the children's home management, it is useful to request a meeting with your contact person or someone else in the management team at some point during the first two weeks. During this meeting, you can ask if they would like to give you specific duties and times, and if they do not, you can propose what you think you could contribute to the children's home during your time there.

You can also ask questions such as:

- Which group of children would you like me to focus on?
- Are there areas of the building/compound that you would like me to focus on or stay away from?
- Do you have any particular need for someone with my background in (fill in the expertise/experience that you have to offer)?
- How many hours a day should I work?
- How many days a week should I work?
- Is it possible to get time off to attend language classes?
- Can you give more information about the children's home (when it started, how it got started, etc.)?

There are some chidren's homes – not many, thankfully – where they decide to use volunteers structurally to either solve their staff problem, or to reduce the expense of caregivers' salaries. In these places, volunteers, who are usually required to stay for at least three to six months, are put to work as the children's main caregivers. This is not a good situation. In a general sense, it is unfair because it deprives local people of the opportunity to earn a living. However, more importantly, it is harmful for the children.

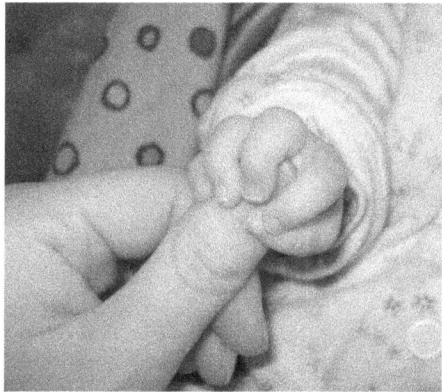

Children need caregivers that they can rely on long-term.

In Part 3, Chapter 3: 'Essential Psychological Needs', the crucial importance of attachment will be discussed in more detail, but here it is brought up to explain why having volunteers as the children's caregivers is a bad idea. Volunteers are only going to be at the children's home for a limited time. Even if that time is as much as six months or a year, it is still very limited. This means that every three, six or twelve months, someone else will be taking care of the children. There are a number of 'minor' issues which make it undesirable to have volunteers as main caregivers, like:

- A foreign volunteer is probably not fluent in the local language
- Most volunteers have little or no childcare experience
- The volunteer may struggle to adjust to the foreign surroundings and as a result not be able to be fully invested in the care of the children
- Someone who comes from the other side of the world is almost certain to get sick more often, and therefore will be unable to care for children from time to time
- A foreigner is not able to make the children familiar with their own local culture

Please put their need above the fact that it is flattering and exciting to be asked to act as a full caregiver.

Even if we leave all of that aside, however, there is still the issue that the children do not have anyone who cares for them long-term, no one who knows their history, who can reminisce with them or predict how something will affect them because of something that has happened in the past. Not to mention the fact that these children get systematically 'abandoned' every three, six or twelve months. This is not the volunteer's fault. But it is the children's experience that whenever you start to get to know someone properly and to depend on them, they will leave. This means that the children will not learn to form attachments and relationships. In fact, life is clearly showing them that it is not possible to form attachments and relationships, because everyone will always end up leaving. This can result in them refusing to make any further attempts at forming relationships, and closing themselves off socially. It is also likely to result in behavioural problems and severe depression.

"On the very first evening there – at a group home for babies and toddlers – the director came to see me. He asked me three questions – which I was just about able to understand and answer, since I was still learning the language – 'Do you know how to make a bottle?', 'Do you know how to cook food for small children?' and 'Are you afraid to stay alone with the children at night?' The answers were two times yes and a no. The conclusion was 'she will do'. Three days later the caregiver of the group home went on holiday for 15 days and I was left in charge. I was able to cope, but they really had no way of knowing that, based on what they knew about me."

So, for the protection of the children, please do not agree to take on a role as a principal caregiver. It is probably a good idea to enquire before you go if that is the kind of role that the children's home has in mind for you. It is perfectly all right to help out as a caregiver's assistant or to take a principal role in a different area – such as the medical team, the fundraising team and so on – but the children's principal caregivers should be people who are going to be around for a much longer time, preferably many years. This is to allow the children to form attachments and to learn to depend on trusted adults.

Accept Any Training Offered

When you think of what you will be doing as a volunteer, the picture in your head likely entails diving straight into things, surrounded by children and making their lives more worthwhile. Sitting through more or less useful training is probably not part of this picture. Particularly if you are volunteering during a gap year between high school and college, the last thing you want to do is sit through training. However, if the children's home offers you the opportunity to attend any kind of training – whether it is a training especially held for visiting volunteers or whether it is held for most of the staff – I would strongly advise you to take it.

> *Some volunteers sat in on a training I provided for the staff of a particular children's home. Afterwards they told me that they understood many things better now. The training had been about basic childcare, and the volunteers had no previous childcare experience.*

First of all, some of the information may be useful for you, in the sense that it gives an insight into the rules that are used at the children's home. Secondly, the way the training is given and the way staff is addressed can give an idea of the usual way things work at the children's home.

Respect the Seniority of Caregivers

An important ingredient to making your volunteering time enjoyable is showing respect to the caregivers who, generally speaking, do a very hard job for little money and who, most of the time, will have the best interest of the children at heart – to the best of their knowledge and understanding. Even if you see them do things that you believe are wrong, try not to be confrontational, and maybe request more information about the situation from your contact person, rather than criticising the caregiver in question.

While in certain points you may have more education or experience with how particular childcare situations should be handled, the fact is that there is a lot of information about the specific situation that you are witnessing that you do not have. You do not have the child's full medical and behavioural background and knowledge of the tricks that are effective to get the child to **cooperate**. You may not be fully up to date with the cultural traditions and beliefs that have an impact on the situation. In other words, before you jump to conclusions, make sure you are fully informed. When you discuss the situation with your contact person, you can always make a suggestion about what might be a different and possibly preferable approach. If your suggestion has merit in her eyes, she will likely consider it, and if it does not, she may explain to you why that would not be the best approach in the given situation.

"It's very important to be flexible and to connect/collaborate with the people around you. A lot of times, what you think it's the best is not what is the best for the locals."

Remember that if you are very accusatory towards the caregiving staff, they are not likely to be friendly towards you. In the end, if they want to, caregivers can make your stay very difficult by excluding you, or by telling other staff and possibly even children that you are not to be trusted. You do not have to be everyone's best friend or be insincere about how you feel, but you do not necessarily have to be very vocal about what you disapprove of. You can still treat people with basic respect and politeness, to help maintain a good working relationship. Having an outwardly good relationship with the caregivers also helps your relationship with the children. In the end, the caregivers are the ones who are always there for the children, who have an established relationship with them, while you have 'wandered in from the street'. Children look to their trusted caregivers to find out whether or not they should trust a stranger before they learn to make this assessment themselves. So being seen as accepted by the caregivers will make the children more likely to accept you too.

If she is not handled the right way, she will pinch or hit you; her caregivers know this, and if you listen to them, so will you.

"For reasons unknown one of the caregivers had taken an instant dislike to me. She stayed out of my way as much as possible and only gave grumpy, short replies if I addressed her directly. Very frequently she sent angry looks in my direction. This particular lady was one of the oldest caregivers there and she clearly had a high status among the caregivers. While the other caregivers were friendly to me and tried to talk with me when the older caregiver was not around, whenever she was near, everyone gave me a cold shoulder."

When caregivers give you specific instructions on how to handle a particular child, you should follow them. After all, as mentioned before, the caregiver usually has more information than you do on what a child needs and what works best. If you start to do something with a child and one of the caregivers shouts at you to stop, please do so. Or, if she is giving you instructions that you do not understand, but she seems agitated and worried about what is happening, freeze and stop what you are doing until you have figured out what is going on and what is

A notice like this is not put on a door randomly, it is there to protect the children, so please respect it.

being said. It is better to err on the side of caution than to take a risk with the children. This is to ensure the children are kept safe from unintentional harm.

In fact, the advice I give children's home management about how to deal with volunteers includes the suggestion to make sure that caregiving staff is always made explicitly aware that they outrank volunteers. I add this because of the situations that I have witnessed myself where a volunteer – often with the best intentions – was doing something that could cause serious problems for a child, while a caregiver stood near and was clearly torn, but too afraid to intervene.

"I think through the cultural differences, sometimes suggestions for handling or improving children's development through positioning and strengthening exercises or simply playing with toys in front of them to get them to improve their eye contact and focus were possibly mistakenly interpreted as criticisms or maybe they thought we were wasting our energy on children they thought would not develop normally in the future."

Chapter 2: Work Ethic

As a volunteer, you do not get paid for what you do. In some cases, you have spent quite a lot of money for flights, preparations and cost of living while there, to come and work at the children's home. To some people, this means that they do not really have an obligation to do the work they came to do. After all, they are not getting paid. It is not a real job. However, it is important to keep in mind that you have made an agreement and a commitment to do certain work, to help out in certain ways and to be there for certain hours. Having made this commitment, the people at the children's home – not to mention the children – now rely on you to keep it. The management arranges the duties of the staff in the knowledge that certain things will be taken care of by the volunteers, as agreed. This means that if you decide not to show up because you do not really feel like it, or if you are there but decide not to do the things you have agreed to do, the children do not get all the care they need. In other words, if you do not take care of your part of the agreement, some of the children's needs are not met.

You will not be equally motivated every day, but please honour your agreements for the sake of the children.

There is another effect caused by a casual attitude to your commitment to go to the children's home that you might not realise exists. This is the effect on the children. In most cases, children living in a children's home, with no family of their own and often a shortage of caregiving staff, already have a very low opinion of themselves. They may feel that their circumstances are something they brought upon themselves by not being good enough. Or they may feel that their circumstances are proof that they are not worth much. A volunteer coming to the country and then regularly not showing up when he was supposed to is an example of those circumstances. Or showing up, but not showing an interest in the children. Or not doing the things needed to meet their needs. By the children, all of these things are likely to be seen as 'further proof' that they are not good enough. That they are not likeable, and that no one cares about them. Obviously this is not at all the message that you want to pass on to them, but it is one that you might accidentally bring across if you do not properly commit.

The volunteer was scheduled to and had agreed to spend the afternoons in the baby home, during his stay. One afternoon he was found stretched out on the rug on the floor, listening to music on his MP3 player. He did not so much as look at the babies. There was little room left on the rug for the babies to play on the floor, with him stretched out on it.

This is certainly worth seeing, and there is nothing wrong with taking a few days away to do so, but make sure the balance is right, or book a separate holiday.

There is nothing wrong with wanting to see more of another country and taking some time to do so while you are there. However, if what you really want is a holiday in that country, then face that fact and book a holiday instead of a volunteering trip. It is also entirely possible that there are other volunteering opportunities where they are very happy just to have a few hours of help here and there, leaving you with a lot of free time. That may suit you better, if you prefer that kind of thing. The main point, which has been made before, is that if you do not want to make a real commitment to doing what you agree to do and to showing up when you say you will be there: please do not volunteer in a children's home. It will not be of help to the children, and it may be of real harm to them.

So in short, even though you are not getting paid for what you do, you should still adopt a good work ethic for the well-being of the children.

Be Reliable

Making sure that you are where you are supposed to be at the time that you are supposed to be there is the starting point of reliability. Of course, there are likely going to be days on which you are unavoidably held up, or on which you are unwell. You cannot prevent that. However, you can make an effort to keep these kind of days to a minimum, as well as to let your contact person know as early as possible that you are delayed or that you will not be coming, so that arrangements can be made for someone to take over your duties. Naturally, the demand for punctuality is only as relevant as it is locally in the place where you volunteer. In some places, when someone says that they will give you a lift to your children's home every morning because they are going that way anyway, this may not always mean that the lift will be available at the same time every morning. Or there may be mornings when a detour is made to pick up someone else or to drop something off for someone, adding considerably to the driving time. Just make sure, if you are relying on semi-reliable transport, to let your contact person at the children's home know

You can hardly expect these little ones to take care of themselves while they wait for you to arrive.

that this is the case, so they can take this into account when making arrangements. For example, in a case like this it is probably not a great idea to put you in charge of making sure that all the children are dressed correctly in their school uniforms and have brushed their teeth before going to school, when half the time you cannot manage to arrive before the children have left for school.

A volunteer, who, theoretically, was supposed to work at the children's home whole days to help out with the youngest children, usually did not arrive until shortly before lunch. She would sit down on the sofa and talk to one of the adults present, or play with her phone, until it was time to have lunch. She ate with the other volunteers and after lunch went outside to smoke. After about half an hour, she would return and sit on the sofa again for an hour or more. If a child approached her, she would talk to him. Then she would leave again for the day.

The same goes if you are planning to take some time off to see more of the country, or just to rest a bit. It will be very hard to make sure the children's care will continue smoothly if you announce that you will not be coming tomorrow because you are going to travel for a week. Give as much notice as you can: as soon as you know when you will be taking time off, let your contact person know. Or better yet, discuss with your contact person when would be the most convenient time for you to take off early on in your volunteering, so that everything continues to go as smoothly as possible.

Be Responsible
Just like you should honour the commitment you make to the times that you will be present, you should also really take on the responsibilities that you have agreed to. If you have agreed to make sure that certain things will be done, then do them. If something happens that makes it impossible to do so, let someone know. Ask for help to make sure that something is being done to remedy the problem or

to find an alternative solution together. This is also a part of being reliable.

A volunteer had agreed to spend three days a week at the children's home from 9.00 a.m. to 5.00 p.m. She was asked to spend those days helping out the caregivers in a particular room, so that she would get to know the babies there and they would get to know her. She agreed to this. However, on the days that she came to the children's home, she could usually be found in the – already overcrowded – office for several hours. She would be working on her CV or other things, on her laptop. In the end, management added a new rule to the list of volunteer rules: volunteers were not allowed in the office, unless called in by management.

Being responsible also means acting like a grown-up around the children. You can play games with them, have fun and joke around. However, in the end, they are not yet aware of all of the consequences of their actions, while you ought to be able to predict when things are getting dangerous (see Part 3, Chapter 4: 'Developmental Stages of Childhood' for more information about how thinking ability develops throughout childhood). This means that you may need to help protect them against themselves from time to time, and stop them from doing something that could seriously harm them or one of the other children. In other words, take responsibility for the children's well-being to the best of your abilities.

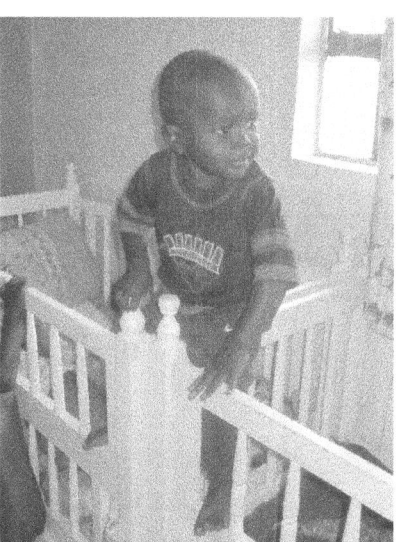

He does not understand the risk of this position and needs you to protect him against himself and keep him safe.

Sometimes, taking responsibility for a child's well-being can take a form that you might not expect, namely: holding back on your expression of affection. Most volunteers will have their favourites, once they have been in a children's home for a while. These are children whom they have a special bond with. In itself there is nothing wrong with this, but it is important not express this special fondness by always taking 'your' child's side against others in arguments or by giving 'your' child lots of extras – no matter if it is food or gifts or time playing with your phone – that the other children do not get. This kind of favouritism has a number of unfortunate effects that are not intentional, but they are still real. Favouritism gone too far can happen among the regular staff of a children's home as well as among volunteers, and the result is the same.

This particular children's home mostly took care of babies and most children only stayed there for a few months before they went into foster care. However, there were four children between eighteen months and three years old. One of these children was three years old and he had been at the children's home since he was very small. The office staff had known him for a long time and was particularly fond of him. So, several times a week, this boy was allowed to come into the office and watch TV there for a while. Sometimes he was given extra treats and at times he was taken along when someone had to go out to buy things. The other toddlers looked longingly after him, whenever he was taken out of the room and the older ones would cry and be very upset at being left out. The little boy himself was becoming more difficult to handle as well, because he knew that the office staff had a soft spot for him and that if he threw a tantrum, he would usually either get what he wanted, or something else to make up for not getting what he wanted.

The first effect is that the other children will feel left out. This is more than just a feeling of disappointment. Children living in a children's home generally already have very low self-esteem and feel like they are probably there because they are not good enough – even if they will not say it out loud and may laugh loudly if you suggest it to them. Seeing that another child is clearly favoured more than them will make these feelings even stronger. They may see it as proof that they are not good enough, that they are not lovable. Because look, you chose the other child over them! That must have a reason.

The children's home director of a home that was particularly struggling to get enough funds to feed the children properly had one big favourite among the children. It was a four-year-old boy, who had arrived as a tiny baby, who seemed unlikely to survive long. She had helped save his life, by personally caring for him in his early days, even letting him sleep with her. This bond had stayed intact. While the other children were expected to just be grateful for what they were given, this boy was always given more attention, as well as special snacks. One of the older children would be given money – from the director's own pocket – to go and buy a snack for the boy. When the child got back, the snack was given to the boy and all the other children in the room would watch him eat it, almost drooling as they did so. This little boy did not have any friends among the other children.

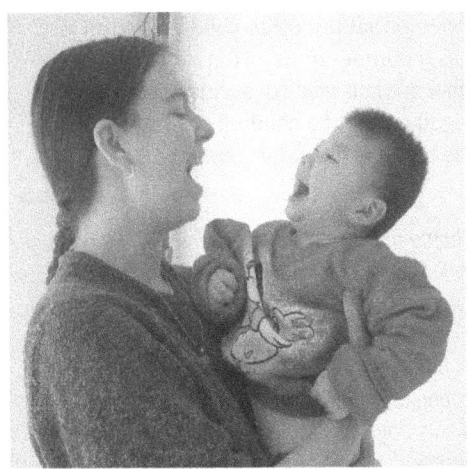

The last time with one of the favourites.

The second unintended effect can be that when you give your favourite child extra treats, it may make the other children very resentful and jealous. At moments when you are not there, or are not watching, the other children may turn against your favourite, taking revenge for the way they were excluded. So, in effect, you painted a bull's eye on your little favourite and made him the target of anything from being excluded from the group to having his treats taken from him, or even to bullying or beatings. This was never what you had in mind, but it is something that you need to be careful of and that *you* need to be responsible about.

Giving one child a little more attention than the others is fine. Giving one child a tiny little extra on one occasion, if it is not very noticeable, is also not the end of the world. But for the sake of all the children, including your favourite, please do not be very obvious in giving extra attention and extra treats to just one or two children.

Another aspect of being responsible is being aware of the health risk you may pose to the children in certain situations. Just like you are more likely to get sick with relatively harmless bacteria when you are very far from home, simply because you have never been exposed to them before, the same goes the other way around. This is to say that if you are in any way feeling unwell – even if it is nothing more than a cold – when you arrive in the country, please do not go to visit the children's home. If you have no choice, keep your distance from the children and do not touch them until it has passed completely. Because, just like you are more likely to get sick more seriously from bacteria and viruses in a country far from your

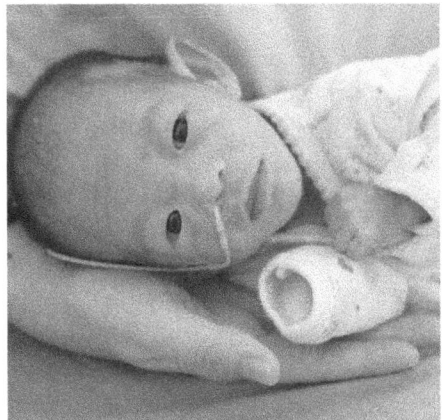

Catching a cold would most likely kill this little one, no matter how lovingly you are holding her while you pass the virus on to her.

own that you have never visited before, the children will have the same problem if you introduce a virus or bacteria from your own country among them.

If you will be surrounded by small babies or medically **fragile** children – that is to say children who have serious medical conditions or whose immune system does not work well, for example HIV+ children – ideally, you should quarantine yourself. That means not going to visit the children for at least a week after first arriving in the country. This is to wait out the incubation time of whatever you may still be carrying from home and make sure you will not get ill and start spreading it after a few days. If you work with this group, you should also change your clothes before coming into contact with the children whenever you arrive after traveling – not after only commuting to the children's home, but any time you have spent a considerable time away, in contact with the outside world.

Working with small babies or medically fragile children, you should also take the day off any time you get sick during your entire stay. Even if it just is a minor cold or manageable diarrhoea. Because passing your minor cold to a child whose immune system is weak may end up with it developing into life-threatening **pneumonia** in him. Your minor diarrhoea may cause serious, and again possibly life-threatening **dehydration** in a baby. In Part 3, Chapter 7: 'Dehydration and Malnutrition', more information is given on the possible effects of diarrhoea.

In a particular baby home, caregivers were made to wear facemasks if they had a cold, because sending them home was not an option. During cold and flu season many of the babies got sick and one of the volunteers was worried about catching something from the babies. She asked if she could wear a facemask to protect herself. This was not allowed. It was explained to her that for the babies it is quite unsettling to have someone walk around with half their face hidden. At times, for the safety of the babies, this is inevitable. However, it should only be done to protect the babies from others, not to protect others from the babies. Any adult too worried about being infected has the option of not coming to the baby home. The children do not have that option.

It is incredibly frustrating not to be able to spend time with the children, especially when you do not feel all that bad. However, it can literally be a matter of life and death, and you are there to make the lives of the children better, not worse. You can always ask if there might be something you can help out with in the office while you have to stay away from the babies. As a rule of thumb, you are no longer **contagious** when you have been free of symptoms for 24 hours or, in the case of a serious bacterial infection, 48 hours after you have started taking **antibiotics**.

Responsibility also involves being aware of how you act and what you do around the children. As we have mentioned before in Part 1, Chapter 3: 'Cultural Preparation', and will expand on in the next section, you are a role model. The children look up to you and will try to copy any kind of behaviour and language they see and hear from you.

 'Not in Front of the Children'
There are three sides to this: The first is you being a role model and being aware of that what you do will be copied. The second is being aware of the –unexpected – impact that being excluded in small ways can have on the children. The third one has to do with talking about the children and the situation they live in.

 Role Model
Children are still learning about how the world works, and they copy adult behaviour while they try to figure out how things should be done. We often think that the majority of what children know comes from what we tell them and what they read about in books. It is certainly true that children learn a lot from what we explain to them and from the reading material we provide them with. However, the vast majority of things that a child knows and is able to do, she has learned through observing the behaviour of other people, particularly the adults around her, and through her own experience and practice.

Stacking some stones into a wall for fun while I was waiting for something started a trend among the children straight away.

'Do as I say, not as I do' is often the wish of people who are raising children. They feel that it is okay to use rude behaviour, and think that if they just tell the children not to act like that, all will be well. But children observe adult behaviour very closely, thinking that what they see is what it means to be a proper adult. They are unable to judge if someone is a good or a bad role model. They try to copy any behaviour they see in adults around them, trying to get every detail of it right, so that they can be just like the adults they know best. In this process, children pay much more attention to what they see adults do than to what they are told. Being a caregiver, even as a volunteer, means being a role model. The children around you will do all they can to copy your behaviour. So maybe it is a good idea to think about the role model that you show them with your behaviour, not just with your words.

In a home for mentally retarded children, a group of volunteers comes to spend the afternoons playing with the children. The group of volunteers are friends and most of them are in their early 20s. They have a lot of fun on these visits, both with the children and with

each other, joking and playing. At one point, a campaign was started to reduce the violence and aggression amongst the teenagers at the home, many of whom were regularly hitting, biting or kicking others. So a zero-tolerance approach to any aggression was started with 'time-out' as a consequence for breaking the rules. One afternoon, a few of the volunteers were joking with each other and one of them slapped the other one on the shoulder for fun. It had to be explained to the volunteers that they were role models and that the children would not be able to understand the difference between hitting in anger and hitting as a joke. So the volunteers were asked not to hit anyone, for any reason, while they were among the children, to help enforce the rule that hitting was unacceptable behaviour.

Children who grow up in a family get to observe the roles that men and women have in the world, in the community and in a family, from the day they are born. They see how men and women interact amongst themselves and between the sexes. They see how elders are treated. They see how people with a different status to their own are treated, relative to their own position in society. The children get to see these things day in, day out, and they take in this information to slowly start to act like the adults around them as much as possible. This is a preparation for their future lives as adults.

They live cut off from the world, and any chance they get, they spend looking out the window at the outside world.

Children who grow up in a children's home usually grow up cut off from the world and society. Until they reach school age, their world begins and ends with the confines of the grounds of the children's home. Even when they do go to school, where they meet teachers and classmates, they still do not come into contact with the concept of family, or with their place in society outside of the classroom and the children's home. The caregivers and other adults in these children's lives usually mean well, but they are more concerned with keeping the home running smoothly than with the child's emotional **development** or well-being. These caregivers usually position themselves in much the same role as a teacher: someone who is to be respected and obeyed, at a distance from the child, while volunteers come in as their temporary friends, with somewhat

Children imitating the way adults work on the building site on the compound.

strange habits and ways of doing things. None of these are effective role models to prepare the children for life in the outside world, but the children are not aware of this and will take what they can get.

So if you spend several months working with children in a children's home and you become one of the significant people in their lives, be aware of how you act. Help the children make sense of how the world works in a way that will help them cope with life in their culture.

Children will particularly copy the behaviour of adults they trust and admire. As you can imagine, the cool, fun volunteers who are there for a short while to give them a good time can count on more admiration than the 'stuffy' caregivers who are always there and who make them do their **chores**. This poses a bit of a problem, because the volunteers are almost always foreigners with a different cultural background, so copying their behaviour is not necessarily the best way to learn appropriate behaviour for the local culture. This becomes an even greater problem when the volunteers do not adapt to local culture, or if they show behaviour or standards that would be frowned upon in most places.

> *When I went to the toilet area to empty a potty, I found two volunteers kissing there. It could have been any of the children coming through that door and seeing them.*

It suddenly becomes a lot harder for the caregivers to teach the children locally appropriate behaviour and moral values, if what the children's 'heroes' do goes against everything they are being taught by their caregivers.

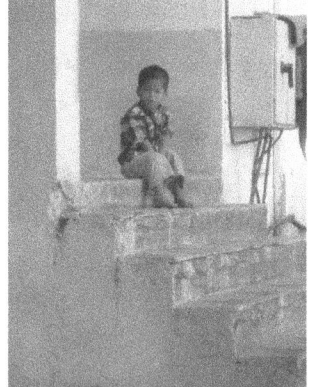

Children can easily feel excluded and then withdraw to avoid disappointment.

  *Exclusion*
It is not always easy to realise what will make the children feel excluded or deprived. A lot of things, such as eating a dry cracker or playing a simple game on your phone, would not draw any attention from any group of children at home. They are used to it and they are used to getting better than that. You would have to come up with something fancier to make them want a part of it.

However, the fact is that the children in these children's homes, in many cases, have very little of anything. Their meals are usually very basic and sometimes do not even cover what we would consider the basics such as fruit and milk – let alone eggs or meat, even in non-vegetarian places. There are often very few toys to play with, and no electronics.

Three volunteers had worked hard for several hours, making improvements to the children's home, when they came into the common room for a break. They sat down and took bananas from one of their bags, which they ate. They were completely unaware of the fixed way in which the children in the room stared at those bananas, occasionally smacking their lips. In the mind of the European volunteers, these were just bananas, not candy-bars, not something most children would be interested in sharing, in their experience. However, these children lived in a place that was struggling to provide three very basic meals a day for them, they almost never got something as extravagant as fruit.

So it is advisable to err on the side of caution and presume that anything you are eating and they are not and anything that you are doing and they cannot, will make them feel envious and deprived. As a rule of thumb, only eat and drink whatever everyone is having while you are surrounded by the children. And leave playing with your phone, camera or tablet until you are not surrounded by children, unless you are willing to risk letting everyone have a go. Remember that it really is a risk to take with expensive equipment and a large group of enthusiastic children.

There is one exception that you often cannot escape: special hospitality extended to you by the management of the children's home. You are their guest, and often people want to make sure that you feel well cared for and are well fed, even – or sometimes, especially – if the quality or amount of food available to the children is lacking.

Hospitality cannot really be refused without causing great offence.

This is something that you cannot really decline, because to do so would be a great insult to your host. And while you can try to share whatever extras you are given with the children, this will not always be allowed.

Part 2: Getting to Work

The children received porridge in the morning and either rice or a cornflour-based substance with beans for lunch and dinner. Very rarely there were green leafy vegetables instead of beans. That was all the variation they got, because the children's home could not afford to buy anything else or more. However, when I arrived, a stew of potatoes and two other vegetables was made by some of the older girls and served with rice, paid for by the children's home director out of her own pocket, to be eaten by her and me. I tried to feed some of the smaller children who were hanging around from my plate, but was told not to, they would be cared for. They never got vegetables with their meal that day, though.

Discussing Circumstances

It is only natural that you discuss the situation in which the children are living and the way things are different from what you are used to from time to time. Particularly if there are other foreigners. However, you should not do this in front of the children, or when children are near enough to hear you. Even if they seem to be engrossed in their play, they hear more than you would think. Even if you use a language that you do not think they can possibly understand, it is surprising how much children can still pick up on; they seem to sense the undercurrent of emotions and meaning that run through a conversation.

Two visitors came to the children's home and the children's home director sat and talked with them, surrounded by playing children. She told them the story of a girl who was now six years old, who had been severely beaten by her family, before she came to live at the children's home. Then the child was called and made to show her scars to the visitors. The visitors showed a lot of compassion and made a nice donation. The girl looked thoroughly humiliated.

The same goes for discussing individual children's backgrounds, behaviour and prospects. Again, this is something that cannot always be avoided because caregivers and children's home's management staff often do it themselves. However, you can try not to bring it up yourself or to encourage it. Try to make a point of saying something positive about the child, praising an accomplishment or saying something like 'we all have difficulties in our past, but we

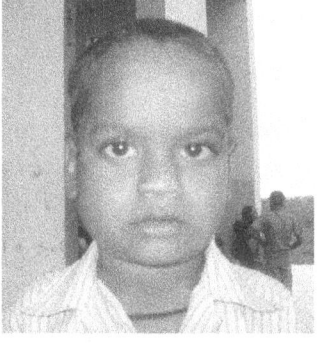

Children can very easily start doubting their own worth.

can make our way past them if we try', when something like this is brought up despite your own efforts.

We were waiting outside the dining hall for the bell to ring to indicate that dinner was ready, and a teenage girl who had recently arrived at the children's home was hanging on my arm. A manager joined us and asked me if I knew the girl's history. Since I had been working with this manager for quite some time already and he understood that my first aim is always to protect the children, I was able to answer: 'No, and you should not tell me while she is standing right here, even if she does not speak English'. The manager smiled and nodded.

It is hard to bring across just how humiliating it is for children to have their bad circumstances or the questionable behaviour of their parents discussed with and by other people. Again, this has a big impact on the child's self-esteem and self-worth. She may feel that she probably deserves anything bad happening to her because of who she is and where she comes from. This feeling will get stronger every time the story is repeated.

Big donors are a group that can often be very insensitive to this issue. They want to feel good about the donation they have just made. What better way to feel good about yourself than to emphasise how badly off the children were before your generous donation?

All the children from the children's home were assembled to listen to the introduction and the speeches of two people who had just made very big donations to enable a new building to be built. The children had been instructed to listen attentively, to smile and to applaud. What they had to listen to was a speech about the amazing work done by the children's home, how it had plucked these children out of the gutter. How these children came from nothing, were nothing. And now, living in the children's home and with the help of generous donors like themselves, they had a life and a future ahead of them. Several heads of children hung down by the end of a long speech that repeated their worthlessness again and again.

I would like to suggest to people who do this, to just say that with their money the children's lives will be *even better*, rather than pounding on and on about the children 'being nothing and having nothing'.

Respect the Rules
Aside from showing respect for people, big and small alike, the rules are also to be respected. Most children's homes will have rules of

conduct. Some will show you a list of rules specifically for volunteers, and in some cases you will simply be asked verbally to do or not do certain things. These rules are there to protect the well-being of the children and the staff, not to annoy you or to make your life difficult – even if that can be an unintended side-effect. So, in the interest of the children, please obey any rules that you are given.

An example of a set of rules for volunteers that new volunteers are asked to read and sign when they arrive in a particular children's home:

Rules for Volunteers

- *Tell us the times and days that you will be volunteering and commit to really being there*
  Years…………..Months…………..Days……………… (If you plan to go for any trips or travels kindly tell us the duration two weeks before the date of departure so that we may re-assign your duties).
- *Your duties and responsibilities will be assigned to you by the management, take responsibility and ensure that they are taken care of all the time.*
- *Feel free to voice your opinions, complaints, ideas directly to the management at any time. Remember that we value your contribution towards the betterment on the project.*
- *If you have problems with the staff or any of the children, please discuss this with the management so that the issue can be resolved.*
- *Donations are always appreciated, but please discuss anything which you want to give to the children – including snacks and meals – with the management and make sure it is authorised before giving it to or even discussing it with the children. This is in order to make sure that the interest of the children is not accidentally overlooked.*
- *Please do not discuss the children's 'terrible situation/background/circumstances' in their presence, in any language. It is amazing how much the children can pick up on and how big the impact of such things is on them.*
- *Please do not drink alcohol or smoke before or during your time with the children at the centre.*
- *Please report any health issues of any of the children to staff members when you discover them.*
- *Any activities taken outside the centre e.g. medical check-ups (unless it's an emergency), taking children to cyber cafes, taking children to academic trips etc. must be discussed with the management beforehand. Any expenses incurred will be taken care of by whoever initiates such activities.*

- Any events organized (e.g. watching movies etc.) must be done so after receiving authorization from the management.
- Do not hit any of the children for any reason.
- Please listen to the staff when they give you instructions with regards to the children or the rules of the home.
- Do not make photos of the children public (including posting them on Facebook) for any reason unless explicit permission has been given to do so, in order to protect the children's rights to privacy.
- Do not make promises to the children which you are not 100% sure you can, and are allowed to keep.
- Except for sharing lunch, please do not gather/sit around with more than 4 volunteers in the common room since this is very disruptive to the children's daily structure and their freedom of movement.
- Please avoid using bad language while in front of the children As a volunteer you are a role model for the children, so please be aware of your behaviour and how it is likely to affect the children.
- Please wear decent and appropriate clothing when you come to the children's home.
- Don't eat anything in front of the children unless they are all having the same thing too.

The request to change from your shoes into slippers is for the children's protection and should be obeyed.

Even if the children's home does not present you with a set of rules like these, keeping these in mind is still a good idea to help you promote the well-being of the children. The rule about not making photos of the children public is there to protect the children's privacy and dignity and to ensure that children's 'orphan' status is not exploited to make money.

Part 2: Getting to Work

Chapter 3: Donations and Treats

Many volunteers will raise some money for the children's home that they are going to visit before they go. Some volunteer organisations and children's homes even request or require that you do so. It is a great way to help out the children's home, because there is really no such thing as a children's home not struggling to find the money to provide everything the children need.

The first thought – of both donor and receiver of the donation – is usually that all donations, in any form, are welcome. After all, it is all the little bits together that help make up a solid whole. The popular sayings go that 'beggars can't be choosers' and 'one should not look a gift horse in the mouth'. However, in practice, donations can in certain cases cause problems, particularly if they come with a lot of strings attached. This is why I advise children's homes to think carefully about whether accepting a donation under certain conditions is worth it, or if in the end it will cause more problems than help. In the latter case, they may be better off refusing the donation, however strange this may seem to the generous giver.

In a particular children's home, more than 60 children were looked after by one caregiver. The children's home could not afford to hire more staff. This meant that older children were expected to take care of younger children and that there was little or no supervision most of the time. Two volunteers came for several months and had raised quite a lot of money to help out the children's home. This money was used to install indoor toilets and to paint all the dorms in cheerful colours. Worthy causes, but not really the highest priorities.

Examples of problems with donations are:

- Putting strict conditions on donations: putting restrictions on who can use the thing that was donated and how exactly it should be used, or very precisely laying out what the money is to be used for when this may not always be the cheapest or most needed option, can make accepting a donation more troublesome than helpful, however well-intentioned the conditions are.
- Wanting to sponsor one particular child: this is fine if the children's home has a set-up where all or almost all children have a sponsor and, by putting together the sponsoring money for all children, all of them get what they need. However, this is not the case in all children's homes, and in a place where no such system is in place, you cannot really provide one

Chapter 2: Work Ethic

You do not want to create a situation like this.

child with the good food, nice clothes and new schoolbooks provided by the sponsor, while the other children go without these things, having to watch the difference between themselves and the 'chosen' child, this would have the same effect as the favouritism mentioned in the previous chapter.

- Funding only 'cool' things: most donors and particularly fundraisers are eager and excited to provide money or materials for things that will cause an immediately visible improvement in the lives of the children, for example installing toilets, painting the building, new clothes for the children and in some cases – if the diet is very poor – providing some food (though this is already harder to get donations for). These are things that you can take before and after pictures of to show to everyone who has contributed, and everyone will feel really good about themselves. It is not bad that these things get done. However, often the much greater need is finding a way to pay for a properly balanced diet for the children, paying for electricity and water, paying for firewood, and a big one: paying the caregiving staff. These are not 'sexy' things and you can find almost no one willing to contribute to them, yet *nothing* will make quite as big a positive impact on the quality of life of the children as making sure that there are enough caregivers to give them proper care and attention and making sure they are well fed.
- Creating victims: the instinctive reaction when you see the situation in the children's home is often to 'get it all fixed'. That is to say to hand over the money, or arrange for improvements to be made, and to start fundraising to help solve more issues. While this is understandable, and in a certain way admirable, it is not always the best way to go. You run the risk of becoming a 'cash cow' for the children's home. While the children's home risks making itself depend-

ent on you, instead of taking proper charge of their situation themselves.,. So, please think of ways to donate that will help build a sustainable foundation that will enable the children's home to take charge and do things for itself rather than making donations in a way that will weaken its independence.

A former volunteer who still made regular donations to cover children's school fees wrote an email to the children's home. In it, she mentioned that she had heard that the diet and hygiene standards at the home still left a lot to be desired. She wrote that she was disappointed by this. The care manager of the home was very angry about this email. She said: 'In December we had no money, NOTHING to feed the children. And did she send more money for food when we needed it?! Then how can she complain?'

Problems with donations do not exist because the donor is trying to be difficult. The donor is genuinely trying to help and may not be aware of the difficulties that his decisions or conditions are causing. He just wants to make sure that his money is being put to good use, to the best of his knowledge. But his knowledge may not always be complete. This is why in this chapter I want to raise the issue of donations and how to donate responsibly, to help you avoid some of the **pitfalls.**

Discuss Donations with Management Before Giving

Before deciding what to do with your donation money, it is a good idea to talk to someone in management, to find out what *they* feel are the greatest needs. Once you have been told, you should take some time to think for yourself about whether a contribution to that need would help strengthen the children's homes independence, or whether it might lead to dependency.

If you want to undertake a particular project with the money that you have brought over for the children's home, please discuss this with your contact person before you take any steps to get started on it.

Initially the volunteers wanted to have sitting toilets installed with their donation, but locally this is considered more comfortable and suitable.

While in itself your plan may be admirable and seem to make a lot of sense, it is possible that you do not have all the information needed to make the best decision. Something

Chapter 3: Donations and Treats

that seems like a great idea may have already been tried and failed in the past. Or it may not be culturally appropriate. Or it may be quite low on the list of priorities, while the things at the top of that list keep being overlooked by donors.

Volunteers had noticed the problem of rats and bedbugs in a certain children's home. Wanting to help out, they hired and paid a pest exterminator to come and deal with the problem. They had not mentioned this to the children's home's management. While the management was grateful for the help offered by the volunteers, they were sad to see so much money being wasted on an exterminator who was more expensive than most and who in the past had already proven to be unreliable and ineffective.

In a children's home struggling to feed its children the most basic food, meat, eggs and milk were far beyond what they could hope to afford. The option of buying some chickens was raised by a volunteer, so that there would be a regular supply of eggs and, once a chicken stopped laying, meat as well. This seemed like a very sensible, long-term solution. However, when the plan was discussed with management it turned out that this had already been tried more than once in the past and somehow they had never been able to keep the chickens alive. The chickens kept getting ill and dying, and no food had ever come out of it. So this plan was abandoned.

Some children's homes will prefer you to hand over the money so that they can spend it on what is needed. This is often the case if in the past they have learned from experience that they are unlikely to be able to cover the basic running costs of the children's home if they do not do this. In the past, volunteers may have put their money into projects, rather than food and salaries. It is up to you to decide, after having gotten to know the management a little, whether you are confident that the money will be used well if you hand it over.

If you intend to do more fundraising after you return home, please discuss this with the management first and agree in advance what the money will be used for, as well as the methods of fundraising that the children's home agrees to be associated with. Also make sure you check if you are allowed to use the photos you have taken during your stay for fundraising purposes.

Some volunteers know before they leave that they will be involved in building or improvement projects at the children's home, and they will raise money specifically for this. They may also consider

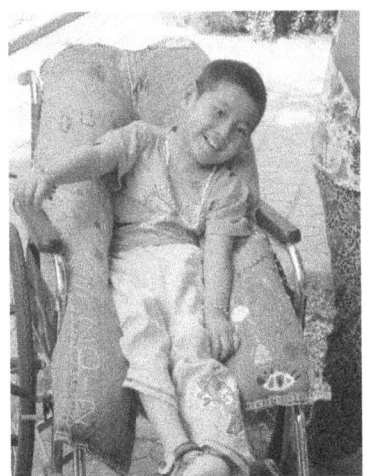

Second-hand jeans filled with cotton or foam and sewn shut make great positioning aids for children who need them, and they can be used in a lot of ways.

buying certain materials at home and bringing them along to be able to get started straight away. This is rarely a good idea. First of all. materials bought locally are generally cheaper and it helps the local economy to buy there (though you may need to bring a local person with you to make sure you get reasonable prices). Secondly and more importantly, materials from another country are not always compatible with local materials, and if something breaks later on, local repairmen may not be able to fix something of a foreign make and the whole thing may need to be replaced, leading to higher costs in the end – or even to the abandonment of the whole thing.

Donations are not always in the form of money. It is also possible to bring useful things with you, such as clothes, toys, books or medical supplies. These are usually very welcome. When you go about collecting the materials that you are planning to bring with you, make sure that they are in good shape. Occasionally, the attitude of 'having something is better than having nothing' is foremost in the donors mind, but this is not entirely true. It is not very respectful to give someone toys, clothes or other things that are broken or dirty. Although you are giving away things that people get rid of because they do not want them anymore, make sure that they are in the kind of condition that you would not be ashamed to use in public.

Also make sure it is a sensible donation, something that will really be of use to the children, not just a way to get rid of old things without guilt. And if you give something to the children, make sure there is something for everyone.

Visitors handed out bags with treats to 120 children. Each bag contained several kinds of sweets, some biscuits, a chocolate bar and crisps. However, there were not enough bags for all of the children. When the mountain of bags was almost gone, the forty or so children who had not gotten anything yet, were starting to look worried. The last ten bags were handed out. The visitors looked around and noticed that quite a few children did not have anything yet. They shrugged apologetically and handed the left-over children a packet of biscuits each.

Just like with money, talk to someone from management before you start handing out the things that you have brought with you for the children. Allow someone from management to make sure that the donation is appropriate for the children and the circumstances they are in, and to make sure that there is enough for everyone – and enough may not only have to do with the total amount, but, for example, also with the ratio of boys' and girls' clothes, or clothes for the right age groups. It is also possible that, for example, all the children have been given new clothes by another donor quite recently and that this is not the best moment to add more onto that. Management may feel that it would be better to store the clothes for now and bring them out at a later time when the current batch of new clothes is starting to wear out, or when children are growing out of the clothes they have now.

Children waiting for the clothes to be handed out by the volunteer.

A volunteer had brought stuffed animals to give to the children. However, there were four times as many children in the home as she had stuffed animals to hand out. So the management decided not to hand the toys out, but to keep them aside, until the combination of several smaller donations would allow for all the children to be given something.

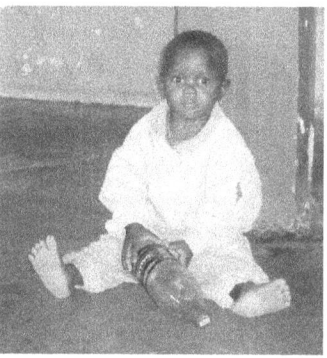
Something does not have to be a toy to provide hours of fun.

For the donor, it is very gratifying to see the delight on the faces of the children while a donation is being distributed. However, a situation like that may not always be in the best interest of the children. In some children's homes, volunteers are allowed to hand out the things they brought themselves. However, in some places this is not the way it is done. This may be because of the large number of children, because of the ages and abilities of children, or simply to avoid jealousy and fights over individual items. Instead, the management may place any donation in their storage and will bring out items when there is a need for them.

Think Carefully About Treats and Donations

In the previous section, we discussed how to handle large donations of money or materials, and the thought that should go into it. There are likely to be moments when you would like to make smaller contributions as well, in the form of buying small treats for the children or organising activities and outings. As you become familiar with the children and the way they live, you will realise that – even if you are only a poor student – relatively speaking, you are quite rich, particularly considering the favourable foreign exchange rate. Doing something small to brighten up the children's lives is a good idea.

A group of volunteers decided to hold a crisps and guacamole night for the children. The volunteers would make the guacamole themselves, a fun way to spend the afternoon. They had already bought all of the supplies, before announcing the plan to the children's home manager. The manager felt she had no choice but to let it go ahead, though she did say she was sorry that she did not know they would spend so much money on something like this. Because, for the same money, more than one entire meal could have been prepared for all the children

Again, first of all, discuss any plans you have with management and get permission and an agreed time and place to do what you are planning before taking any practical steps. Secondly, just like with the larger donations, try to put some thought into what would be the best kind of treat. For the thought to be most useful if you put it in the context of the child's living circumstance, rather than your own memories of what you wanted as a child.

I stayed for a longer time in a children's home and saw several of short-term volunteers pass by. On several occasions, one of the volunteers would go out and buy some treats. Usually, they would buy sweets or biscuits and a sweet drink. As a result, the children actually got sweets and sweet drinks quite often. However, the children's home was struggling to find money for anything but the most basic food and in practice these children never got anything like fruit or milk. When at one point I managed to convince a volunteer to buy fruit and milk instead of sweets and a sweet drink – something which cost the same – the children were just as excited about the treat, and they got some desperately needed nutritional value out of it, too.

Thinking back to your own childhood and thinking of things that were treats then and what you wanted most is a natural thing to do when trying to think of what children would most enjoy. However, while children are children everywhere, circumstances play a big part in determining what is considered a treat. Oddly enough, sometimes a treat to the children in a children's home may be the exact opposite of what a treat was to you when you were young.

Chapter 3: Donations and Treats

Some volunteers organised a video night for the children, on a Saturday night – the only night that no one had school the next morning. This had been approved by management, on condition that it would not go on too late. However, half an hour before everything was supposed to finish, a new movie was put into the recorder and when time came to stop, of course, the children wanted to finish watching the movie. One of the volunteers pleaded to let them, after all they did not need to get up early the next morning. Seen in the context of her European childhood, this idea makes perfect sense: when she was young she had to go to bed early every night, but on Saturday night she got to stay up late and watch a movie, as a treat. However, the lives of these children were very different. Every evening they had dinner after 8 p.m., after which they would start their homework and tuition, bedtime was when they were completely done. It was very rare for anyone to be in bed before 11 p.m. In the morning, they had to get up between 5 and 5.30 a.m. to make sure they were ready for school in time. And the older children also had school on Saturday morning. This meant, that all the children were sleep-deprived all the time and Saturday was in fact the only evening when they had a chance to go to bed early and catch up on sleep. Staying up late was not a treat here, but a further attack on their health, depriving them of sleep even more.

Again, as discussed in the previous chapter, taking responsibility plays a role here. When giving the children a treat, you want to brighten their day a little, not cause problems or put them or their health in danger. So, it is important to be aware of circumstances that may come as a surprise to you, but that do actually put children at risk.

Many of the children were playing upstairs in the playroom, when word got out that downstairs, in the kitchen, a volunteer was handing out snacks. In a moment, a stampede broke out, all the children ran for the staircase as one, pushing each other out of the way. A two-year-old boy got knocked over and trampled in the rush: the bigger children were too excited to notice him.

So in short, by all means, do organise treats and outings; they mean a lot to the children. But discuss it with the management and put thought into what would be the most appropriate treat or outing for the children in their situation. And if you are choosing to organise an outing, make sure that you are aware of all possible costs involved, so that you do not end up with nasty surprises at the end. Because, whether you checked out the costs thoroughly or not, you are still going to have to be the one to pay for them, as the children's home will not be able to afford to.

Careless Use of Gifts

It is not uncommon for a volunteer – or some other donor – to hand out wonderful – and seemingly sturdy – toys and books, only to find that by the end of the week hardly a trace of them is to be found anywhere, except perhaps a broken off piece here and there. The toys and books were received with great enthusiasm. They were played with vigorously, passed from hand to hand, ripped away from smaller hands, taken apart and in the end, destroyed.

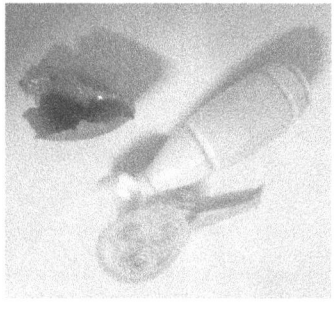

The remains of some toys that have been thoroughly enjoyed for a short time.

This gives the impression of ingratitude, something that I have heard the occasional volunteer and many a caregiver complain about: 'the children are ungrateful, they just destroy the lovely gifts that they were given'. The complaint is extended to the fact that they do not take care of their clothes or their schoolbooks, they just leave things lying around.

On the face of it, this seems like a valid complaint. However, it is not quite fair on the children. The reality is that it is very rare for children who live in a children's home to have any experience with private property. Everything that is there is there for everyone. Even if a particular volunteer says 'this is yours', their experience is that this is only temporary. Sooner or later someone else is going to get their hands on it – either by force or by taking it when it is lying somewhere – and *if* it ever gets seen again, it probably will not be intact anymore. These children have never had the experience that when you have something for yourself and you take good care of it, it will last longer and you will be able to enjoy it longer. Their experience is that one way or another, it is going to be destroyed by the end of the week. So what is the point of being careful with it?

Showing off their new schoolbags, bought locally by a volunteer together with one of the managers.

Much of what seems like wanton destruction on the surface, is in fact only curiosity and exploration. Taking something apart to find out what is inside it and how it works, only to find out that you are not able to put it back together again. Or using something in a way that it was not made to withstand and finding out that this will break it. Or, quite simply, the continuous use of dozens of pairs of

Chapter 3: Donations and Treats

hands for hours and days, which pretty much equals the use of one pair of hands for a year or more.

While it is very disappointing to see this happen with the gifts you brought, it is important to remember that the children still got a lot of fun out of it, even if it was brief. As a visitor, it is not possible for you to change this situation. It is something that can only be addressed by the management by making a sustained effort to teach children about private property – a lesson that is going to take quite a lot of time, and a large amount of 'property' to be learned. In any case it might help you to be prepared to see this happen. If caregivers complain about the children's behaviour in this respect, maybe you can explain to them that it is not badness, but a natural consequence of the way they live that is causing this.

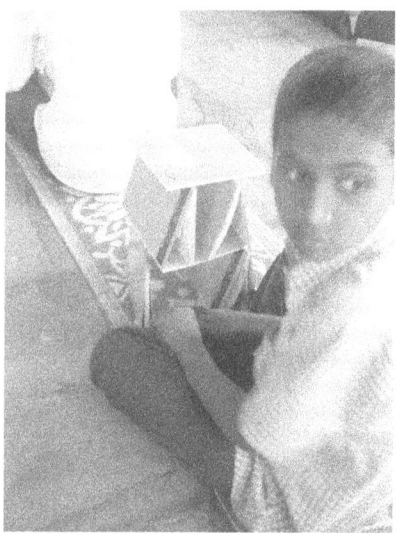

Using things in ways they are not meant to be used, which will end up damaging them.

Conclusion

So in short, in order not to cause disappointment and feelings of worthlessness in the children and to protect their well-being:

- Put thought into the things you give the children's home and the children, making sure it is in good order and of real benefit to them.
- Discuss donations, treats and other plans with management before you go ahead with them or bring them up in front of the children.
- Do not make any promises to the children that you are not absolutely sure you are able to and will be allowed to keep (the next chapter will go into that in more detail).

Finally, I would like to mention one low-cost, high-impact option for a donation: giving the children's home a copy of *Children Everywhere* and *Sick Children Everywhere*. These are the institutional childcare manual and the medical manual for children's homes, which give lots of information and advice on providing optimal institutional childcare and on how to keep the children healthy.

Chapter 4: Interaction with Children

 Only Make Promises You Know You Can Keep

One of the main reasons why I keep hammering on discussing donations, gifts and plans with management before you start handing them out or talking about them with the children, is to avoid enormous disappointment for the children. If management decides that, for whatever reason, the things that have been handed out are not suitable for the children and the children have to give them back, it will be a terrible blow for them.

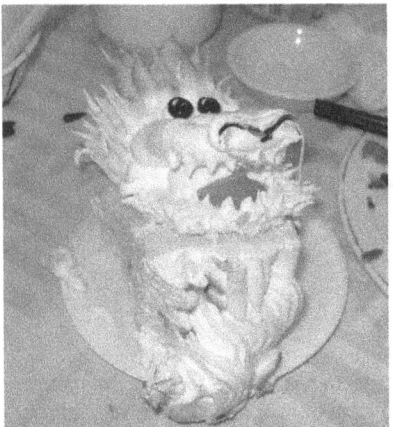

Even a birthday celebration should not be mentioned unless you are sure it will happen.

The same goes for excited discussion about an outing you would like to organise for them. When you discuss this with the children, they will probably take for granted that the outing will take place, while you may only be in the early stages of finding out if it is possible. At a later stage in the planning, you may find out that management will not allow the kind of outing you are proposing, that it is not possible to organise transportation for such a large group, that not enough caregivers and volunteers are available to properly supervise the children while they are out, or that the total cost of the undertaking is beyond your budget, and you may not have any choice but to abandon the whole idea. If the early plans were discussed with the children, then to them the cancellation of the plans will be much the same as having received a gift and having to give it back again. This can very easily lead to thoughts of 'we never really get anything because we are worthless' and blaming themselves: 'If I had been good, the outing would not have been cancelled.' This was not at all your intention, of course, and you do not think it was the children's fault at all, but that will not change their perception.

There were plans for a corporate sponsor to make it possible to take a group of mentally challenged children to the zoo. Initially the trip was tentatively set for a Friday, but this still had to be confirmed. One of the volunteers mentioned to the children that they would be 'going on the bus' – this was the way the children usually spoke about outings among themselves – on Friday. The excitement was indescribable. Then the trip got postponed for several weeks. That Friday, every few minutes, one of the children would ask a caregiver if they were going on the bus, and had to be told 'no'. They visibly deflated on hearing that. A few of the children gave it another try by asking 'tomorrow?' Again, they had to be disappointed, no bus tomorrow either. Shoulders slumped again.

This is why I want you to think very carefully before you make promises of any kind to the children. In the majority of cases, the children are more used to being disappointed than to having people keep their word. Making sure you are careful to only give your word when it counts will mean a lot to them. So, before you make any kind of promise – and preferably also before you make any mention of an intention to give them something or organise something for them – think very carefully and make sure that you:

- Will be able to keep your promise
- Will be allowed to keep your promise
- Can afford to keep your promise
- Are sure that the likelihood of outside influences interfering is very low

Even when you are extremely careful, you cannot always avoid breaking a promise and disappointing the children. During one stay in a particular children's home, I had prepared the children well in advance that on Wednesday the 25th I would have to start the long journey to the airport, so that I could fly home on the 26th. Particularly in my last week, this often came up, and I reassured children that I would still be there for several days. Then on Monday at 5 p.m. I was called to the office and told that there would be no car going to where I needed to go on Wednesday. However, the next morning at 5 a.m., a group of people would be going to somewhere near the airport and they could drop me off. So suddenly, instead of having a day and a half left, I only had 12 more hours. Telling the children about this was one of the hardest things I had to do during that stay.

There is one promise that almost every volunteer is asked to make by the children, and sometimes staff too, and it is one that you need to be particularly careful to avoid: the promise to come back again. It is a promise that many volunteers are quick to make, and one that very few (are able to) keep. As the moment of leaving approaches, you will be at least as sad to leave the children behind as they are to see you go. In many cases, you will feel that leaving is unbearable unless you have the prospect of returning. This is why the promise is easily made, in all sincerity.

However, when you return home, after a while life takes over again. There are many reasons why volunteers end up not going back, and most of them are more or less out of their control:
- Not having the money to pay for another expensive trip
- Being extremely busy with a new study, with lots of papers and exams to prepare for
- Having started a new job, needing to settle in and not having a lot of vacation time

- Having started a new relationship and being consumed by it
- Taking a relationship to a new level – such as marrying and having children, not leaving time for long trips abroad
- Becoming involved with different charitable work, or deciding to volunteer in a different children's home or a different country

For the most part, these are things that you do not plan for, but that happen anyway, and take your life in a different direction. They make your stint of volunteering seem like a worthwhile, but remote, past experience. The strong desire to go back and hold those children again fades. This is not true for everyone, but it is true for a large part of volunteers, however unlikely it seems when you have just left.

Having to say goodbye and desperately wanting to believe that you will see her again.

Meanwhile, in the children's home, the children are wondering if they will see you again and after a year or so, they will give up hope, thinking that they have been forgotten and are not worth visiting again. Of course, you have not forgotten them, you never will. But this is their experience. All of this sounds quite depressing. This does not mean that you should put everything aside to make sure you will go back, that would not be fair. Life happens and you move on and grow. That is a good thing, no matter whether or not the children's home in which you volunteered continues to be a part of your life. The point is not to put your life on hold after you have volunteered. The point is, simply, to be very, very careful what you promise. No matter how sure you are at the moment of leaving that you have to come back.

"It was horrible. The last days I've visited all the different projects of the NGO to say goodbye to everyone and to exchange contact details. I tried to be formal and professional, but when I saw all the children waving goodbye I couldn't stop crying... The hardest part was that I didn't know for how long I had to say goodbye and that I couldn't promise the children that I would come back within a certain time."

You are certainly welcome and free to promise *yourself* that you will be back, and then to wait and see whether that will be possible. This will in all likelihood make leaving just a little bit easier. However, please do not give the children an unconditional promise unless you have already booked your flight and arranged your visa – another issue for the list, sometimes you may try to get back, but be unable to get another visa to do so. Instead, tell the children that you love them, and that you will miss them. If it is possible and you are really going to follow through, you can tell them that you will stay in touch and you can say that you hope you will see them again, but be careful not to make a promise.

> *Whenever I leave a children's home, I tell the children and staff that I hope I will be back to see them, but that I do not know when this will be.*

Unfortunately, it is harder than you might think to keep from making a promise, because you will almost always be pressed for one. Not just a promise to return, but also a commitment on when you will be back. This last thing is an even harder promise to keep, so should be avoided even more diligently.

Why Talking to Children Is Important

It is very important to communicate with children of all ages, from newborn onwards. Even when they cannot talk or communicate themselves, you talking to children and explaining things to them serves several very definite purposes:

- Talking to a child is giving him attention. This fulfils some of the essential need for affection and attention that exists in all children and which is particularly urgent in infants and **toddler**s. This will be explained further in Part 3, Chapter 3: 'Essential Psychological Needs'.
- In order to develop thinking processes, children need to develop a language to think in, and this development starts with being talked to. It does not make a lot of difference whether this is spoken language, sign language or tactile sign language – a sign language that children who are deaf-blind can feel on their hands – as long as they are offered a language in which they can develop their thought processes. Language development will be explained further in Part 3, Chapter 4: 'Global Developmental Stages of Childhood'.
- Once toddlers start to understand what you are telling them, having things explained makes them feel

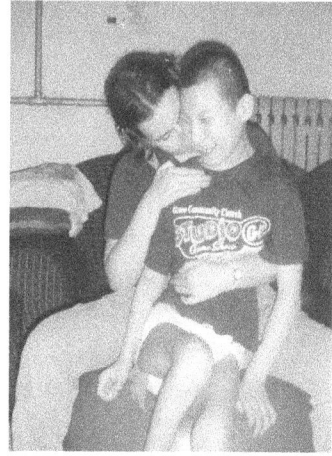

Normally quiet and withdrawn, she is laughing at the attention she is getting; though she is unable to talk, she enjoys being talked to.

more safe and secure. If difficult or big things always come completely out of the blue, it gives a child a feeling of complete helplessness and vulnerability. If this happens often in a relatively short space of time, he is likely to become very stressed and nervous. After all, if there is no warning, and no way to predict that unpleasant things will happen, they could happen at any moment. Maybe even right now… or now… or now. The child becomes very tense, ready to deal with the impact of whatever it is that might be coming down at any time. This is not a healthy way to live.

Of course, life throws misfortunes out of nowhere at everyone from time to time, and we have to deal with that. However, more often than not, there are some warning signs that help us prepare for what might be coming. There are also signs that indicate, quite reliably, that nothing major is likely to happen for a while. Especially in the life of a young child, there is not a lot that cannot be predicted by the adults around him. The problem is that many adults do not bother to warn the child, either because in their eyes it is obvious what is coming, because they cannot be bothered to explain it, or because they expect crying or a tantrum ahead of the event and prefer to postpone having to deal with that until it is inescapable.

Talking to children gives them attention and validation.

However, the long-term benefit of having a child who does not feel like life is waiting to ambush him around every corner far outweighs the short-term inconvenience of having to deal with a toddler who is fighting the idea of an upcoming event that he wishes would not happen. Plus, if you make a habit of explaining things to a baby from the start, before you can even be sure he understands what you are telling him, he is likely to already feel more secure and trusting once he reaches the toddler stage.

Lying to Children

Adults all over the world lie to children. The aim is usually not to deceive them; the adult simply tells the child what they think she wants to hear in order to prevent crying or tantrums. The problem with not telling children the truth is that, in the long run, there are a lot of consequences that are not usually taken into account. First of all, if you lie to children, they learn from your clear example that it is acceptable to lie, and they will follow your example.

Secondly, telling a child something that is not true, making a promise you have no intention of keeping, or a promise you do not know you will be able to keep may prevent or put an end to tears at that moment. However, once the child realises the truth, which they usually do eventually, the discovery will bring on the tears or a tantrum anyway. In other words, the lie did not get rid of the issue: it only postponed it.

Thirdly, as children start to realise that what you say is often not true, they learn that you cannot be trusted. That what you say does not need to be taken seriously, because you will apparently say anything at all. By regularly making promises that you do not keep – it does not matter whether this is because you were never going to or because you did not think through whether it was possible – children will learn to only believe things when they happen, and will not be so easily calmed down or bribed with promises anymore. Even when you make a sincere promise that will become reality, they will only believe it when they see it.

If you make threats that you have no intention of seeing through in order to get something done – such as taking away or destroying toys, leaving the child behind alone in the street, or getting other people to punish her – this will become clear to the child very quickly. Once the child realises that the warnings you give are nothing more than empty threats, she will push you to prove yourself. Any further threats you make will become a joke, and it will be your own fault.

At a train station, a child was being very difficult and refused to listen to his father. This led to dangerous situations, such as him running away into a large crowd of people to get to the escalator. After a while, his father had had enough and threatened to call the police if the boy would not listen. The boy still did not listen and the father pretended to call the police on his mobile phone, saying they could come to get a little boy, who would not listen to his father. This did not have much effect either. A few moments later, a police officer happened to pass by, while patrolling the station. The father pointed and warned the boy that the police had come. No effect. Then the father took the boy by the arm and dragged him towards the police officer, who ignored them completely and walked on. The father was left to deal with his son by himself, and with the result of having made too many empty threats in the past.

Empty threats can cause more problems than just a loss of credibility for the person who makes them, depending on what threats are made. For instance, in a medical situation I often hear caregivers, and also doctors and nurses, make threats such as: 'If you don't stop crying, I will give you an injection.' Apart from it being untrue, this threat also serves to strengthen the fear of doctors and needles. It is likely that the child will become even more uncooperative in the next medical situation she finds herself in.

Pain is another issue that caregivers rarely tell the truth about. Caregivers are often confused when a child starts crying when a doctor wants to listen to her lungs and heart with a stethoscope. After all, it does not hurt at all, and they told the child so up front. In this case, what they said happens to be true. But how is the child supposed to know that? After having been told that getting an injection or having a broken leg set would not hurt, how is she to know that you are telling the truth about the stethoscope?

Lying about dangers – something that happens very often – is particularly dangerous. Even though it is usually done to protect the child, it is too great a risk to take.

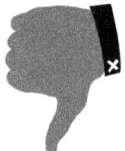

There is a hot stove in the room, which the children need to stay away from. The caregivers always tell a child that the stove is hot, even if it is not at that particular moment. This is done to make sure the child always stays away from it, which seems like the safest thing to do. However, one day the little girl decides to go and find out for herself what 'hot' means, and if it will really hurt when she touches the stove. The moment she decides to try this out, it is summer and the stove is completely cold. She approaches the stove very cautiously, expecting something to start hurting at any moment. But, since nothing happens, she comes closer and closer until she puts both her hands on the stove and it still does not hurt. Suddenly, she is discovered by a caregiver and taken away from the stove quickly, while being told: 'Do not touch the stove, it is hot, you will hurt yourself.' This is very confusing, because she has not hurt herself at all.

The stove is dangerous when hot, but lying about it being dangerous when it isn't hot puts the child at risk.

Several months later, this little girl makes her way over to the stove again while her caregiver is not watching. This time she is not cautious, because she already knows that nothing happens when you touch the stove: she tried it before. Just before she reaches the stove, her caregiver screams that she has to get away from the stove or she will burn herself. That is what she was told last time, and nothing happened, so the little girl confidently puts both

> *her hands on the stove anyway. She lets out an enormous scream. When her caregiver reaches her, she has to pull at her hands to release them from the burning stove, some of the skin comes off her hands, and straight away both the palms of her hands start to cover with big blisters.*

The child will learn from experience that your warnings need to be taken with a large pinch of salt. Therefore, she is more likely to ignore a future warning and plunge headfirst into danger. So, she is at greater risk after your warning than she was before being lied to, despite good intentions.

> *Instead of lying, you might tell the child that sometimes the stove is hot, and that it is dangerous to touch it at any time, because you cannot see from the outside if it is hot or not. This can be illustrated by asking the child if she can tell if the stove is hot from a distance, at a time when it is lit. She cannot. You can carefully approach the stove together with the child, and allow her to experience the radiating heat, without going close enough to burn her. This way she learns how to assess the danger herself, while continuing to trust you.*

Fourthly, lying to children can deprive them of an opportunity to learn something important. For example, when one of the children is chosen to go out with an adult, the caregivers tells the other children that the child is going to somewhere 'horrible' such as the doctor's office, to spare the feelings of the other children and to avoid causing jealousy, but also to prevent a tantrum.

Instead, if other children ask, let them know that the 'chosen' child is going for an outing. It may cause protests and tears, but it also teaches children

Most of the time lying to children is well-intentioned, to prevent this. However, it is still not a good idea.

something about taking turns and not always getting what you want. Explain that another time it will be their turn to go, and then this particular child will be staying behind – and make sure this is true!

In a particular medical children's home, the standard practice was that when a child was well enough and no longer needed specialist care, he would go into local foster care until an adoptive family had been found for the child. A week before adoption would take place, the child would be removed from the foster family and placed back in the children's home. This was done to allow the child some time to grieve over the loss of his foster parents, before having to make the next big adjustment: settling into a permanent new family. Most of the children would cry most of the time, for three or four days, and then they would start to come to terms with the situation. It was heart-breaking to see a child so sad, and at times the caregivers would say literally anything to try to cheer the child up a little and to make him stop crying. Though it was done with the best of intentions, this sometimes went too far. Caregivers would try to comfort the child by telling him that his mother would be coming back soon – meaning the foster mother, the only mother the child could remember. The child would, in fact, never see this foster mother again.

Take a moment to think about when this child has been adopted, is starting to bond with his new family and cries when the adoptive mother goes out for some shopping and the adoptive father tells the child: 'you mother will be coming back soon', what is the child likely to think?

Instead of telling the child that his mother will be back soon, just to stop the crying, you will be helping the child a lot more if you explain the real situation to him. Even if this will not put an end to his tears right now. It will help him deal with the difficult transition from the foster family, whom he knows and loves, to the adoptive family, who are complete strangers to him – and who in many cases look weird and talk in a strange way. You could say to him:

'Your (foster) mummy and daddy did not want you to go either. They love you very much and they are very sad that you are not living with them anymore. But they cannot take care of you their whole lives. The reason why they have let you go is that they know that there are a mummy and daddy who are able to take care of you your entire life. They want to take care of you and love you so much that they are coming all the way over here to make you their little boy. Your (foster) mummy knows that even though right now it is very sad, letting you go with this new mummy and daddy will make you the happiest for the rest of your life. On Thursday your new mummy and daddy are coming. They have been waiting for a long time to finally meet you and give you a hug. They are so happy that you will become their little boy.'

Chapter 3: Donations and Treats

Thinking of what might help children deal best with the difficult things they need to go through and learn is a more sensible strategy than to only think about how to make your life easier right now at this minute. In the end, making your life easier at one moment will end up making your life – or that of the next person dealing with the child – a lot harder in the long run regardless of what it will do to the child.

Chapter 5: Special Needs

Introduction

This chapter will give some insight into three medical conditions:

- Mental retardation
- HIV/AIDS
- Seizure disorders

One of the reasons why these three in particular have been chosen is that it is not uncommon to meet children with one or more of these conditions in children's homes. In other words, it is not unthinkable that you will be confronted with one or more of them. A second reason is that these are three conditions that scare quite a lot of people, mostly because they do not have a complete understanding of the issues and how to deal with them.

Yes, these children are HIV+, but that is no reason to be afraid of them.

Having a simple explanation of what the conditions are, what this means for the child's life and how you can handle children with the condition respectfully and responsibly, you will hopefully be less wary of interacting with any children who have these conditions. This way, these children will also be able to benefit from the extra attention and excitement that you provide, to brighten up their day-to-day lives.

Dealing with a child who has one of these conditions is a lot less scary than you probably think. First and foremost, you need to remember that you are still simply dealing with a child. They are not medical conditions on legs: they are children who want to laugh, to be held, to play, to try out new things and to discover the world.

Mental Retardation

Many different terms are used to talk about mental retardation that are said to be friendlier or more politically correct. Examples are 'learning difficulties', 'developmental delay' or 'mentally challenged'. Without wishing to offend anyone, I choose to continue to use the original term that is also still widely used by doctors: mental retardation. Just to keep everything clear and simple. Because while I am aware of the negative feeling attached to the word 'retardation' for many people, I feel that this is simply due to the way it has been used. Only a couple of decades ago, 'mental retardation' was the more politically correct term. In another decade or so, 'learning difficulties' is likely to have been given the same nasty after-taste, simply because of the group it refers to and the way any term referring to that group ends up being used as an insult.

They really won't mind very much what term you use, as long as you treat them with respect, or better yet: affection.

Although the impression is often created, it is not true that the world is divided in three categories of people: the incredibly smart, the normal, and the retarded. Often, someone who is considered brilliant because of their extreme expertise in a certain scientific area is all but helpless when it comes to dealing with ordinary, everyday things in life. While on the other hand, there are people who are severely mentally handicapped, who are unable to learn to read or write or even to dress themselves, but who have an amazing ability to do one particular thing that few other people of any intelligence level are able to do.

In a home for mentally challenged children, the caregivers told me that they did not do activities with the children and did not spend time teaching the children how to wash and dress themselves or how to behave, because the children were too stupid to understand anyway. When I looked around I saw that quite a few of the children had a mental age range between six and ten years, which gives them the ability to learn quite a lot of skills and become quite independent. When I mentioned this to a caregiver, she waved it away. To prove her point, she pointed at one of the children who was eating with his left hand. 'Look at that, such disgusting habits. Who would eat with their left hand?'
Well, anyone who was never told that he should only use his right hand for eating might decide to eat with his left hand. When I told the boy that he should not touch his food with his left hand and should use his right hand instead, he did so straight away. You cannot expect children to know things that no one has taught them.

Generally speaking, there are two widely used methods to express the different grades of mental retardation: IQ and mental age. They say something about how much a person is able to understand and how much he can learn when it comes to functioning in daily life. I included a brief overview of the official medical division when it comes to the seriousness of mental retardation using a combination of IQ and mental age.

After that, I will mostly use mental age to explain things, because it gives a more concrete idea of what you can expect a child to understand. Until he reaches adulthood, you cannot know for certain what the maximum mental age a child can reach is. Because while his development is delayed, it does not

Able to help out with daily chores.

always mean that it is stuck at the level that he is at while he is still a child. If the difference between chronological age and mental age is already great, for example an eight-year-old with the mental age of a one-year-old, then it is not likely to develop much further anymore.

IQ stands for Intelligence Quotient, a number given to someone with a certain mental ability. Around 100 is a normal IQ, within a range of about 20 IQ points either way, so let's say 80-120. People with an IQ above 120 are considered more intelligent than average, and people with an IQ below 80 are considered less intelligent than average. However, someone is only considered to have mental retardation with an IQ below 70. What follows are the internationally agreed categories of mental retardation, with the ICD code, (the code of the International Classification of Diseases and Health Related Problems – in this case the code is F followed by a number).

F70: Mild Mental Retardation
Approximate IQ range of 50 to 69 (in adults, mental age from nine to under twelve years). Likely to result in some learning difficulties in school. Many adults will be able to work, maintain good social relationships and contribute to society.

A teenage boy has a mental age of about ten years old. His physical handicap is more severe than his mental handicap. He does not have much strength in his hands and his fine motor skills are not good. His legs are deformed: due to lack of physiotherapy he has contractures at his knees and hips that keep his legs in a permanent 'folded up' position; he cannot stretch them. He is unable to speak, but sometimes he uses inarticulate sounds to attract your attention.

Altogether, this gives the impression that he is much more handicapped than he really is, particularly mentally. He knows this and uses it to manipulate people, particularly volunteers who do not know him yet. He loves playing with a ball, either throwing or rolling it to someone and then trying to catch it when it comes back. When the ball rolls away from him, he will point at it and say 'Aah!', while putting on his best 'I'm a poor invalid' look. Volunteers usually fall for this and will go get the ball for him, at which he gives a triumphant smile.

When I play with him he will try the same thing at the start of the game, but I tell him 'Go on, get it yourself, you know you can do it.' When I say this, he will break into a huge smile with a twinkle in his eyes and he will go after the ball in his squatted shuffle. He appreciates that someone sees through his appearance and values him at the right level, even if it means he has to make more of an effort.

F71: Moderate Mental Retardation
Approximate IQ range of 35 to 49 (in adults, mental age from six to under nine years). Likely to result in clear developmental delays in childhood, but most can learn to develop some independence in self-care and learn to communicate well enough and to learn some things in school. Adults will need varying degrees of guidance and support to live and work in the community.

F72: Severe Mental Retardation
Approximate IQ range of 20 to 34 (in adults, mental age from three to under six years). Likely to result in constant need of support, but can learn to handle some elements of self-care themselves, under supervision.

F73: Profound Mental Retardation
IQ under 20 (in adults, mental age below three years). Results in severe limitation in self-care, continence, communication and mobility. These children will need lifelong help with every aspect of their care.

A large man in his twenties with cerebral palsy had an inner ear infection. He reacted exactly the same as a baby of eight months old – roughly his mental age – might do, by rocking his head violently from side to side against the headrest, to try to do something about the pain and the itching in his head, while crying loudly. He wanted someone to make it go away.

While IQ numbers are rather abstract, mental age can give a more concrete insight into what these categories mean. Everyone has a chronological age: the number of years that you have lived since you were born. Everyone also has a mental age that may or may not correspond to their chronological age. You regularly hear people comment about someone that 'she is very mature for her age' or 'he is very young for his years'. That already is a pointer in this direction. Some people mostly act according to their age, while other people act as if they are older or younger.

Generally speaking, when you come to the two extreme ends of the IQ scale – people who are extremely gifted and people who are mentally retarded –, mental age does not correspond very well with chronological age anymore. Extremely intelligent people often have a mental age that is much higher than their chronological age. They are interested in things that usually only older people like. Gifted children often feel talked down to when they are talked to according to their chronological age, because it seems childish to them. With mentally retarded people, the opposite is the case: their mental age can be considerably lower than their chronological age. You can get a good indication of a child's current abilities and potential if you try to figure out what age his reactions resemble most, without looking at how old he really is.

A teenage boy having fun with a local volunteer.

The most important thing to remember is that the most effective way to interact with anyone at all is to approach him in a way that fits his mental age, regardless of what his chronological age is. So if you have a seventeen-year-old boy across from you who has a mental age of four, you will make more of a connection with him if you initiate a game, like chasing his toy car with your toy car over the floor, than if you try to start a conversation with him about the hot looking new girl band. For each mental age group when trying to think what the children in it need, try to lose the image of the big boy standing in front of you and imagine a child of that chronological age.

Children from the first group, zero to three-year-olds, mostly want to be held, to be talked or sung to, to look at interesting shapes and colours and to hear funny sounds. They may have a basic concept of cause and effect, such as 'if I push this, a sound comes'. They have no idea of consequences such as 'if I break this, it cannot be used again and I will have nothing to play with', nor do they have the empathic ability to realize that something could hurt you, because when they hit or bite you, they do not feel the pain. Their brain has not reached the stage of development that allows them to realise

Chapter 5: Special Needs

A fifteen-year-old boy with some behavioural problems and a mental age of about two-and-a-half years old does not like to be held. You can touch him, or guide him by placing a hand on his arm or back, as long as he can escape whenever he wants. If you really hold his hand or arm, after only a moment the boy will start to fight you. And if you do not let go straight away, he will hit, pinch, kick or bite until you let go. He is unable to speak, and this is how he tells you that he wants you to stop. One day, the boy had poop all over his hands and I took him to the tap to clean him up. To get the poop off his hand, I needed to hold it securely for quite some time and I knew he did not like that. So, when I did not pull my arm back fast enough and he bit me hard, the boy was not to blame. He was just letting me know that he did not like what I was doing and he did not know that he was hurting me. I had taken the risk of that happening myself, and I should have reacted faster.

Children from the second group, three to six-year-olds, are still very physical, but slightly more independent. If they are taught how to and if they are physically able to, they may be capable of certain basic elements of self-care such as dressing, undressing, feeding themselves and washing. They may have the motor ability and an interest in drawing and starting to write, and to build things. They often love stories, both hearing them and telling them, and they are able to play together and share. They have a certain amount of empathy, so some idea that other people have feelings, but only if someone has taught them this.

Children from the third group, six to nine-year-olds, occasionally want a hug or closeness, but on the whole are quite independent. They are capable of self-care, with some supervision to make sure it is done properly, and are able to help others with basic things. However, they will have to be specifically taught to notice that others require help. Usually they have an interest in a wide variety of games and activities. They are trying to explore the way the world works through playing 'house', 'shop', 'school' and so on. Reading, writing and arithmetic ability can start to develop if taught, just like a basic idea of right and wrong.

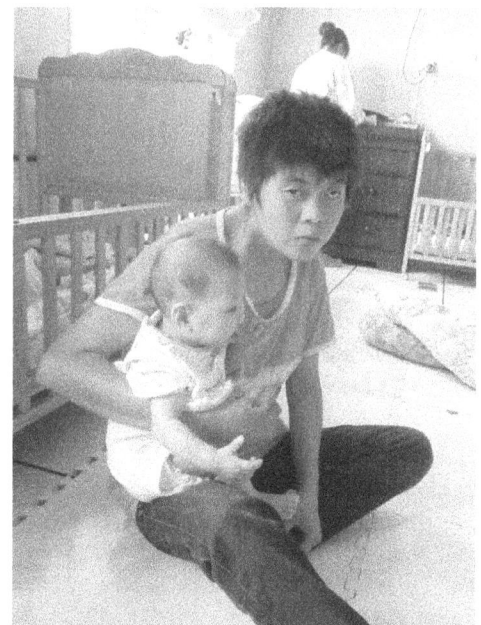

Feeling useful and having something to do by helping out under supervision.

Children from the fourth group, nine to twelve-year-olds, are able to take care of themselves and even to live independently, *if* they have been taught how they should deal with all aspects of life according

143

to very clear, straightforward rules. With supervision, they can also be productive in simple vocational work, and derive a sense of achievement and self-worth out of doing so.

A particular children's home has both a baby home and a long-term care facility for older children with cerebral palsy in the same compound. One of the girls in the long-term care facility is sixteen years old and has a mental age of about eight years old. She does not have serious physical problems. In the mornings one of the caregivers of the long-term care facility walks with this girl to the baby home and makes sure that she washes her hands. Then the girl is led to one of the rooms where babies older than six months are cared for. There the girl spends her mornings, until lunchtime, helping the caregivers by holding babies, playing with them, and giving them a bottle – she is handed a freshly prepared bottle, ready for use. For the babies, it means that they get a little bit more attention. For the caregivers, it means a little bit less work. For the girl, it means that she has something useful to do and that she feels valued.

He loves helping out the caregivers by taking down the laundry; he needs a wheelchair for support when walking.

What separates an eleven-year-old from an eighteen-year-old or an adult is abstract thinking, logical thinking and the ability to predict consequences. This is something that develops during adolescence. Part 3, Chapter 4: 'Global Developmental Stages of Childhood' gives more information about this.

In mildly retarded people this insight – cause and effect on a larger view or a longer time-span – will never develop. Because of this, when you teach children with limited intelligence things, it is very important to put everything in very simple and 'unbreakable' rules. They cannot deal with many options or choices. If you would like to have more information about this subject, there is more information about mental retardation in *Sick Children Everywhere. How to Provide Good Institutional Care. Book 2: Basic Medical Care for Children in Institutions*, Part 2, Chapter 9: 'Cerebral Palsy'.

I do not need to jump off a roof to know that that is going to end badly and that I will more than likely break several bones if I do.
A nine-year-old will not think about any possible danger at all, he will just be fascinated with what it will feel like to 'fly through the air'. And if, by some miracle, he jumps off a roof and does not get seriously hurt, he will take that as proof that it is safe to jump off roofs. The same goes for people with a mental age of up to twelve years old.

The fourth manual in this series will be dedicated entirely to caring for mentally retarded children in children's homes.

HIV/AIDS

HIV is short for Human **Immunodeficiency** Virus. This literally means: a virus that causes the immune system in humans to weaken, or that breaks it down. HIV is a virus that enters cells in the body that have the function of fighting bacteria and viruses in the most specialised way: the **CD4** T-cells. When the HIV has entered these cells, it uses them to make copies of itself. When a T-cell has been entered by HIV, it cannot do its job anymore. The more T-cells are destroyed this way, the weaker the immune system becomes. The test done to check how strong the immune system of someone with HIV infection is counts the CD4 level, which means seeing how many of the CD4 cells are still working properly.

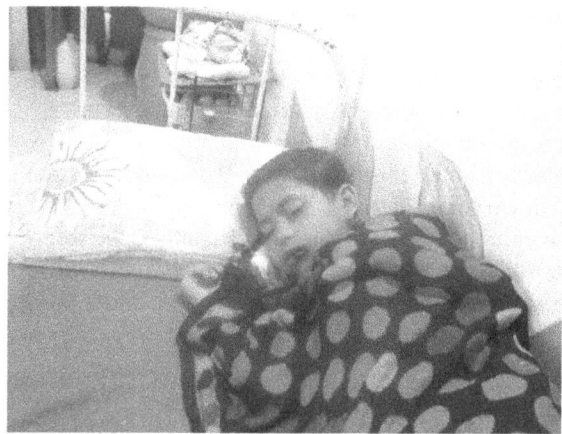

Because she is HIV+, she became very ill, eventually even hospitalised, with what for most people would be a minor infection.

The task of the immune system is to fight off bacteria and viruses to prevent infections and illnesses. When the immune system has been weakened by the destruction of T-cells by HIV, it is not able to fight intruders very well anymore. This means that a person with HIV becomes sick much more often than a person with a strong immune system, and it also means that when someone who is HIV positive – someone who has HIV in their body – gets sick, it will be more serious, because the immune system is unable to keep the illness or infection under control. Opportunistic infections are a big problem for someone who is HIV positive.

Opportunistic infections are caused by bacteria and viruses that are quite weak. They are bacteria and viruses that most people have in their body from time to time, but a healthy immune system gets rid of them before you even notice they are there. They never get a chance to cause an illness. In someone who is HIV positive, they do get the chance: the bacteria or viruses only get attacked very weakly or not at all by what is left of the immune system, and they take the opportunity to cause serious illnesses. That is why they are called opportunistic infections: they grab the opportunity of finding a weak immune system to spread.

The reason people who have been infected with HIV die younger than other people, is that their immune system is broken down so much that bacteria and viruses that would hardly cause any illness in people who have not been infected get a chance to cause an illness so serious that it can kill you. What makes it so hard to find a vaccine or medication to prevent infection or cure someone with HIV, is that the rate of mutation – accidental changes made every time the virus copies itself – is very high. So the virus keeps changing all the time, allowing it to find ways to survive and get stronger despite the medications that are used.

Most children who are HIV positive were born that way. They got the virus from their mother while they were still in the womb, or while they were being born. Not all babies born to HIV-positive mothers get infected by their mother, some of them are born without being infected. Children who are HIV positive, particularly those under five years old, tend to become symptomatic very quickly. If they do not receive ART treatment – a combination of different medications that slows down the HIV spreading in the blood –, 50% of babies born HIV positive will die before their first birthday, and most of those who make it to their first birthday will die before they reach age five.

What Is the Difference Between HIV and AIDS?
Essentially HIV and AIDS are different stages of the same disease. AIDS is short for Acquired Immuno Deficiency Syndrome. AIDS is caused by HIV infection and is the stage where the immune system has been broken down so much that it is no longer possible to strengthen the immune system and improve health. Once someone who is HIV positive reaches the stage where he has AIDS, he is terminally ill. He will not be able to get better anymore and is likely to die quite soon.

> *While officially someone with a CD4 count below 200 is considered to be terminally ill, sometimes you are pleasantly surprised. The first time a teenage boy who was very ill had a CD4 count done, it was 16. There seemed to be no hope left for him. However, he was still started on ART medication, in an attempt to help him. Six months later his CD4 was slightly above 400.*

The point where AIDS is reached is defined by the WHO (the World Health Organisation) as the CD4 level having reached 200 or 20% of the normal level in children over five years old, a CD4 level of less than 20% of the normal level in children between one to five years old, and a CD4 level of less than 25% in children under twelve months old.

How Does It Spread?
In practice, the spreading of HIV does not happen nearly as easily as most people think, especially if you look at the infection risk of cases not involving sexual relations. Through unprotected sex, HIV is passed on very easily. This is also true for using injection needles that have

already been used. However, outside those ways, it is actually quite hard to get infected with HIV.

The common beliefs that HIV could be transmitted through **saliva**, the air or toilet seats are all false. Even when blood is involved, a tiny scratch on a HIV-positive person is unlikely to lead to spreading of the virus. Fairly large, actively bleeding wounds on both the person infected with HIV and the person who is not yet infected with HIV need to come into direct contact with each other for a good chance of passing on HIV infection: a chance, not a guarantee. This is not something that is very likely to happen. HIV cannot survive very long when it is exposed to oxygen.

Spending time playing with and cuddling HIV+ children, just like you would any other child, will not get you infected.

Knowing that I will not get infected through normal interaction with children, I treat HIV-positive children exactly the same as any other child. I let them sit on my lap, I play with them, clean them, change their nappies, eat with them, let them kiss me and dress their wounds if needed. Sometimes they will even throw up on me. In some places, this causes a lot of amazement and disbelief because the stigma of HIV infection is so great. I regularly get tested for HIV, to prove to people that you do not get it like this. I am still HIV negative.

After being exposed to air for less than a minute, the HIV in a drop of blood will have died. Hugging, holding, changing nappies and kissing a HIV-positive child is not going to get you infected. Likewise, there are no reported cases of children infecting other children by playing together, even if they fight or bite each other.

However, since the consequences of infection are serious, it is important to be aware of where risks do lie and to take proper precautions to prevent infection, without being panicky about it. Basically, all precautions have to do with bodily fluids and how to deal with them:

- Wear gloves when caring for a wound or handling anything that has been stained with blood, sperm or fluids coming from

the vagina; poop, **urine** and **vomit** only pose a risk if there is blood in them.
- All cuts and grazes to the skin of both the HIV-positive person and their caregiver should be covered with a plaster or bandage.
- Never re-use injection needles or other sharp objects that have pierced the skin of someone who is HIV positive; it is best never to re-use these items in any case, because sometimes someone may have a contagious infection (HIV or other infections) without knowing about it, and this can spread to the second person using the needle.
- If blood from a HIV-infected person is accidently spilled on the skin of another person, it should be washed off with soap and water straight away.

If care is taken in these situations, the risk of infection with HIV is next to nothing.

What Is the Effect of the Stigma?

The practicalities of preventing transmission of HIV and keeping the child's health in optimal state are very important, but usually they are more or less taken care of. What are very often overlooked are the child's psycho-social needs: the way that he is approached by the people in his environment and how this affects his emotional and psychological well-being. Yet this aspect of the situation is just as important as the other two. Not only to make sure that the child is able to enjoy a happy life, but also to keep him healthy. Studies have shown that depression is seen a lot among people – both children and adults – who are HIV positive. In turn, depression is known to weaken a person's immune system and generally weaken his health. This can make a HIV-positive child even more prone to opportunistic infections, just like a poor diet and poor hygiene.

Celebrating the coming of the first rain should be enjoyed by all, regardless of HIV status.

The stigma attached to HIV and the fear surrounding it can lead to terrible **isolation** and loneliness. It is very important to allow children to express their feelings and questions about their life and situation and to answer them honestly. This is true in general, but especially with HIV-positive children. If these children are not allowed to

Lining up for ART after prayer; they cannot eat for at least half an hour after they take their medication.

ask questions and do not receive honest answers, they will try to find other ways to get information, and that information may not be accurate. This, in turn, may lead to their drawing their own conclusions and becoming even more anxious, worried and possibly even ashamed than there is any need to be. Often adults withhold information from children in an attempt to protect them, but usually this ends up doing more damage than good. Children should be provided with enough information, but not so much that they are overburdened with things they cannot change. For example, telling them that they may be sick more often helps them prepare, while telling them that they may be in a lot of pain is not going to help them and will only scare them. Explain things simply, making sure the child understands.

Finally, the greatest psychosocial need of a HIV-positive child, is to simply be allowed to be a child. To be allowed to play with other children, to explore, enjoy, be held, be hugged, receive love and attention and generally enjoy life. They also need to feel valued, so that they can build up self-esteem. This can be accommodated by allowing the child to do simple chores and praising him when he has completed them successfully. As simple and easy as this may sound, it is often overlooked, and no great effort is made to ensure that it happens. Every effort should be made to ensure this.

I was used to hearing people in the countries where I have projects have very limited understanding of what is and is not a risk when it comes to HIV. There, I expected the stigma. However, when talking to a Dutch doctor about the work I do with HIV-positive children, I was shocked to be asked: 'How do you protect yourself from infection?' I was literally stunned for a moment and could not think of anything other to say than: 'Well, I do not have sex with them and I do not share needles with them.' It saddened me that the stigma is clearly still alive all around the world.

Something to keep in mind when you want to organise a treat or a meal is that children who take ART medication need to take their medicine at exactly the same time every single day. This may also mean that some of their meals have to be at exact times, to make sure they can take their medication at the right time and on a full or an empty stomach, as needed. Depending on the medication they are taking, they may not be allowed to eat anything at all for one or two hours before taking their ART and half an hour to an hour after taking it. It is extremely important that this is done right, to keep their health as strong as possible. So if you volunteer in a place with HIV-positive children, find out which of these rules, if any, apply to those children. Find out about this and take it into account before you plan to hand out a treat, prepare a meal together or plan outings for the children. Plan things in a way that does not interfere with set meal and medication times.

If you would like to have more information about this subject, there is more information about HIV/AIDS in *Sick Children Everywhere. How to Provide Good Institutional Care. Book 2: Basic Medical Care for Children in Institutions* Part 2, Chapter 8: HIV/AIDS.

At 6 p.m. every evening, the children were assembled for prayer. After prayer, at 6:30 p.m. ART medication was taken and dinner was at 7:30 p.m., to allow the stomach to stay empty apart from the medication for an hour.

The holidays were coming up, and one evening several visitors arrived at the end of prayer. When the ART had been handed out, the children were all told to sit back in their rows. The visitors started handing out goody bags full of sweets and other snacks, as well as a little candle. As soon as all of the children had gotten their bag, and had thanked the visitors, they opened the bags and started eating the snacks. Having a snack 15 minutes after taking the kind of ART medicine that most of the children here were taking has roughly the same effect as skipping the dose.

Seizure Disorders

A **seizure** is also called a convulsion or a fit. Seizures are quite common in children. Up to 6% of all children have at least one seizure during their childhood, but less than 1% of children has epilepsy. Just one seizure does not make epilepsy. Epilepsy is a condition where seizures regularly occur over a longer period of time. The reason why children have seizures more often than adults is that their brain is not yet fully developed and still more vulnerable.

There is a lot of false information going around about what causes seizures and what might cure them. So let's start with setting the record straight on a few myths:

- A seizure disorder is not contagious.
- It is not possible to swallow the tongue during a seizure – or at any other time.
- You should not put anything in the mouth of someone having a seizure, because it does nothing to help, and it could cause damage to teeth and gums or choking.

- Putting something metal in their hand will not stop the seizure and may cause cuts to the hand, so do no put anything in the hand.
- You should not restrain someone who is having a seizure.
- You should not keep someone away from water – so not washing them – because they have a seizure disorder; it makes no difference to the seizures and makes a big difference in hygiene.
- You should not put the feet of someone having a seizure in the fire: it will burn them, but it will not stop the seizure.
- Doing work, dancing and going about normal life is not likely to cause a seizure – unless it is done to the point of extreme exhaustion.
- Having seizures is not a sign of the child being evil or possessed.

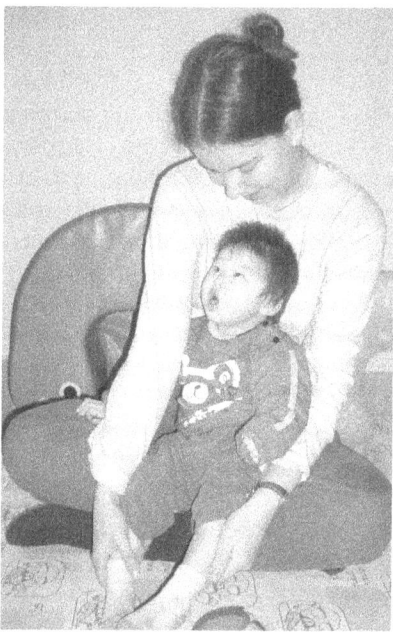

This little guy had spastic cerebral palsy with seizures, but with medication his seizures were under control.

Officially, a seizure is defined as 'a transient, involuntary alteration of consciousness, behaviour, motor activity, sensation and/or autonomic function caused by excessive rate and hypersynchrony of discharges from a group of cerebral neurons.' Very roughly translated: a seizure can be described as being a short-circuit in the brain that leads to strong, not very useful orders being sent to various muscle groups or to other parts of the brain. There are many different kinds of seizures. Some kinds are so mild that they are not easily recognised by someone who is not experienced in dealing with seizures.

It can be something as little as the rhythmic twitching of an eyebrow (not all eyebrow twitches are seizures, but some can be) or a child suddenly stopping what she is doing and getting a dreamy stare for a few seconds, only to continue what she was doing before as if nothing happened when the seizure passes – in fact, the child will probably not be aware that she stopped what she was doing at all. Automatic behaviour, like smacking lips or making chewing movements, could be a seizure or the warning that a seizure is on its way. There can be rolling back of the eyes and jerky movements with arms and legs. Someone having a certain kind of seizure may lose consciousness and fall to the floor. The muscles could go completely limp, or on the other hand they could tense up very, very tightly. It is also possible for the muscles to go tight and then limp over and over again.

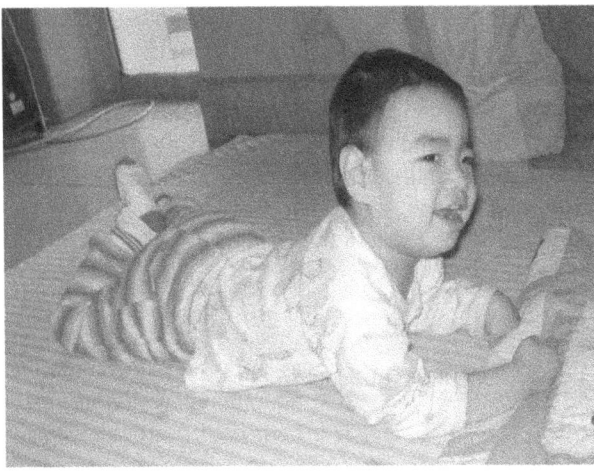

In a severe seizure, the child will lose consciousness and most of the muscles in her body will either tense up – her arms and legs will usually either be spread out completely or pulled all in, almost curling up into a ball – or she may make jerky movements, lashing her arms out and pulling them back in. She may throw her head from side to side and she may be drooling or even frothing at the mouth. It is possible that she will stop breathing and turn blue. A seizure in which a child turns blue can be very dangerous, but there is nothing you can do for the child to help her breathe until the seizure has passed. If the seizure lasts a long time, the lack of oxygen may do a lot of damage. If there is no breathing for more than five minutes, the child could die. Thankfully, seizures where a child stops breathing for more than a moment are very rare, and seizures like this lasting for more than a minute or two are even rarer.

You cannot tell by looking at her that she has a seizure disorder.

A baby with a severe seizure disorder had a few dozen seizures a day. Several times a day, his breathing would stop for a while during a seizure. He had become deaf and blind because of the brain damage caused by the lack of oxygen. Only caregivers and medically trained volunteers were allowed to hold the boy because he had seizures every few minutes, and the person holding him needed to be confident about how to handle him through this.

Another specific kind of seizures is **febrile** seizures. These are seizures that only occur when the child has a fever. Children who have febrile seizures do not necessarily have seizures at other times. However, children who have a seizure disorder already are at greater risk for febrile seizures. A febrile seizure usually occurs together with a high fever of more than 39°C or when the child's temperature rises or drops very fast. Febrile seizures are most often seen in children between six months and five years old. Bringing down and controlling the fever is the most effective way to deal with a febrile seizure. There is more information about this in Part 3, Chapter 6: 'Fevers and Hypothermia'.

Chapter 3: Donations and Treats

What Should Be Done?
If you see a bigger child having a seizure involving unconsciousness and jerky muscle movement, you should make sure that she is lying in a safe place, where she is unlikely to hurt herself. Move her away from danger if she is not in a safe place. However, do not move her unless she is somewhere that is dangerous for her. Let her lie somewhere where she cannot fall down when moving wildly and where she will not bang her arms, legs or head on hard, sharp or pointy objects. Then make sure that no one is restraining the child.

Holding her arms and/or legs will not make the seizure stop. Because the force behind the muscle tightening in her body is so great, holding her tight can lead to serious injury or broken bones. Place a pillow or cloth under her head, to prevent her from banging her head on the ground. If there is nothing available to put under the child's head, put your hand under her head to cushion the blows.

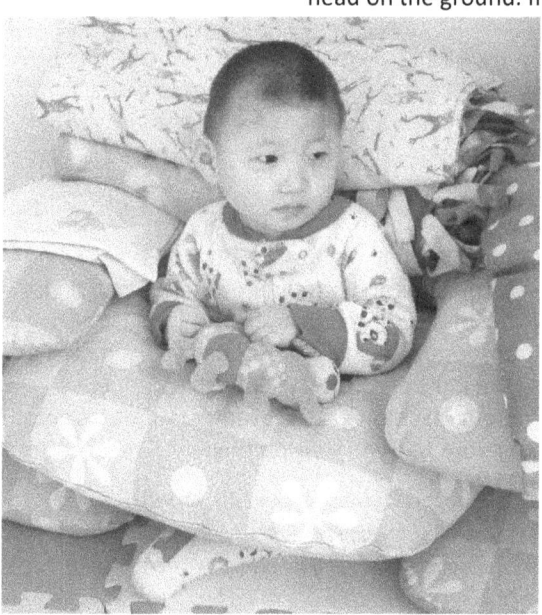

With anti-seizure medication, her condition is controlled and she hardly ever has a seizure anymore.

Do not place anything in her mouth to prevent her biting her tongue. It is possible that she will bite her tongue, but a bitten tongue will heal quite quickly, while there is a danger of her biting down so hard on the object put in her mouth that it breaks, or of the object moving back in her mouth, which can cause her to choke. Because the danger of choking is much more serious than the danger of biting her tongue, nothing should be put in the child's mouth during a seizure. Putting something in her hand will not help put an end to the seizure either, while there is a danger that she might cut herself on what is in her hand when she clenches her fist very tightly.

If the child is drooling a lot or frothing at the mouth, gently try to turn the child's head to the side to allow the saliva to run out of the mouth so she does not choke on it. But do not try to force the head, because this can cause serious, permanent injury.
If the child having a seizure is a baby or toddler, small enough for you to hold without constraining her movements, you can hold the baby through the seizure. If she is drooling a lot, or frothing at the mouth, you can hold the baby facing down, so that the saliva runs down onto the floor and she does not choke on it. Make sure that she has plenty of room to move her arms and legs freely through the seizure.

Then, all you can do is wait until the seizure passes, which usually takes less than a minute or two. While the seizure is still going on, do not leave the child alone. Make sure that there is an adult with her the entire time, until she regains consciousness again. Other people should not be allowed to gather around the child and especially children should be removed from the room – it can be very scary and traumatic for them to see another child having a seizure. Ask for one of the other adults to take the other children to another room or, if that is not possible, to keep them occupied at the other side of the same room.

A nine-month-old girl had many seizures a day while her medication was still being adjusted. Caregivers often had to be reminded that they needed to allow her to move while she was having a seizure. They wanted to hold her tightly to make the twitching stop. When I sat with her, I sang to her through her seizures, but otherwise I did nothing to interfere with her, other than making sure that she did not fall off my lap. This made some caregivers feel that I was uncaring. They gave me angry looks for not doing anything to make it stop. Since there was nothing I could do to make it stop, I focussed on keeping her comfortable and making sure she did not hurt herself.

If a seizure lasts for more than ten minutes, or if the child has not been breathing for four minutes and has turned blue, an ambulance should be called, or urgent transportation to hospital should be arranged if possible. Transporting the child to hospital yourself during a seizure is only possible if the child is small enough to lift her up and transport her without restraining her movements. If this is not the case, it is too dangerous to try to transport her.

A teenage boy falls to the ground and starts making jerking movements. He is having a seizure, something that happens from time to time. His friend wants to help him, so he grabs the boy's arm with both of his hands and leans on him, to try to make him stop moving. Other children go to call a caregiver. The caregiver thanks the friend for his help, but explains that the best thing for the boy is to let him go and allow him to move. She asks all the children to stand back and to go call another one of the caregivers to look after them. She puts a folded up jumper under the boy's head, to keep him from banging it, and stays with the boy until he is conscious again.

After the seizure is over, the child may be exhausted and may only want to lie down and sleep – sometimes for several hours. You should allow her to do that. In any case, it will be next to impossible to keep her awake in this situation. The tiredness after a seizure can last an entire day. It is also possible that the child will be extremely fidgety and restless for several minutes after a seizure. This is a common reaction. Allow the child to pace or sit down and get up again or to fidget, just keep an eye on her safety and that of other children. After a while, she will calm down again on her own. It is also possible, and relatively common, for a child to stay unconscious for half an hour to an hour after the seizure as passed.

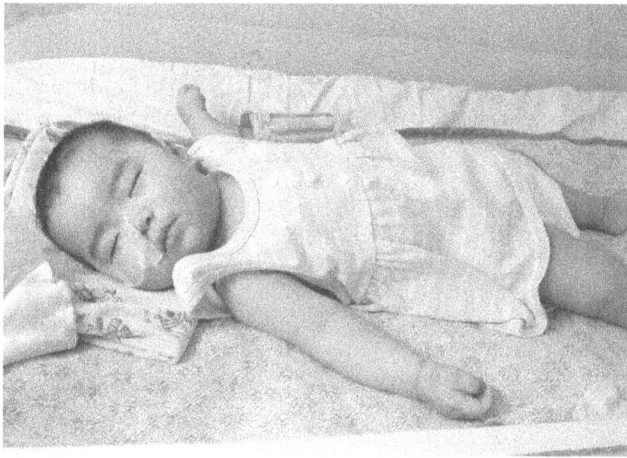

She has seizures very regularly, so she is placed so that she won't hurt herself if she starts moving violently.

So remember:

- Only move the child to prevent her from falling or injuring herself.
- Do not restrain her movements.
- Do not put anything in her mouth or hands.
- Protect her head from banging against the floor.
- Make sure an adult is with her throughout the seizure and stays with her until she is conscious again.

If you would like to have more information about seizures, take a look at *Sick Children Everywhere. How to Provide Good Institutional Care. Book 2: Basic Medical Care for Children in Institutions* Part 2, Chapter 6: Seizure Disorders.

PART 3:
Basic Childcare and Child Psychology

Introduction

This third part of this manual gives a mini crash-course in childcare. It is specifically aimed at care for children in children's homes, which is not always the same as that for children in families. I have used excerpts from the first and second manual for institutional childcare, giving you some of the same information that is given to caregivers and managers of children's homes, adjusted slightly for the situation. In several places it still describes what the 'caregiver' is expected to do or know; in these cases you can look at yourself as a stand-in caregiver in your role as a volunteer. Of course, considering both those manuals are books of considerable size, you will understand that only the most important issues have been picked out to make you aware of them. The subjects included are those that have the greatest impact on the children's health and well-being. This part of the manual explains basic hygiene and safety issues, makes you aware of some child psychology and child development – why children act the way they do – and helps you recognise relatively common and possibly serious problems like fevers, **hypothermia**, dehydration and malnutrition, giving you an idea of what you can do to help these children safely. If you have more than a passing interest in these issues, you can have a look *Children Everywhere* (the institutional childcare manual) and *Sick Children Everywhere* (the medical manual) as well.

Of course, you are not the one in charge of the children's home and it is not your role to decide how things are done there. This means that while the information given in this part helps find the way to best practice, what you see happening around you may be very different, and in most cases you will have no way of changing the situation. Still, this last part of the volunteer manual serves an important purpose. The things explained in the first five chapters of this part should ideally be followed by all caregivers. If that is not the case, you yourself can still make a point of using good hygiene practice, being conscious of the safety of the children and approaching them in a way that caters to their essential needs. This will have a positive impact on the children's lives and may set a good example that starts caregivers thinking. With regards to the more medically oriented chapters, you will generally not be allowed to do much with these. The reason for including them anyway is to make sure that in case you do find that you have the opportunity and inclination to step in, you have the right information available. Sometimes volunteers decide to step in with the best of intentions but an incomplete understanding of the situation, which can lead to dangerous circumstances. By including the medical information I hope these dangers will be less likely to occur.

So while the methods of dealing with various situations described here are generally effective and it would be good if children's homes put them in place, it is important to remember what was mentioned before: you need to respect the management and caregivers and not go against their wishes when it comes to handling the children. So before you go ahead and start disciplining children, or want to start treating a child with a medical issue described here, you need to talk to your contact person at the children's home and get permission to go ahead. Sometimes there may be circumstances that you are not aware of that make it undesirable to go ahead, as it might harm the child more than help him. Also, to be able to help effectively, you need to keep a good relationship with the people who work at the children's home, because going against their wishes may end with you being thrown out. However well your intentions (and you may be right), if the management does not agree that the course of action you propose is in the interest of the children, then throwing you out, in their eyes, may be the best way to protect the children from harm. If that happens, you will not be able to help out in any way anymore. So always look for ways to help and to encourage improvements being made, but do so within the limits set by the children's home. Trying to force change is never effective. It will just stop people listening to you.

However, the aim of Part 3 of this manual is not getting you into trouble for wanting to do more good than you are allowed to. It is to give you an insight into various situations. To make you less scared of encountering these kinds of issues and to make you aware of how you can approach them sensibly.

Part 3: Basic Childcare and Child Psychology

Chapter 1: Hygiene

It is extremely hard to overstate the importance of good hygiene in ensuring children's health and improving their chance of survival. This is generally true in the case of babies and toddlers who are still building up their immune system and are more vulnerable to illnesses and infection than older children. However, it is especially true where children in a children's home are concerned. Many people living close together in itself increases the chance of someone carrying some kind of virus, bacteria or other infection, as well as increasing the chance of whatever one person has being spread to others through close contact. When you add to these factors the fact that children living in an institutional situation almost always have a weaker immune system than children of the same age group who live in families – due to lack of breast milk, enough physical contact and attention as well as a variety of other potential risk factors – you will realise that doing your best to protect these children from infection through good hygiene is a top priority.

General Hygiene

Washing Hands
The simplest, and at the same time most complicated way to maintain good hygiene, is by thorough hand washing with soap. It is the simplest because everyone knows how to do it and it is a very cheap and effective way to prevent the spread of bacteria, viruses and fungi. It is complicated in the sense that is very hard to make people understand how important it is and to make sure that they do it consistently.

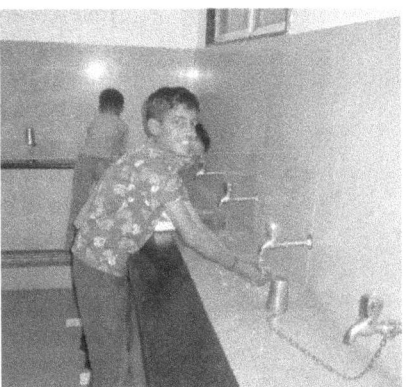

The children have been taught to wash their hands before they eat.

Making sure that hands are washed consistently means that anyone at all setting foot in the children's home should make a straight line for the tap and soap, to wash everything they have come in contact with outside the home off their hands before they touch *any* of the children. Using soap to wash your hands is important, because just rinsing them with water will not get rid of bacteria or dirt that is not very superficial.

Next, and even harder to enforce: hands should be washed in-between handling different children. When you are sitting in the

Chapter 1: Hygiene

middle of a group of children, playing, you do not need to wash your hands between one child and the other. It would be better, but it is not practical. However, before you move to another group or a child from another group, you should wash your hands.

To give a simple overview:
- Before preparing meals or bottles, hands should be washed.
- Before preparing or handling medication, hands should be washed.
- Before handling **sterilised** bottles, hands should be washed.
- After EVERY nappy changed, hands should be washed.
- After every bath given, hands should be washed.
- After handling vomit, hands should be washed.
- After having been drooled on, hands should be washed.
- Before and after touching any wound, sore, rash or child with a fever or other signs of illness, hands should be washed.
- Before and after handling one of the youngest babies, hands should be washed.
- After visiting the toilet, hands should be washed.
- Before and after eating, hands should be washed.

It is time consuming, it is annoying, it is hard to get people to co-operate with and it is hard on your hands. I know all these things, because I practice constant hand washing if the circumstances allow me to. The reason why I keep washing my hands so often despite the inconvenience – and in some cases in spite of the pain – is that I have seen the enormous difference hand washing makes in the children's health. Using hand lotion after washing your hands can help ease discomfort.

An eye infection broke out. There were two groups, separated by a hallway, one consisting of babies and one consisting of toddlers. At the start, one or two of the children in each group had the infection. In the toddler group, it soon spread a lot faster, and within three days two or three of the caring staff also had the eye infection. This solved the riddle: in the baby group hands were washed diligently and the infection was kept relatively contained. In the toddler group, hands were not washed as well as they should be, and the infection did not only reach more children, but also the caregivers who did not wash their hands.

If washing hands with water and soap is not possible because of shortage of (safe) water or a great inconvenience in reaching the place to wash your hands, or many people needing to wash their hands at once, **hand sanitiser** can be used instead.

Nappy Hygiene

It is very important that nappies or wet/soiled clothes are changed very regularly. Both urine and **faeces** literally break down the skin if it stays in contact with them for some time. How often nappies need to be changed, depends on the type of **nappy** used.

These days, most disposable nappies make sure that the contact between skin and urine is minimal. Therefore, it is usually not a problem to let up to four hours go between nappy changes, at least when the nappy is only wet. A dirty nappy (one with poop in it) should always be changed as soon as possible, as faeces acts more aggressively on the skin than urine. If you use cloth nappies (they should preferably be made of absorbent cotton), there is no barrier between the urine and the skin, plus the nappy tends to become saturated more quickly. Therefore, cloth nappies ought to be changed every two to three hours at least. Clothes should be changed whenever they are wet or soiled. In either case, unless the baby's bottom is already red or the skin in the nappy area is broken, you can usually leave changing nappies longer, at night. How long mainly depends on how absorbent the nappy you use is. In cases of a bad nappy rash it is advisable to leave the baby with a bare bottom for at least a few hours a day, to let the skin dry and heal.

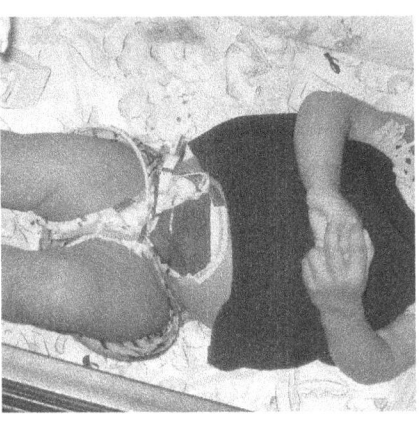

A thin cloth nappy like this does not absorb much, so clothes and bedding need to be changed after every wee.

Cleaning Bottoms

Whether you use disposable baby wipes – preferably ones without any kind of perfume, because the perfume can lead to allergies – a washcloth with water, or by holding the baby's bottom under the tap and washing it there with your hands, it is extremely important that you wash the baby's bottom very thoroughly every time she has pooped. Just wiping the baby's bottom with a dry cloth or toilet paper, or

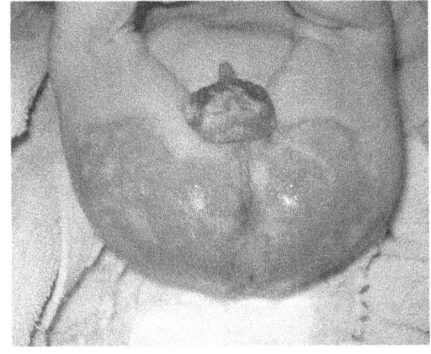

The result of not changing often enough and not cleaning well enough; it can get even worse than this, if you let it.

with the nappy you have just removed, is not enough. The material that you use to clean the baby's bottom needs to be damp in order to effectively remove all remaining poop. Whenever the nappy area is very damp after removing a wet nappy, it should also be wiped clean and dry.

Lack of properly cleaning a baby's bottom can literally kill her, eventually. Remains of faeces on the skin will continue to eat away at it. This will cause slight redness at first, which will steadily get worse, in a process that progresses exponentially faster if it is not stopped by proper care. The redness will get livid and become very painful. Then the skin will break, and weeping sores and blisters will appear. This will progress to open, bleeding wounds, which will get infected when the bacteria from the faeces enter them, and this can – and is highly likely to, if nothing is done – lead to Septicaemia: a blood infection that can be **lethal** if not treated promptly. This is why it is so extremely important to clean the baby properly after she pooped, every time, and to take action straight away if a nappy rash is starting to develop.

When cleaning a girl after a dirty nappy, make sure you wipe front to back, to prevent faeces from being wiped up into the vaginal and urinal openings, and possibly cause infections there. Both with boys and girls, make sure you check all the hiding places. This is not sexual assault: it is proper hygiene. Little boys tend to hide some of their poop between their penis and their scrotum, so check and clean, but do not pull back the foreskin. Another hiding place is under the scrotum, so check and clean. Girls sometimes manage to store poop in between their labia, so this also need to be cleaned to prevent irritation and skin break-down.

After a training session on basic childcare in a children's home for staff and volunteers, one of the volunteers came up to me. She told me that she never knew that girls are supposed to be wiped from front to back. Even adding little bits of new knowledge can make a big difference in the health of the children.

When you use a bowl of water (make sure the water is safe to use; if there are a lot of water born parasites and such in your area, strain the water through a clean cloth and boil it before you use it to wash children, and their bottoms) and a clean cloth to clean a bottom, avoid dipping the soiled cloth in the water again. Use a different cloth for the second 'round'. Otherwise, poop will get into the water and may be smeared onto other bottoms, increasing the chance of spreading infection.

If you are applying any creams, especially when more than one child uses the contents of the tube or jar, apply the cream with a cotton swab, not with your finger. Use a new cotton swab every time you want to get more out of the tube or jar. This prevents bacteria getting into the cream and spreading onto the next child. If the baby has a nappy rash, zinc oxide is the most effective barrier. Applying a generous layer of zinc oxide will prevent the skin from coming into contact with urine and faeces, thus allowing the skin time to heal. If there is no zinc oxide or other barrier cream, very fine corn flour can also be used.

Do not put fingers in jars of cream.

If the rash on the baby's bottom is not a red area but separate red dots, it is likely to be a fungal infection rather than a regular nappy rash – especially if the baby has thrush (white patches on the inside of her cheeks and on her tongue) in her mouth too. In this case, a doctor should have a look at the rash, so that an appropriate antifungal cream can be prescribed.

When you put the clothes back on the baby, check that they are still dry and that nothing has leaked out of the nappy onto them. If there is any wetness or staining, the clothes should be changed.
Finally, ALWAYS wash your hands after you finish changing a baby's nappy, for your health as well as theirs.

Bathing
It is very important for health and hygiene that children are kept clean. Mouths and hands should be wiped regularly with a damp cloth throughout the day. The whole face, neck, and nappy area should be given a wash at least once a day. If enough safe water is available, all children should be given a bath at least twice or three times a week. If this is not an option, giving them a full body wash using a cloth and water that has been thoroughly boiled – and cooled – could be an alternative.

If there is plenty of water and time available, having a daily bath is good. However, more than once a day – as I have encountered – may be excessive. It is inadvisable to use soap on the whole body more than once a day. Soap dries out the skin. Especially with babies, whose skin is even thinner, using soap very often can cause skin problems.

Do not, under any circumstances, leave a child under four years old

Chapter 1: Hygiene

Having the basin on the floor is a safe way to bathe.

alone in a bath. Children up to eight or nine years old should be within hearing range of an adult while they are in the bath. A baby or toddler needs only a couple of minutes and a couple of centimetres of water in order to drown. What many people do not realise, is that there may not necessarily be a big splash or a scream to warn you that something has gone wrong.

In a particular children's home, the little children were bathed in a small baby bath that was put on a slightly unstable stool, to bring it to a height that was easier on the caregiver's back. The caregiver had a habit of putting a baby who was able to sit up by herself in the bath, and then go to one of the bedrooms to get clean clothes for the baby to sleep in, while the baby was allowed to play in the water.

One evening I was giving this baby a bath in the same construction. At one point the baby decided to try if she could stand up. Pulling herself up changed the balance of the bath and caused it to shift, which in turn caused one of the legs to break off the old stool on which the bath was placed. I was just in time to catch her. If no one had been standing beside her, she would have crashed to the floor, together with the bath and the remains of the stool, and might have gotten hurt very badly.

A few things become clear in this example. First of all, even if a situation has not caused any problems for quite some time, it does not mean that something will not suddenly happen. Especially when it involves a child who may decide to try out something new at any moment. Secondly, while it is a good idea to try to find a way to spare your back while caring for a baby, only do so if it can be done in a very secure way, not on an unstable stool.

If you realise that you have left the baby's towel in the other room, and there is no one you can call to get it for you, it is better to take the baby out of the bath and bring her with you, dripping wet – if she is very small, hold her against you for warmth, even if this means you get wet – than to leave her in the tub by herself, while you run to go and get the towel.

Grooming

Making sure that nails are kept short is an important part of children's hygiene, both your nails and those of the children. Dirt and germs gather underneath fingernails – and they are very hard to get out from under those tiny nails – and get **transferred** onto food and into the mouth. As well as that, babies and children with long nails are more likely to scratch themselves or others, either by accident or on purpose, and break the skin, which in turn leads to a greater chance of infections.

Children should be checked for lice very regularly, and treated for it if lice are found. There is no shame in having lice. In fact, in any place where a lot of people live close together, it is extremely hard to avoid getting them. However, steps should be taken to eliminate this problem as much as possible. Aside from the annoying itch, which can make children quite difficult to deal with, there is a risk of infection if scratching reaches the point of breaking the skin. Some children might have an allergic reaction to lice, leading to rashes, skin scratched open and infected wounds. Also, do not be under the illusion that it will be possible to make sure that the lice will not pass from the children to adults. If the children have lice, the adults around them will get them too and vice versa.

Dental Hygiene

Brushing teeth is also part of the cleanliness of a child, although at first teeth are very few and really tiny. They do, right from the start, come into contact with foods and liquids that can damage them. That is why it is very important to start brushing the baby's teeth right from the moment the first one appears.

> *When I ask if the babies' teeth are being brushed, I often get a surprised reaction: 'but he only has 4 teeth!' Well, that makes 4 teeth that need brushing.*

You can use a small toothbrush, but even a piece of gauze wrapped around your finger will do. In some countries special toothpaste is available for children under six years old, who tend to swallow everything they get in their mouths, instead of spitting out the toothpaste. If this is available where you are, you can use a tiny amount of it – about the size of the child's pinky nail. If it is not available, just

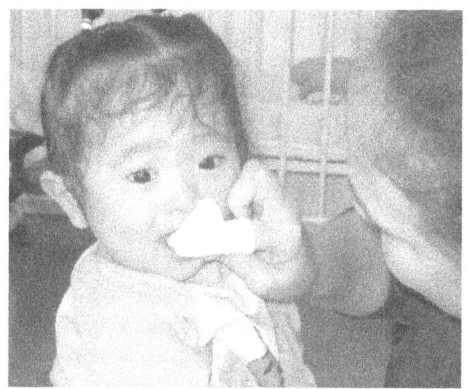

brushing with a toothbrush or gauze with water also works well. Babies and small children should not use adult toothpaste. The amount of fluoride in it is not safe for them to swallow. Until about six years old, children need help to make sure their teeth are brushed properly. You can let the child start the brushing himself, if he wants. But then, you will need to go over all the teeth again, with the toothbrush, to make sure nothing was missed.

It is a good idea to clean the tongue when you are brushing the child's teeth. This too can be done with a little bit of wet gauze. The tongue houses quite a lot of bacteria, which can move back to the teeth after brushing if the tongue is not cleaned as well.

Brushing teeth with wet gauze wrapped around a finger.

Food Hygiene

In any kind of institutional situation, it is of the utmost importance to uphold very high food hygiene standards. Not only with regard to the preparation of food, but also with regard to the bottles, bowls and plates, utensils and eating surfaces. Having a lot of children close together will always promote the spreading of any disease or infection, but no methods of spreading these is quite as effective as through the objects that they put in their mouths.

It is important to:

- Always wash your hands before preparing a bottle or any other food.
- Thoroughly wash your hands immediately after having handled raw meat, fish or eggs.
- Make sure that work surfaces, cutting boards, bowls, pans and anything else that will be coming into contact with the food are clean before using them.
- Make sure that all the food you make is cooked through and through.
- Regularly clean the fridge, containers and any other locations where food is kept.
- Store food that spoils fast in the fridge or freezer and throw it away if it has been left outside the fridge or freezer for too long – or if a power cut has let things in the fridge or freezer warm up or thaw.
- Throw away food if insects, larvae, eggs or mould are found in dry-stored goods.

All these measures are to prevent food poisoning and parasites, which, especially in the case of babies and toddlers, can lead to dangerous medical problems quite rapidly.

Bottles are sterilised in these devices, but boiling them works too.

Where babies are bottle-fed, all bottles, nipples and caps should be thoroughly washed with soap and a brush after every feed. If bottles are shared by all children, they need to be sterilised after every use as well. Even in situations where all babies have their own bottle and nipple which are both clearly marked with their name, to avoid any mistakes, bottles for babies under five months old should be sterilised after every use. At times when the temperature is high – 26°C and over –, bottles, nipples and caps should be sterilised for all children after every time they have contained milk, even if they do not share bottles. For babies over five months, when it is not hot, bottles, nipples and caps should be sterilised at least twice a week. Sterilizing can be done with sterilizing equipment, or by boiling the items in water for five to ten minutes.

When the child starts eating solids, bowls, cups and spoons should be thoroughly washed with soap after every use. Every child should use a separate bowl and a separate spoon.

A caregiver would feed three or four children from the same bowl, using only one spoon. When she was offered one spoon for each child, she said she would not use the other spoons, because not doing so would save on the dishes having to be washed. One of the four children had a throat infection, and this was known. When the other children also got the throat infection, much more time was needed to take them to the doctor and care for them than it takes to wash a few more bowls and spoons. And the cost was also considerably higher.

Very, very few babies and toddlers eat without making a mess. If spilled food is left where it falls, it can start to rot or a mould will form. Then a child may pick it up, eat it and get ill. So, it is very important to thoroughly clean the area where the eating has taken place. That includes the floor, the wall, the chair and table – not to forget the little ridges where food gets trapped– and possibly toys or other things that a child may have grabbed while her hands were still covered in food. A quick wipe is usually not enough to get it all clean; check that everything has really come off.

Making an effort to uphold good hygiene standards can literally help save lives. And it will help keep you healthier too.

Chapter 2: Safety

Especially once they start moving around, children have an almost limitless capacity for getting themselves into trouble. This is not out of malice or stupidity, but simply out of curiosity, a sense of adventure, and a lack of understanding of danger. If you explain to them why something is not allowed, whenever you tell them they cannot do something, their ability to predict what is dangerous or unacceptable will – very slowly – grow over time.

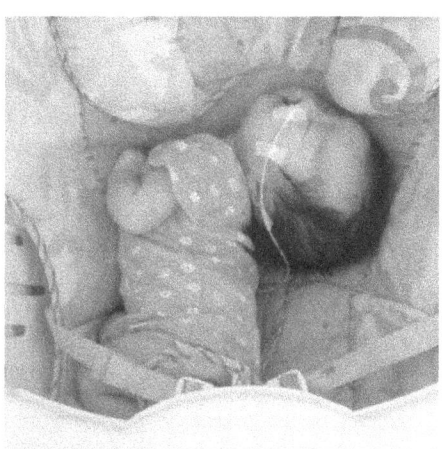

Safety is also about not putting a newborn in an upright seat, where she will end up like this.

If you do not give them an explanation, or simply say 'because I'm telling you!', it will take a lot longer for them to find out what is dangerous and what is not through trial and error. Unfortunately, error can have very serious, dangerous consequences.

Safe Surroundings

Children's curiosity about their surroundings and their amazing ability to get at, onto, under, around, and behind things, make it very important to create a safe environment where they can explore without being in constant danger.

A two-year-old girl wanted to see who was coming up the stairs, so she crawled over, stuck her head through the banister and then stood up. Unfortunately, the wooden banister was sculpted with the openings between the barriers going from wide to narrow to wide. So, once she stood up, her head got stuck in the narrow part, with her ears preventing her from pulling her head out. It took a while to calm her down enough to be able to move her head down to the wider part, where it could come out.

Providing basic safety requires:

- Removing any objects that are small enough to be put entirely in a child's mouth and that they can choke on.

- Removing objects with sharp edges or spikes, or objects that come apart in small or sharp pieces, including building materials and heavy or sharp tools.
- Removing anything that might be toxic or unhygienic from children's reach.
- Closing electrical sockets, either with a special safety device or by taping them closed whenever there is no plug in them.
- Moving electrical wiring out of sight and out of reach.
- Restricting unaccompanied access to stairs, kitchen, and other rooms where a lot of dangerous things can be found.
- Securing cupboards, wardrobes and toy shelves, so they will not fall over if a child attempts to climb on them.
- Keeping medication and medical equipment outside of children's reach at all times, preferably locked away.

Making a situation safe does not always require a complicated, expensive solution.

Supervision

Even in an environment where most dangers have been removed, small children should never be left entirely alone. A child of under three years old should have someone check visually on what she is doing every five minutes or so while she is awake, at the very least. And no child under five years old should ever be out of hearing range of at least one adult, awake or asleep.

The lid to cover the keys of the piano was always kept open to prevent children from being able to lift it up, with the risk of it crashing down again on their fingers. Standing in front of the piano, the toddlers were not able to reach the lid. However, a little girl just short of two years old decided to try if she might not be able to reach the lid from the side. She succeeded. The lid fell closed on the tip of her finger and chopped it off. The girl had to be rushed to hospital. After this incident, the lid was duct-taped to the body of the piano to prevent further danger.

That all children are healthy when you leave them behind does not guarantee that they will not get ill or hurt themselves while you are away, even in a relatively safe environment. Trying to climb out of bed may go wrong, even if a child has done it successfully many times, or a child can choke on something. The more general unexpected dangers are also never out of the question, such as a house fire or an earthquake. In all of these cases, if help is immediate, the result may turn out not too serious, but if the problem is not discovered until an hour or more afterwards, the consequences can be extremely serious.

I was able to grab one of these children just in time to stop him falling head first into the hole with the spikes when a ball rolled into the hole and he wanted to reach down to try to grab it.

Children who are too young – or too handicapped mentally and/or physically to save themselves or take action to get help – should always have an adult close by. And no one – adult or child – should ever be locked in a space without someone being right outside the door to let them out in case of an emergency.

While it seems self-evident, it still needs to be mentioned: never leave a child on her own on an elevated surface – such as the changing table, table top, a bed without high sides, a garden wall, a step ladder and so on. While on the one hand, most people are aware of the risk, on the other hand it really is hard to realise exactly how little time a child needs to come crashing down from something. Even when she is only a few months old, or if she is generally quite capable of doing what she is there to do. Accidents usually happen when someone has been closely watching the child the whole time, but then had to step away for just a very short moment. Even if you do not stop paying attention, you may be surprised.

I was changing a baby on the changing table. He was about four months old and had just started rolling over, but only over his left side, which on that changing table would have brought him over towards the wall. I took one step back to open one of the drawers below the changing mat and grab a clean pair of pants for him. The next instant, I held him in my hands. He had rolled over and fallen down so quickly that I did not realise what had happened until after I had caught him – these reflexes come with working a lot with small babies.

So, whenever a baby or toddler is on an elevated surface, an adult should be not just nearby, but no further than at arm's length of the child, so that she has a chance of being caught if she decides to do something dangerous. The reason why very small children do things like this is a combination of a lack of understanding of the danger, and an infinite trust in adults that they will catch them and make things right, no matter what. So the child puts the burden of responsibility and never-ending vigilance on the adult.

An eighteen-month-old girl who was never any trouble, walked over to see what the caregiver was up to. While she was watching the caregiver take care of something, the little girl held on to the door on the side of the hinges. The caregiver had not noticed her being there and when she was finished what she needed to do, she closed the door and the little girls fingers were caught between the door and the doorpost on the other side. She only very narrowly escaped broken bones, but still needed a trip to the hospital to have her hand treated.

Precautions

Always strap babies and toddlers in when you put them in buggies, car seats or high chairs. Even if you have no intention of leaving their side. First of all, something unexpected may happen that may lead to you having to 'abandon' the child you were looking after to help out with something more urgent, especially in a situation where there are a lot of children together. Secondly, your attention only needs to be distracted for a couple of seconds – while stirring food in a bowl with your back turned, or while very quickly walking over to the sink to grab a cup – for a child to suddenly take a head dive. This can even – or perhaps particularly, because you expect it less – happen with a child who is usually very quiet and unadventurous.

Allowing these children to watch a working digger from such a short distance is not a great idea.

Always place hot items, such as cooking pots or cups of tea, completely outside the reach of the children. Every year, many children get burned very seriously because they pull at a kettle or pan and have the boiling contents poured over them. Children who pull at tablecloths may be scalded by the contents of a teapot or have everything that stood on the table fall on top of them. Cups of hot tea or coffee seem the most innocent, yet might do the most damage. A child pulling your arm while you were just about the take a sip might get burned when the contents of the cup spill, or a child who wants to imitate you may grab your hot beverage while your back is turned or while you are distracted, and either take a big gulp of a liquid that is far too hot, or be unable to manage the cup and spill the contents all over himself.

The caregiver had just made a cup of tea for herself, when she was called over to help with one of the children. She placed her cup on the windowsill and went over. A little boy of about eighteen months came over to investigate. He was just able to reach the bottom of the cup. He gave it a few pushes and then it fell down, pouring the scalding hot tea all over his belly. He needed treatment for the burns on his belly for several months.

All of these things can cause very serious burns, which in turn can lead to dangerous infections as well as almost inevitable scarring. So even though it is inconvenient not to be able to drink a warm drink while you are holding a child, or not to be able to keep your cup within easy reaching distance, it really is worth the trouble to bring down the risks of very serious injury.

He's enjoying it, but does not understand the danger of standing this close to the fireworks, let alone on his bare feet.

Also make sure that the children are not able to enter the kitchen unsupervised. Small children need to be taught, under close supervision, to recognise the danger of things that are hot or that burn. They should not be left to discover such things by themselves, because they may not live to benefit from the lesson. The same goes for matches, lighters, knives, and other dangerous utensils and tools; they should be stored where children cannot possibly get to them.

A tour of the living spaces – as well as the areas around the house, especially those where children play – should be made very regularly. While walking around, you need to discover which of the things lying around and the situations you encounter might pose a danger to the children. When you find something that could be dangerous, everything possible should be done to change the situation into a safer one.

It is important to be aware of the limits of a child's ability to predict consequences. Up to about thirteen years of age, most children are unable to predict that there is a certain chance of something going wrong, especially if the danger lies not so much in the initial picking up of an object, or the climbing onto something, but two or three steps further down the line. Part 3, Chapter 3: 'Global Developmental Stages of Childhood' will give more information about this.

Part 3: Basic Childcare and Child Psychology

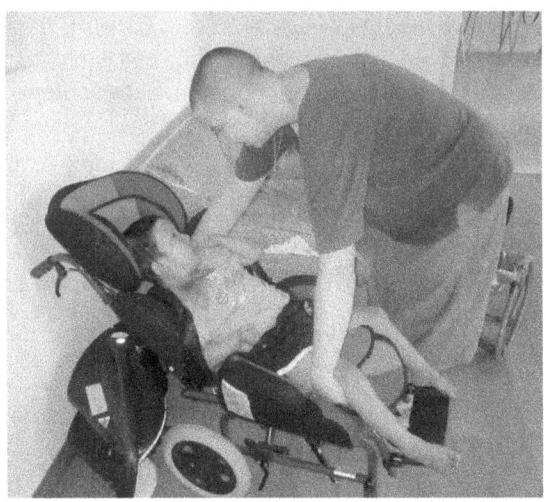
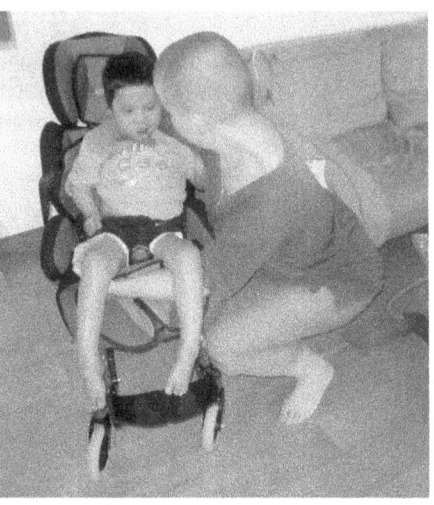

Your safety is also important: picking up a large child like this will hurt your back if you do it regularly.

If you keep your back straight both when lifting and when putting down, you will be fine.

At Diwali all of the children, aged three to eighteen years old, were given a bag of fireworks to set off. The only instruction given with this was not to set them off in certain areas of the compound. The next few days were a chaos and mayhem of children setting off fireworks all over the compound, for the most part unsupervised. One boy got something in his eye and many children had burns to their hands and feet – mostly from grabbing a sparkler just after it had gone out, or stepping on it with bare feet.

When I asked why it was organised like this, I was told that the previous year the fireworks had been set off under controlled and supervised circumstances, in a large circle with the children surrounding it. But the children had said they wanted to be free to do it themselves.

Of course that is what they want! But since they do not understand the consequences and dangers of handling fireworks, it is the role of adults to protect them.

Chapter 3: Essential Psychological Needs

Things like food, hygiene, shelter, sleep and safety are generally acknowledged to be essential basic needs: things that children require to be able to survive and **thrive**. These are the things that most people running a children's home strive to provide to the best of their knowledge and ability. It is much rarer for people anywhere in the world to realise that affection, attention, physical contact, stimulation and attachment are needs that are just as basic and essential. Relatively few people know that a child's survival can depend on these things too.

In search of even closer physical contact, he has burrowed himself into the volunteer's shirt.

This chapter aims to give a better understanding of why this is the case, what exactly the impact of lacking the above mentioned things is, and what is required to provide adequate care in these areas. To keep things clear, what are generally considered to be basic needs will be called 'practical needs' (all basic essential needs, except for affection, attention, physical contact, stimulation and attachment) and the complete set of basic needs will be called 'essential basic needs' (practical needs plus affection, attention, physical contact, stimulation and attachment). Of course, as a volunteer you are not in a position to turn the care system of the children's home around. But hopefully, an awareness of these essential needs will give you a better understanding of the difficulties these children face and, in turn, this may shape your personal attitude towards the children.

The Difference Between Care in a Family and Care in an Institution

For the child, what is the difference between care in a children's home and care in family? The answer seems obvious: the child misses her parents and she is not surrounded by family in a children's home. In a way, the answer really is this simple, but it becomes more complicated when you start looking at the *effects* of not having your parents and family around. Let us first have a look, in some detail, at the ways in which life in a children's home is different from life in a family.

A child in a family is surrounded by love and affection. This is very often not said in so many words, but it is still clear to anyone from the way parents talk to their children, give them attention, touch them and look at them. In most families, there is quite a lot of physical contact, especially when children are small. Babies are held and carried around, on a parent's arm or in a sling of some kind. Toddlers

Even without words, the love and bond between mother and children is clear.

get to sit on a parent's lap during mealtimes and on other occasions. Older children regularly get a hug, lean against their parents' legs or hold their hand in the street. In many countries, children and parents share closeness at night too: they sleep in the same bed, or in the same room. All these things together make a child feel safe. She feels that she has someone looking out for her, protecting her and keeping her from harm. Most of the time, the natural love and pride that parents feel for their children are expressed without it being consciously noticed by anyone.

Caregivers in a children's home do not have this natural bond with the children in their care, so the love does not come automatically and it is certainly not expressed without anyone realising. In a children's home, caregivers are doing a job. They are usually kept busy trying to meet the child's practical needs, such as making their food, keeping them clean and washing their clothes. This often leaves little time for holding children and giving them real attention. So, important parts of what a child needs as she is growing up are met in a family, where hardly anyone notices that they are fulfilling those needs, while in a children's home these needs are often simply forgotten because of the heavy workload. This is why it is important to think about the children's essential needs, and try to do something about meeting them consciously.

The caregiver never picks up or holds any of the six babies and toddlers that she cares for, except to move them in and out of bed, lift them onto the changing table or put them in their seats for dinner. On his first visit, a visitor presumes that this is because she is too busy to find the time to hold the children between cleaning, cooking, and other chores. So when the visitor is sent outside to watch the children playing there, he picks up one of the smallest children from

the blanket on the floor and holds her in his lap, while giving the other children attention and allowing them to lean against him. This way, he feels, he is able to contribute something that is usually lacking, without any cost to the caregiver. However, when after some time the caregiver sticks her head around the door to check on them, she tells the visitor sharply to put the baby down and to let the other children get on with their own play. It will only get them used to being held and getting attention and that will make them become difficult and demanding. The children need to learn to do without those things and then they will be fine, she claims.

It is true that if, for a long time, a child received – almost – no attention at all and is then given some attention, she can become more difficult, demanding more attention. However, this is not a sign of her being spoiled or of her being better off without attention. It is a sign that the child recognises a glimmer of hope that her essential needs may be met, and the instinct to start fighting for them kicks in.

Children without families also need to feel that they have someone they can depend on long-term.

In a family, a child has a primary caregiver, usually her mother or grandmother. This is a person in her life whom she knows will always be there and who can be relied on – if the parent goes away for a while, the child soon learns that it is only for a short time. A bond is formed with a primary caregiver, and with other people who are always around in a child's life. For example, her father, brothers and sisters, and maybe uncles or aunts, or grandparents who live in the same house or nearby. These relationships, which are formed at a very young age, teach the child how to form a relationship with someone and how to keep it going without anyone even noticing. These lessons are needed later on in life. They are important for forming and maintaining future relationships of all kinds.

In a children's home, there are usually few adults taking care of many children. This means that the caregivers are very busy and do not have much time to spend with each child. Plus, caregivers in children's homes quite often vary from day to day and from year to year.

This can be because:
- A caregiver leaves her job and someone else takes over
- Caregivers work in shifts and are only available at certain times
- The children's home is divided into different age groups, requiring children to move from one group to another when they reach a certain age
- Caregivers are moved around between groups and dorms

Also, even when caregivers do live at the children's home and are available around the clock, they often look after so many children that a distance is created between caregiver and the individual child. All of this means that there is no primary caregiver for the child to depend on. The adults vary frequently, and there is no chance for real bonds or relationships to be formed.

A caregiver lived together in the dorm with 17 children, aged one to six years old, for whom she was responsible. She did try to take time to sit with individual children and play with them or talk to them from time to time. However, it was very rare that she would find that time. With getting the children dressed and ready for school, keeping the dorm clean and tidy, giving the children baths and helping them in the toilet, hand-washing their clothes and caring for them when they were ill, answering the many urgent calls for help every hour and making sure that the children took their medication, there simply were not enough hours in the day.

In a family, children are part of a group. They have parents, maybe brothers and sisters, and other extended family around them. Seeing the daily activity around them and being a part of the group and the activity teaches children things and stimulates them. Children are allowed to play in and around the house, to explore their surroundings and learn from their explorations. They are taken along with their mother or father on outings to the market, to the field, or to visit neighbours or relatives who live further away. Children in a family help out around the house with chores, and they are taught how to do a good job at them. These children play with toys, household items, or things they find in the road. By seeing their parents, aunts, uncles and neighbours live a regular life, children learn about how the world works and what their role in it will be when they grow up. They learn about the duties and rights of men and women, of parents, and of people from their own social status. In play, they try out their understanding of these roles by playing 'house', 'shop', and so on.

In contrast, the routine in a children's home is generally inflexible and unchanging. Outings, or exceptions to the fixed routine, are very rare. Children in children's homes do not usually see realistic role models of adult life. The only examples they know of adults are their caregivers, who are almost always women; very few men or male role models are around. The children do not see and learn from people going about their regular lives in the way that the children do when they grow up in a family. In a children's home, what children see is people doing their job, and keeping

Though life in a children's home is also group life of a sort, it does not have the same strong bonds.

order and discipline. These people are more likely to be annoyed with difficult circumstances than to be enjoying life. Or the children see foreign volunteers who look different, talk differently, behave in strange ways and disappear again quite soon. This does not teach the children much about what their adult life will be like and how they should behave as adults, when the time comes.

Many people will react to this knowledge with the remark: 'Yes, of course that is unfortunate, but really, none of us have it all, how much worse can this be than the disappointments we all have to face in life?'

The answer to that question is that it is much, much worse than the disappointments most of us have to face. The answer is that it can, in fact, in extreme cases, be fatal. So, let us take a look at the effects, particularly the long term ones, of the differences between growing up in a family and growing up in a children's home.

The Impact of the Difference Between Family and Institution

Receiving affection, attention and physical contact is part of our essential basic needs, from birth onward. Especially in children's homes, these needs are often forgotten or pushed way down the priority list as a luxury. They are not a luxury. Children who do not receive affection and attention become emotionally scarred and in some cases even mentally or physically handicapped, if they survive.

Children show an actual **physiological** response to lacking attention and affectionate physical contact. The production of growth hormones decreases, which means that the child only grows very slowly, and may even stop growing and developing altogether. The immune system becomes less active, and in babies it can even stop working completely. When outside influences – such as not receiving enough food, not receiving healthy food, or not receiving attention and affectionate physical contact – weaken the immune system, this means that it does not have the power to properly fight off the bacteria that attack the body. This means the child will get ill much more quickly than other children. If he has a wound, the chance of it getting infected is much higher. Any illness that the child gets is almost certain to get much more serious, possibly even dangerous, than it would in a child with an immune system that works properly. In children who are HIV positive and others who already have a weakened immune system, having it further weakened by lack of affection and a friendly touch puts them at an even greater risk of getting sick, as well as of illnesses becoming life-threatening.

Physical Contact
Children have an essential need for affectionate physical contact. This is taken for granted in families – babies and toddlers are carried around, older children get to sit on parents' laps or lean against them – and often (all but) absent in children's homes. When a baby or toddler is held regularly, it makes him feel safe. It is this sense of security that tells his body that all is well, and that stimulates the body to produce all the hormones needed for a normal development and for good health. Lack of physical contact is one of the reasons why children in children's homes are smaller than most children their age, why they are ill more often and why they develop more slowly than children their own age who live in a family.

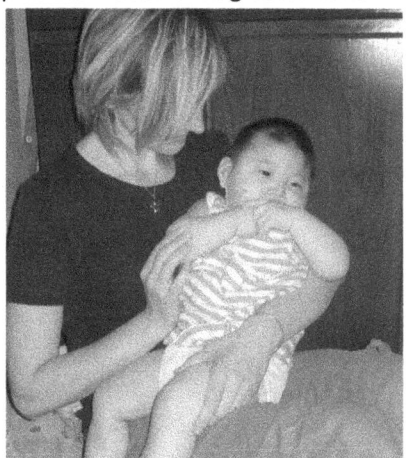

A simple and enjoyable way to help a child's brain develop and her body grow.

In the first half of the 20th century, in many European cultures, showing affection to children was seen as something pointless, if not indeed the cause of many problems. Harry Harlow, an American psychologist, took a different view and set about proving it. In one of his experiments (his most famous), he removed rhesus monkeys from their mothers only a few hours after birth and gave them a choice between two different 'mothers'. One was made of soft terrycloth but did not give any food. The other was made out of wire and provided food through an attached bottle. The young monkeys showed a strong preference for the soft 'mother', snuggling up to it, which made them feel like being held, over the wire 'mother' that only provided food.

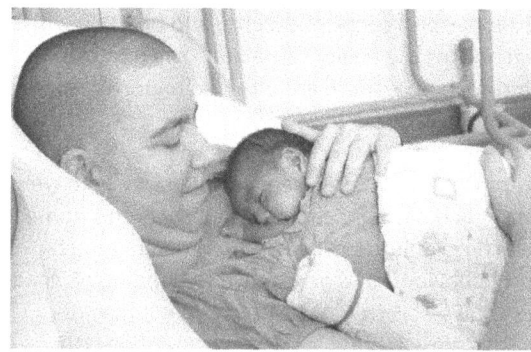

A lot of research has proven that giving premature babies 'kangaroo care' (holding them skin-to-skin) helps them grow and develop better and stay healthier.

Children under three years old need to spend several hours a day being held by an adult. Older children need to have the opportunity to sit on someone's lap for a while from time to time, or to hang against them or hold their hand.

Although children's need for physical contact and attention is so great that they will settle for any kind of physical contact or attention they can get, if they are starved of these things, this is in no way an invitation for sexual contact with children. There are no circumstances under which sexual actions towards a child or physical contact with children for personal satisfaction of the adult are acceptable! No form of sexual contact is ever in the best interest of the child. In fact, it invariably damages them psychologically and possibly physically and developmentally as well.

An eighteen-month-old girl was the size of a four-month-old. She was badly neglected by an overworked caregiver. When I was there, while I played with the other children from her dorm I would have her lying on my lap. I made a kind of sling out of a scarf and during prayer assembly and such occasions I would put the girl in there. She would be asleep within moments, feeling safe while held against my body.

Attachment

The ability to form relationships – attachments – with people is something that is learned at a young age. Usually, with a child who lives in a family, you do not even notice that he is learning anything, because he simply picks up the ability from having a role in the normal family situation, from having his needs met, and from receiving the love of his family members. Nobody needs to explain to a child in a family what relationships are and how to go about forming them; in fact, it is not even really possible to do so. The child gets to experience all kinds of relationships, and through this he learns how to form bonds with other people.

Children who do not get the experience of forming a special bond with a certain caregiver who is always there for them, who can be relied on to meet their essential needs, and with whom they feel completely at ease and completely safe, do not form the links in their brains that make the forming of such bonds happen automatically later on. This can make it difficult, or for some children even impossible, to form any kind of normal relationship later in life.

Having experienced a long-term sense of security and bonding with people at an early age makes the ability come naturally to most people. But in a children's home, there are often no opportunities for a small child to form these bonds.

Two problems are often seen in children who have spent much of their childhood in a children's home. These problems are called 'indiscriminate attachment behaviour' and 'resistance to bonding'. A child who shows indiscriminate attachment behaviour has such a great need for positive attention and affection that he will not care what risks might be involved in approaching strangers. He will go up to anyone and everyone and be open, trusting and affectionate, without making a difference between people he knows and strangers. In children who live in a family and who have bonded with their parents from an early age, you see a resistance toward approaching strangers from about nine months of age onwards. This mistrust of strangers is a system that is built into human beings to keep them safe. Because after all, you do not know if a stranger can be trusted or not. In a child with indiscriminate attachment disorder, the need for attention and affection is so much greater than the need to stay safe that this built-in safety mechanism is thrown aside.

Flocking around, craving attention and physical contact – after they improved my appearance by rearranging my scarf. Any stranger will do.

Asking for positive attention by showing off skills and endearing you.

> *During projects in children's homes, the children usually come running up to me the moment I walk in, even the very first time, when they have no idea who I am. They will grab my hands, try to climb on my lap, touch my hair and lean against me.*
> *When I go home with one of my colleagues who work at that children's home to meet her family, her children are very curious about me and stare at me. I look different, very tall and with a different colour skin and hair. However, these children will keep their distance. They will not approach me until their parents' behaviour towards me and the way I act have reassured them that it is safe. Then they will cautiously come closer.*

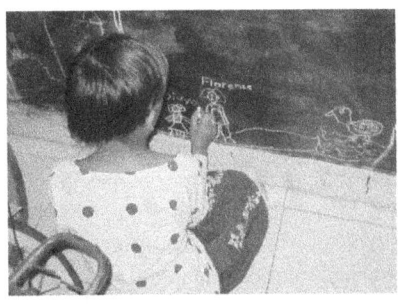

Visitors who come to a children's home are often endeared by the way children flock towards them, grabbing their hands, trying to sit on their laps. This is seen by most people as a sign that the children are open and welcoming. In fact, it is a clear sign of indiscriminate attachment disorder. Children who have shown indiscriminate attachment behaviour for several years may continue to do so even after they have been placed in a permanent adoptive family. Even though they now have a secure home with a primary caregiver and lots of affection and attention, they are so used to the absolute necessity of getting attention and affection wherever you can get it, that they may be just as likely to walk up to a stranger in the shop and hold his hand, as they are to go to their adoptive mother.

During one of the projects I was in a situation where an eighteen-month-old girl was in very poor condition. To be able to give her the one-to-one care she needed, to have a hope of surviving, a teenage girl was more or less made her foster mother, under supervision. The teenager did a fantastic job taking care of the little girl and she helped her become healthy and happy. It was more than two years before I was able to visit the same project again and none of the younger children really remembered me anymore. When I arrived at the dorm where the little girl stayed, all 18 other children came pouring out of the room to hug me and hold my hands and try to sit on my lap, even though they did not know who I was anymore. The little girl followed after them much more slowly and kept watching me from a distance. Because she had had a chance to attach to her 'foster mother', her healthy fear of strangers was not thrown overboard and she made sure I could be trusted before approaching me, much later.

A child who shows resistance to bonding has given up hope that someone will provide him with attention and affection. Rather than risk being disappointed and rejected – yet again –, he prefers to not even attempt to bond with other people and he rejects their efforts to bond with him. He is convinced that even if they try to bond with him now, they will find out he is not worth it in the end and they will abandon him. So, instead, he withdraws within himself, making as little contact as possible with the outside world, to protect himself from any hurt that he is sure will come.

Carried around in a scarf; the tiny girl is actually eighteen months old.

Not having an opportunity to form a secure attachment to a primary caregiver in the first three years of life also has serious physiological and behavioural effects. For example, a child can only learn self-control and empathy in a close relationship. If he does not get this opportunity, he is very likely to become impulsive, anxious and even aggressive or violent when he is older. Lack of secure attachment in combination with exposure to repeated and/or prolonged traumatic stress (which can be something as simple as a baby being afraid after hearing a loud noise and no one coming to comfort him, or not receiving any physical contact or attention) changes the makeup of the brain and the nervous system for the worse.

Giving Attention

Attention is not just something children like, it is something that they really need. They need it to make sure that their brain develops as it should, and to make sure that they develop self-confidence and respect for themselves and for others. In fact, children need attention so desperately that when they get no attention at all, or not enough, they will try literally anything to attract it. This behaviour is built into all of us.

To start out, the child will try to attract positive attention by being affectionate, showing you his '**possession**s', and showing off his skills. If this does not work, he will settle for negative attention because the need for attention is so deep that a child will prefer any kind of negative attention – including physical abuse – over no attention at all. To attract negative attention, a child will use bad behaviour, such as damaging objects, hurting himself or others, being extremely disruptive, or anything else he can think of, to get you to pay attention to him. This will happen even when the attention he gets this way is nothing more than being shouted at or being beaten to make him stop doing what he is doing. Unless positive attention is given, there will be no end to the child's bad behaviour and ultimately, there will be no limit to what he will be prepared to do to get just a little bit of much needed attention.

In a home for mentally challenged children, one of the problems was that there were many bits of glass in the outside area where the children played. It was almost a sport for the children to find bits of glass and hide them in their pockets. Some of the children would cut themselves with the glass, to see what would happen, some would threaten others with this weapon and some would put the glass in their mouth and chew it. To improve safety, an effort was made to get rid of all of the glass and any glass found in the possession of any of the children was confiscated. Some of the children discovered that searching for glass and then handing it over was a good way of getting some extra attention. However, one of the children was not satisfied with this, and he figured out that he could get even more attention if he showed that he had glass and then made the caregivers chase him, to take it off him and reprimand him.

To put a stop to this behaviour, I gave him attention when he came to hand over the glass, but would ignore him completely when he made it clear that he had the glass and that I had to come and get it. The boy was not happy with this at all: he had lost that precious attention. The solution he came up with was to stand in front of me and put the piece of glass he had to the throat of another child. He was clearly entirely willing to push it in, if that was what it took, thus forcing me to do something about the situation. Anything to get some attention.

To avoid getting into this downward spiral, or to break it, it is essential that the child receives positive attention. Part 3, Chapter 5: 'Discipline' will give more information about 'Breaking the Cycle of Negative Attention Seeking'. Spending 'quality time' with a child can consist of playing together, reading a book out loud or talking about his experiences, without any intrusions. I would define quality time as time in which a child receives attention, is listened to, gets positive re-enforcement of his qualities, and is held, hugged or allowed to sit right next to the adult for physical contact. However, it does not need to be a separate time. Children can also receive valuable affection and attention in combination with physical contact at mealtimes, or while being involved in little chores, done together with a caregiver or volunteer.

Showing an Interest in the Child

Parents want to hear what their children have been doing, who they were playing with, and where they went, out of genuine interest in their children's lives.

This seems like a small thing, but it has an enormous effect on children. It makes them feel that they are real people, worthy of someone who listens to them. It gives them a sense of self-confidence and identity.

Showing an interest and dividing attention between children.

Children who live in children's homes also need someone who will listen to what they have to say, to ask how they are, what they think about things, and to look at the small 'treasures' that they have found. This is essential both for brain development and for emotional well-being. Especially when a child is feeling sad, she needs someone to listen to her and to help her deal with the situation. This can be done, for example, by explaining the situation or by reassuring her about it.

Balancing Praise and Reprimand

In a family situation, there is normally a natural balance between **reprimanding** a child when he does something wrong and praising him when he does well or helps out. This balance comes from the underlying, ever-present love and pride that parents feel for their children. In a children's home, the divide between children and caregivers is often much greater. When caregivers have a lot of children to look after, there is no room for forming relationships, and the caregiver's child-raising efforts concentrate mostly on correcting bad behaviour. Praising and showing gratitude for good behaviour does not seem like a very high priority, which usually means that caregivers spend most of their time reprimanding children, without praising them.

Receiving praise and gratitude is not just something pleasant. It is just as important as having bad behaviour corrected. It is by receiving praise and gratitude that children will develop positive motivation (in other words, their own wish to do good things) and self-confidence, instead of negative motivation, which only leads to a child trying to avoid being caught and punished, rather than trying to do something good or well. Praise and gratitude have a part equal to reprimand and discipline when it comes to helping children to become well-mannered and well-behaved.

Stimulation

For children's brains to develop as they should and to prevent children from withdrawing completely into themselves, children need stimulation. Stimulation is varied input through all of their senses: hearing, vision, smell, taste, and touch. The need for stimulation, just like the need for attention, is so big that every child has built-in mechanisms that will start working if she does not receive what she needs, as a way of protecting herself.

"In most of the cots lie babies, or so they are called. The youngest is about a month old, but the oldest might well be two or three years old. It is very hard to say, growth and development are all stunted. Almost all are lying down, unable to sit or stand. Or, perhaps they have learned that anything other than lying quietly is undesirable. Almost all those over the age of ten months lie rocking back and forth. Their head or their entire body. If they are not sleeping. Sores on their heads from banging against the bars of the cot. Some with their faces pressed against the bars, their neck at an uncomfortable angle. One little boy grates the paint off the bed with his teeth."

Children who receive no stimulation, who are left in a single place that always looks the same, without objects to play with and without people to interact with, will start to rock themselves endlessly, or even bang their head against a hard surface or pull out their own hair, all of this with the single purpose of feeling something, experiencing something. Without stimulation, a child will not learn anything and may even lose the skills that she already possessed.

Some examples of stimulation, all of which are needed in children's daily lives are:

- Freedom to move around and explore the surroundings
- Being talked to by other people
- Receiving affectionate physical contact
- Having a varying range of objects to play with

When very little of interest happens, everything out of the ordinary becomes entertainment.

Not only the size of the child and her health are influenced by whether she receives enough touch and stimulation. The development of the brain is also strongly influenced by the presence or lack of touch and stimulation. There is a measurable difference in brain size between children who live in families (and thus are exposed to regular physical contact and freedom to play) and children who grow up in a situation with many children to few caregivers (where physical contact and freedom to play and develop is extremely limited to non-existent). The brains of children in institutions have been shown to be 20-30% smaller than those of children in families. Stimulation, various experiences, physical contact, and being talked to from a very early age all together determine how well the brain is prepared for future learning and how well the two halves of the brain can work together and make sense of the information they are getting.

Stimulation of all kinds leads to the creation of synapses and pathways in the brain. These are the links between different parts of the brain that are needed for it to function well. Lack of stimulation – which includes being held, seeing, hearing, feeling, tasting and experiencing a variety of

Colourful surroundings are a form of stimulation, but not if the surroundings always stay the same.

things – not only prevents the making of new synapses and pathways, it also leads to the destruction of existing connections. Only connections that are regularly used are kept intact. Young children need safety, affection, conversation and a stimulating environment to develop and keep important synapses. When a child reaches the age of ten, the phase of rapid brain growth and the development of neural connections is completed, and it will stop. This means that for the foundation of the brain, what has not been created by then, or what has already been lost, cannot be regained anymore. So, if these things do not happen when the child is small, it is too late, and the child will simply have to live without what has not formed or been kept intact early on.

I regularly get complaints from people in children's homes all over the world, about children who have lived in a home with many children and few caregivers for several years. The complaints are always very similar: the children are badly-behaved, ill-mannered, disobedient, disrespectful, rebellious and ungrateful. It is said in a way that makes it seem like these are somehow exceptional children, very bad ones. And they ask me how they can make the children behave better.

It always saddens me when I hear this. Because the behaviour seen in these children is the natural and inevitable result of being raised without getting attention, affection, a chance to form attachments, proper stimulation and positive role models. There is nothing inherently wrong or bad in these children. Any child put in that position would either turn out that way, or not survive.

These are some pointers towards some of the psychological elements needed in proper childcare. While you are unable to make structural changes to the way the children are cared for, you can make a point of allowing children to sit in your lap, to hold a baby in your arms for an hour or more a day, to compliment children and praise them for their little accomplishments, to talk to them and listen to them and to simply play with them. Having a spark of these things in their lives, even from an outsider, will mean the world to the children.

Chapter 4: Global Developmental Stages of Childhood

In this chapter I will give a basic overview of how children develop from birth to eighteen years old. This will give you an idea of what children in certain age groups can be expected to understand – their psychological development –, what they are able to do – their physical and motor development – and what the essential needs specific to their developmental stage are. Having this basic information may help you understand why children behave and react the way they do, and maybe also help you show more patience for the things they are not able to do yet.

  Birth to Eighteen Months

Psychological
The child explores the world around him mostly through his mouth and through touching things. The child learns to tell the difference between his primary caregiver – if he has one – and other people. Eye contact, touch and positive, affectionate care are essential for healthy development. A child who gets the care and stimulation he needs, at this stage, learns to trust that the world is basically okay and will develop a basic confidence in the future. If the child does not experience trust and is frustrated because his needs are not met, he may end up with deep feelings of worthlessness and mistrust of the world.

Physical
The body grows extremely fast during this stage, as does the brain. Motor development also happens quickly. During the first eighteen months, a child will learn to:

- Grab and hold on to things and pass them from one hand to the other
- Keep his head and body steady and upright
- Roll over from his belly to his back and the other way around
- Stay sitting up when put that way and later sitting up himself without help and moving in and out of a sitting position
- Crawl
- Pull himself up to standing by holding on to someone or something
- Stand without help or holding on to anything

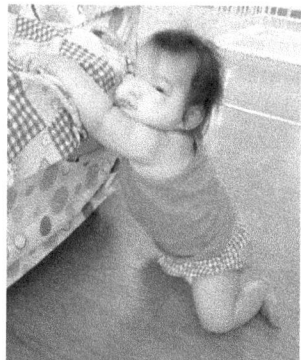
Learning to pull up to a standing position.

- Walk while holding on to furniture – this is called cruising
- Walk without help
- Pick up things between his thumb and index finger
- Feed himself using his hands
- Put things into other things and take them out again
- Smile
- Babble – this means talking without using real words
- Say the first meaningful words

Essential Needs

To make sure that a baby is able to stay healthy and develop normally in the first eighteen months of his life, a few 'care ingredients' are needed. It is very important that someone holds him for a total of several hours per day. Not only while he is being fed, but also at other times, to let him experience touch and attention. These two things allow the baby to start developing trust and a feeling of safety, and it allows the foundation for the ability to form attachments to be laid. Experiencing physical contact and attention are necessary for all future development. This is also essential for good health and growth. To develop normally, a child also needs to have eye contact with his caregiver and have someone talk to him.

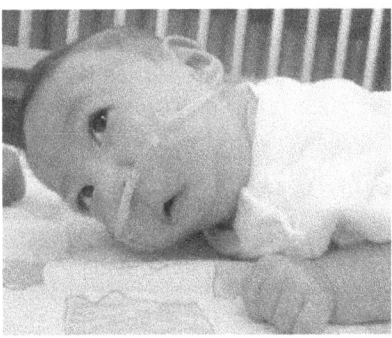

Daily belly time to strengthen the neck muscles.

The first step in the motor development of a baby is to learn to bear the weight of his head and keep the head still, without wobbling. If this is not learned, he will not learn any further skills either. It is by being taken out of his bed several times a day and being held for a while, that he will start to practise all these things. Being allowed to play on a mat on the floor also allows him to practise. From one or two months old onward, all babies should spend at least 10-15 minutes a day lying on their bellies, not swaddled, while they are awake. This will help them learn to lift their heads and strengthen their necks, upper bodies, and arms. From this age, a baby should also spend at the very least half an hour a day lying on a mat on the floor, on his back, not swaddled. This gives him the freedom to wave his arms and legs and strengthen them and to look around, at something other than his bed. Once the baby starts trying to hold a toy, give him one to play with, so he can practise his skills with that too.

As the child starts showing signs of trying to learn a new skill, such as sitting up without help or crawling, encourage him and make sure that he has room to practise these skills. If given enough freedom of movement and stimulation, most babies will continue to discover the world and develop their abilities by themselves. However, a baby who is left lying in his bed most of the day is more likely to get sick very often and his development will be more and more behind that of other children of his age. It is even possible for a child to lose the ability to do something that he had already learned to do, if he is always kept in his bed and does not get stimulation or attention.

Eighteen Months to Three Years

Psychological

The child learns a lot of skills that lead to greater independence, such as feeding and dressing himself and becoming toilet trained. Self-esteem is built, more control over the body is gained and the child learns right from wrong.

He discovers the meaning of the word 'no' and starts experimenting with using it himself. When a toddler experiments with the meaning and use of the word 'no', he can be very difficult to deal with for a while. Suddenly, he goes from being very cooperative to saying 'no' to almost everything. It is important to remember that this is not because the child is bad or because he is trying to make your life harder for you. He is only trying to make sense of his new understanding of the possibility of agreeing or disagreeing with things.

A two-year-old girl has learned to say 'no'. Now it is always her first answer when asked a question. When asked: 'Will you give him one of the blocks to play with?' she answers with a definite 'No!' About 20 seconds later she hands the boy a block.

During this time, he also starts building his self-esteem, that is to say the idea he has of his own worth. If he builds up high self-esteem, this means that he feels he is a good person who is able to do and learn things and is worthy of other people's compliments. If he has low self-esteem, this means that he does not think he is worth much, that he does not think he is good and that he is more likely to believe people who criticise him than those who give him compliments. A child in this age group can be very vulnerable. If he is shamed in the process of toilet training or while learning other major skills, he may feel humiliated and start to doubt his abilities.

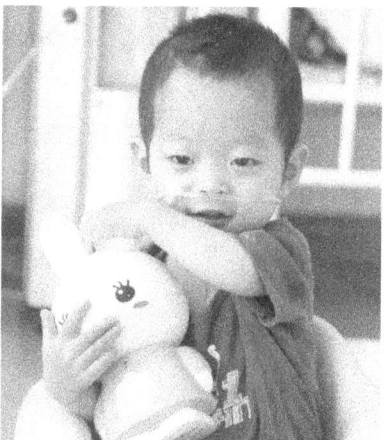

When he got back from hospital, he latched on to the Miffy musical toy and would not let any other child go near it; when it had to be plugged in to recharge, he would scream.

This, in turn, will lead to his suffering low self-esteem and giving up on trying to learn things.

At this age, the beginnings of empathy are starting to develop. This means that the child starts to understand that other people have feelings. He starts to realise that it is possible for someone else to experience a feeling, even if he does not feel it. This starts with the child learning to recognise when other people are upset. He may also become emotionally attached to toys or objects, for security. This can mean that he will become very upset when he is not allowed to keep a certain toy with him all the time, because he thinks he needs it to stay safe.

Physical

During this stage, growth of body and brain has slowed down a little, but it is still faster than during following stages. The fast growth of his body does not always take place in complete harmony, and this can sometimes cause pain. These pains are called 'growing pains'. It is not a result from playing too much, as some people think, but from muscles growing faster than bones, or bones growing faster than muscles for a short while, before the other catches up. This creates a tension. This pain usually only lasts for a few hours and it is more common in the evening. Vision becomes fully developed at this age and **attention span** becomes longer. Up to his third birthday, a child will learn to:

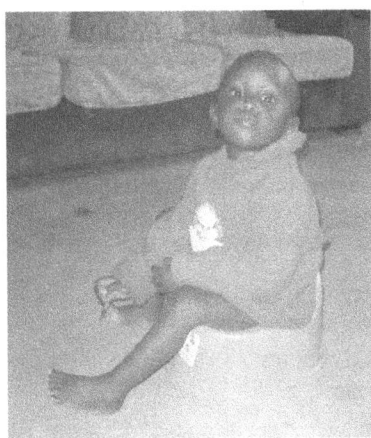

Potty training usually happens at this age; if it is made enjoyable, it tends to be more successful.

- Climb stairs, up and down
- Understand the order in which puzzles and other complex toys should be used
- Kick a ball without losing balance
- Look through a book one page at a time
- Run
- Pick up objects from the floor while standing, without falling
- Use the toilet or a potty to relieve himself
- Put on and take off clothes (as long as they do not have complicated buttons or ribbons)
- Express his needs in words, using two to three-word sentences

Essential Needs

To prevent the toddler developing low self-esteem or feeling very ashamed, it is important to use a lot of praise and compliments for good behaviour, rather than focussing on punishing or shaming him when he behaves badly. Low self-esteem may seem an unimportant matter, but it can lead to the child being unable to stand up for himself when he is older, or, alternatively, to very difficult behaviour and aggression, which are used to cover up feelings of not being good enough. It can also lead to poor results in school and work –

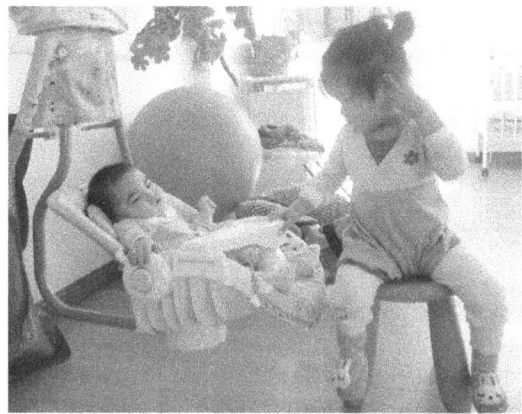

Wanting to help.

because he feels he is not good enough, he may not even try – and even to depression and ill health later on in life. This makes finding a balance between correcting bad behaviour and praising good behaviour very important.

It also points out the importance of recognising which behaviour can, in all fairness, be called bad. When a child accidentally wets his clothes, or gives the wrong answer to a question, this is unfortunate and undesirable, but it is not bad. The child did not intend to do something wrong. He did the best he could, but failed. The failure in itself is already a kind of punishment. If this is made worse by also being punished or shamed, the child might give up trying to be good, or give up trying anything at all, because he is scared of making a mistake and being punished.

A two-year-old boy who knew me well had not seen me for a few weeks because I had been in a different location. When I came into the children's play area, he came straight over to me. He was extremely excited. In fact, he was literally shaking, because he could not think of a way to adequately express his joy and excitement at seeing me again. After looking at me for a moment, trying to figure out what to do, suddenly he bit me in the chest really hard, leaving a mark through my clothes.
Though it was an act of aggression and he had to be told that he could not do that, in essence, it was mostly an act of love.

Another important part of the care of children of this age is talking to them. Spending time talking to a child and listening to what he has to say achieves two things at the same time:

- The child gets positive attention, which makes him feel good about himself and allows him to increase his self-esteem.
- It is essential for a child's development of language and speech to talk to adults. It is through hearing adults talk to him, using correct grammar and words, and through trying to find the right way to say what he wants to say, that a child learns how to use language properly. A child who does not get spoken to and who does not get the chance to express himself may only develop very basic speech, or may not even to try to speak at all.

The development of the other skills mentioned in the list, and skills that were not mentioned there, all depends on whether or not a child gets the opportunity to practise that particular skill and receives encouragement for his efforts to try to learn the skill well. In other words, if a child has never seen a ball in his life, he will not have the ability to throw it properly. So, a child needs some freedom of movement to explore his surroundings and practise his skills, and a variety of different objects to play with over time to allow him to develop a good set of skills. This should be combined with attention, being talked to, and being encouraged and praised in his efforts to try new things.

Physical contact is also still very important at this age. Although the child is becoming more independent, taking off on his own to explore the world around him, he still has a deep need to be able to come back to you and sit on your lap. Getting this physical contact and finding this feeling of safety with you will give him the confidence and ability to go out and try things on his own.

Three to Six Years

Psychological
The child likes to copy adult behaviour. Toys and objects are used to play out what the child understands of adult life. This is practise for her future role. She will also start to take initiative in play situations. That means that she will suggest a game to play, or make one up herself and guide you through how it is done. This is a step beyond always waiting for you to tell her what to do and how to do it.

Around this age, the word 'why' is discovered as a way of finding out how the world works. For a while, the child may react to any answer given by asking 'why' again. Sometimes even without listening to the answer, just in order to ask the question. However, if you help the child discover the proper use of the word 'why' – by answering seriously when she seems to want to know the 'why' of something, and not reacting when she is only going on asking 'why' for no reason – she will find it very useful in exploring the world around her. If you do not know the answer to her question, it is all right to tell her that too.

> *A three-your-old boy asks me why I have no hair. I answer:*
> *'Because I take it off every week.'*
> *'Why?'*
> *'Because it is more practical like this.'*
> *'Why?'*
> *'Because I do not get lice like this.'*
> *'Why?'*
> *'Because lice like to live in hair.'*
> *'Why?'*
> *'You would have to ask the lice that.'*

If the child finds herself unable to do what she is trying to do, or if her efforts are regularly blocked – for instance because she does not have the freedom to try out things or explore – she can get very frustrated, and may even feel guilty for trying. The child's self-esteem is still mostly influenced by how the important people in her life treat her and what they tell her she is worth. In other words, a child of this age who gets reprimanded a lot and does not get any praise will have low self-esteem, while a child who receives a good balance between being corrected and praised will have a much higher self-esteem.

Physical
During this stage, a child is physically very active. Although she can sit still and pay attention to something for some time now, it is still quite difficult for her to do for more than about half an hour at a time. Again, growth has slowed somewhat, but is still impressive. Up to her sixth birthday, a child will learn to:

Impressive climbers, who may not know any fear.

- Skip, hop and jump with good balance
- Cut out pictures with scissors
- Balance while standing on one foot, after some time even with her eyes closed
- Tie her own shoelaces
- Use cutlery, other simple tools, and pens and pencils
- Learn and sing songs
- Count to 10
- Name colours
- Speak in sentences and use the past tense

Essential Needs
Like in the previous stage, getting positive attention, encouragement and room to play and explore are essential for healthy development. At this age, a child moves from learning the basic structures of her language to learning to speak in a more subtle way, such as by using different tenses and expressions. A child who does not get spoken to and who does not get the chance to express herself, may only develop very basic speech, or may not even be inclined to try to speak at all.

Physical contact is still important. While the child may spend a long time playing by herself or exploring things, she will come back to experience the comfort of sitting on the lap of a trusted adult. Having

Part 3: Basic Childcare and Child Psychology

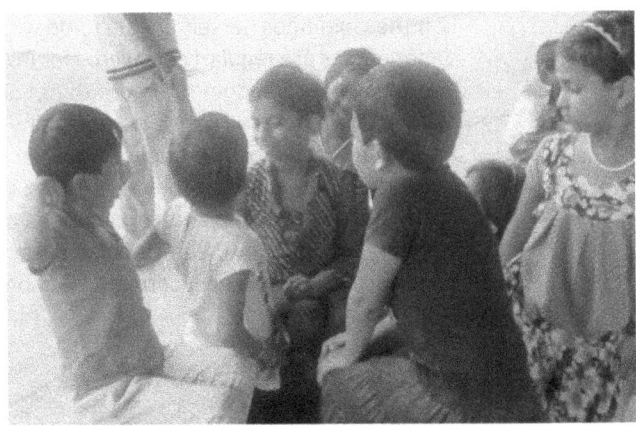

Exploring friendships and forming little gangs.

the opportunity to do this will make her feel more secure, which will both help increase her independence and her health and development.

The development of the other skills mentioned, and skills that were not, all depends on whether or not a child gets the opportunity to practise the particular skill and receives encouragement of her efforts to try to master the skill.

Six to Twelve Years

Psychological
The child starts to become more and more involved with children of her own age, and less dependent on her caregivers. She starts to find out how relationships work by building friendships with people her own age. If the child has low self-esteem or feels she is worth less than her classmates or friends, this can lead to very deep feelings of worthlessness and self-hate. The child needs to be helped in the process of making friends if she is having trouble doing it on her own, and she needs to be encouraged and stimulated to feel good about herself by praising her when she does things well.

Children this age have a tendency to forgive the people they love easily and to find excuses for them even if they have clearly done wrong. On the other hand, they are very readily inclined to look for blame in themselves, even for things that are completely out of their reach. In the song 'Family Portrait', P!nk describes the reasoning of a young girl whose parents are fighting a lot and getting divorced. This part is where the girl pleads with her father not to leave: "I'll be so much better, I'll tell my brother/ Oh, I won't spill the milk at dinner/ I'll be so much better, I'll do everything right/ I'll be your little girl forever/ I'll go to sleep at night" Of course, the parents' fights have

nothing to do with her spilling milk or not going to sleep straight away, but the reasoning of a child of this age will almost always go towards finding blame in themselves for all circumstances.

At this age, the child develops an ability to learn, create, and accomplish many new things. She starts to discover what she likes doing best and how to go about doing those things. By learning these new things and becoming able to perform tasks and chores, she will feel she is contributing to the world. This gives the satisfaction of doing something productive and useful. Allowing a child to explore this and praising her accomplishments and attempts to help out are important at this time, to stimulate this feeling of satisfaction.

Capable of helping out with a lot of practical things, but still in need of guidance and support.

Physical

During this stage, skills that were learned before are improved and new ones are tried out.
A child usually learns to:

- Read and write
- Do arithmetic
- Use language to really communicate, not just to express wishes
- Understand and deal with rules – in the early stages without room for exceptions, later with more flexibility
- Understand concepts of space, time, and dimension
- Understand how her behaviour affects others

Essential Needs

Like in the previous stage, receiving positive attention, encouragement and room to play and explore are essential for healthy development. At this age, a child starts to discover things such as hidden meanings in metaphors and expressions, and she starts to realise that language can be used to present your point of view in a certain way. A child who does not get spoken to and who does not get the chance to experiment with these extra layers to the use of language, may only develop very basic speech, or may even not be inclined to try to speak at all.

If the rules she lives with are random or not consistently applied, she will not find it easy to learn the true meaning and sense of rules. And if no one explains to her, gradually, how her behaviour affects other people, she may never completely understand.

Physical contact still has a role at this age. Becoming more and more independent, at times the pre-teen might reject physical contact initiated by the caregiver. This is a way for her to show how big she is, and it should be respected. However, this does not mean that all physical contact is unwanted. Rather, gradually, the child will start to take the initiative in when and what kind of physical contact is wanted. Occasionally, a larger child might still want to sit on your lap. Generally, though, physical contact will shift to hand holding, or her sitting or standing next to you and leaning against you. Even though the amount of physical contact needed has become less, it is still very important for children of this age to receive some physical contact from caregivers.

Twelve to Eighteen Years

Psychological

At about twelve years old, what is known as 'the teenage years' begin. This is a period in which both the children's bodies and their minds take the step from childhood to adulthood. This process can be quite difficult, both for the child and for the people around him. The changes taking place are so great that they can cause a lot of confusion in the child. When, at times, he does not know how to deal with the changes or how to control the things that are happening in his body and mind, he

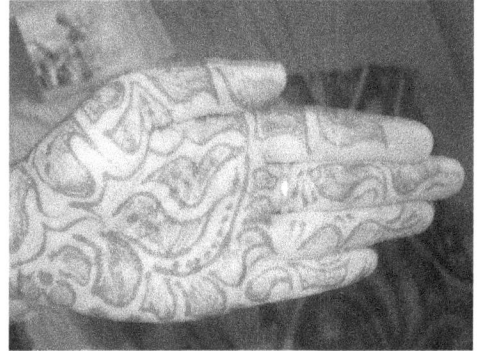

The skills of a teenager can sometimes be quite impressive.

may suddenly show very bad behaviour, which confuses his caregiver, because he never behaved like that before.

At this stage, the child starts to become even more independent. This means that how he feels and what he does are no longer mostly dependent on what other people decide for him or tell him. Life is now getting more complex for the child. He starts searching for his

Putting on a brave face during a confusing time.

own identity, separate from the people who raised them. He also works on completely understanding his interactions with other people and how to behave in these interactions. He develops his own ideas on what is right and what is wrong. The child searches for a philosophy of life at this age and usually thinks in easy, rounded ideas without contradictions or doubts, rather than in terms of experience or reality.

In order to start forming this own identity and these own ideas, the child feels the need to distance himself from his caregivers – this happens in families as well as in children's homes. He is less likely to take things said by authority figures as automatically true, because he wants to think it through for himself and make up his own mind. This can lead to heated discussions and arguments, which caregivers can perceive as simple stubbornness, ungratefulness or disrespect on the part of the child. In fact, it is his attempt to take his life into his own hands, rather than depending on support. The situation is complicated even more by the fact that teenagers almost always feel they are more mature and more in control than they really are. This makes them resent any attempt on the part of their caregivers to protect them or hold them back a little, while it may still be very much necessary to do so at times. Many children go into a period of withdrawal from responsibilities at this stage. A child may leave his room/living area messy, not do the chores he is expected to do, and refuse to give anything consideration except for what he wants to do. This can drive his caregivers to despair. While it is important to remind him of his responsibilities, it is also important to realise that this is just a phase that will pass again; it is not badness of the child.

A teenager needs to be given both the opportunity and space to discover who he is, and still receive support and guidance and the opportunity to talk about their worries and insecurities. If he does not have this, it can lead to a lot of confusion and anxiety. This can make his final step into adulthood, when it is time for him to take care of himself, very difficult and problematic.

Physical
While, for some time, the child had been growing a little slower than when he was very small, suddenly he will have a growth spurt again for a year or two. With girls this usually happens somewhere between the ages of eleven and fourteen, with boys usually between the ages of thirteen and sixteen. This growth spurt can make a child seem quite clumsy, because he will hardly have had time to adjust to the changes in his strength and size before his body changes again.

Self-conscious about an unfamiliar, changing body.

Apart from just getting taller, their bodies also change from children's bodies into the bodies of men and women. If children have not been given any information about the changes that will be taking place and what they mean, they can become quite worried about them, and even very afraid or ashamed.

With the changing appearance of their bodies, which they are not used to, and the new smells their bodies suddenly produce, teenagers can be very insecure about their bodies and about how they look. Many are convinced that they are not good-looking, no matter what others think or say. This is one of the reasons why many girls, but boys as well, can become very preoccupied with things that they *can* control about their appearance, such as their hairstyles, their clothes, and their accessories – caps, jewellery, and so on. Some teenagers can also become completely obsessed with personal hygiene, wanting to shower or wash several times a day and use all kinds of fragrances. This is usually because they are afraid that the smells produced by their body, which were not there when they were children, mean that they are dirty or that other people will think they are dirty. Reassuring the teenager that this is normal and that the process is the same for all children his age – who will not seem as 'dirty' to him as he does to himself – will help him overcome his fears and doubts.

Sexuality becomes an issue during the teenage years, and this is something I advise children's homes about. However, as a visiting volunteer, this is a subject you should stay clear of. Or, at the very least, discuss with management if they are all right with you discussing it with the children and if so, in what way. This is because sexuality is always surrounded by a lot of cultural rules and possibly taboos. While I believe it is very important to give teenagers information about this subject, I think it is at least as important to respect local customs surrounding it.

Although a teenager's size is starting to approach adult standard, with all the growth and changes going on in his body, he still needs more sleep than the average adult. Most teenagers need 8-10 hours of sleep per night in order to have enough energy to concentrate in school and do well.

Mentally
During their teenage years, from the age of about twelve, children start to develop new ways of thinking:

- Thinking hypothetically – this means thinking through the possible outcomes of something that has not actually happened.
- Thinking logically – this means thinking while using only the 'cold', rational parts of your brain, not allowing feelings to get in the way of a decision that you are making.
- Thinking abstractly – this means thinking about things that have no real shape or structure; they are concepts, such as 'love', 'hostility', 'dedication'.

Teenagers also need someone to depend on through their growing independence.

All of these ways of thinking were not possible when the teenager was younger. He needed concrete examples to be able to understand things. Emotions and rationality were a mixture in his head that he could not separate. And it was too hard for him to predict what would happen if he had not already experienced a particular situation. During the teenage years, these new ways of thinking develop slowly. This is not something that happens from one moment to the next. The child will go through periods of not being able to keep emotion out of any of his thoughts and decisions, while at other times he will start to be able to make logical decisions. Thinking abstractly and theoretically are also things that are learned gradually, with a lot of trial and error.

Essential Needs
At this stage, the child tries to make sense of his own identity, the complexity of the world around him, and the idea that quite soon, he will be forced to take the step from being cared for, to taking responsibility for his own life. This thought can be exciting and terrifying at the same time. The process is made more difficult by the fact that the child's body is changing and that he has to deal with all kinds of new things happening to him over which he has little

control. Hormones can cause him to suddenly – and temporarily – become very emotional or over-sensitive at times. While at other times, a previously unknown wave of aggression may wash over him, which he will have trouble dealing with or controlling. It is important for caregivers to be aware that these things will take place in any teenager's life, and to provide guidance about how to deal with this.

Teenagers need a certain amount of freedom to make their own choices, under guidance, so that they can learn how to make their own choices in a safe environment. This will make it a lot easier for them to take the step of going out into the world and taking care of themselves. If they have to go from always having to do what they are told to having to decide everything themselves in one blow, they are likely to make a lot of mistakes during the learning process. It can have big consequences when they are fully dependent on their own decisions, while still learning how to make them.

On the one hand, teenagers need some freedom to keep certain thoughts to themselves. On the other hand, they need to know that there is a responsible adult available to talk to who will listen to them, keep their issues **confidential**, and offer advice rather than judgement. If such a person is not available, chances are that the teenager will try to get information in less reliable places, become misinformed, or even just go ahead on his own, without information, because no one warned him.

So this is not an easy time, but it can certainly be rewarding to help a teenager grow into a responsible adult.

Chapter 5: Discipline

Discipline as described in this chapter is a subject that is useful to know something about when you to go a children's home to volunteer, but that you may not necessarily be allowed to put into practice when you are there. As always, respect the people working at the children's home and their wishes concerning what you are and are not allowed to do. Whether or not you are allowed to use all the things you read about in this chapter, you will still benefit from having an insight into the subject and a way of shaping your own approach to dealing with the children.

Setting Limits

She just wants to play with the funny door and the buttons on top: she does not know the bad effects of cutting off another child's oxygen supply.

Children explore the world and try to figure out how it works. They are searching for limits, to get an idea of the framework within which their existence is placed. Some people find it very hard to set limits for children, because they feel the child's freedom will be reduced or because they feel 'the poor child' has already been through so much difficulty that she should be allowed a little extra freedom. They are also held back because children tend to rebel against new limits. The outcry of the child is taken as a sign that the limits set are unfair, or unbearable.

In fact, the screaming and crying is done to test how solid and dependable the newly discovered boundaries are. Of course, like people of any age, children too try to see if they can win a little bit more than what is offered. However, that does not mean that they actually do not want the boundaries or that they want them to keep shifting. If the child succeeds in pushing the boundary a little bit further every time she tries, that is a scary experience for her. It means she cannot find a solid framework within which to feel secure. Every time the child wants and needs to lean on something, the wall moves a little bit further away. So, there is nothing secure and dependable for her to lean on. Children actually need and want to have limits, however much they act like they do not.

The caregiver of a two-year-old boy provided the children in her charge with haphazard rules: what would be allowed one day, would be 'strictly' forbidden the next and vice versa. This way she tried to assert her authority over the children. 'Strictly' only applied in so far as none of the children protested. If a tantrum was thrown, she would sternly say 'no' another couple of times and then give in. The little boy knew this very well and played her, very clearly.

One day he had a complete meltdown and interestingly enough this was not in protest against something he was not allowed. His entire manner and behaviour made it clear that he was practically begging for limits to be set. He was screaming in desperation, looking very confused. He was demanding things he did not even want and would scream even more no matter whether the answer he got was yes or no. He did not want to win. He very clearly wanted to be stopped. He kept making more and more outrageous demands in the hope that somehow he would finally cross the line and would run into something solid to hold onto. Unfortunately, his caregiver did not see it that way. She just saw it as behaviour typical for the child and his being wilfully difficult. So she did not give him what he needed most of all: dependable limits.

Total freedom brings with it total responsibility. Set rules tell you what you cannot do and thereby provide the framework within which you can move freely and safely. If no adult will clearly indicate what you can and cannot do, or the rules are changed as soon as you give the slightest indication that you would rather not comply – in short, with nothing to stop you – the decision of what to do and what not to lies on your shoulders. Children's shoulders, and especially toddlers' shoulders, are far too narrow to bear this kind of responsibility. Even more so when you consider that they do not even have full knowledge of what is dangerous or not, so they are by definition unable to make informed decisions for themselves.

A boy of two-and-a-half years old has lived in a particular children's home since he was one month old. The transition from treating him like a baby – trying to give him what he wants – to treating him like a toddler – setting limits and giving him clear rules – has only partly taken place. He is smart and curious. He likes to pick up objects that adults use, to study them and try to use them. The problem is that this is sometimes very dangerous, because some of the objects regularly used by adults are sharp or contain medication for one of the other children, which could poison him if he would taste it – and he certainly tries to do that. If it is noticed that he has picked up something like this, he is told angrily not to touch these things. The caregivers ask him

Chapter 5 : Discipline

why he is so bad, they have told him again and again not to touch these things and he still does it. The little boy begins to cry and one of the caregivers picks him up to comfort him.

This is a smart little boy. Although he does like to look at the things he is not allowed to touch, he has discovered that if he is 'bad' and gets told so and then starts to cry, the caregiver – who is usually too busy to spend much time with him because she has other, smaller, children to look after – will pick him up and hold him until he decides to stop crying. The reward for touching things that you are not allowed to touch is much too great to stop doing it. Especially since the little boy does not understand that the drawback is danger.

While failure to set limits can lead to the derailment of all children, especially if they have problems with self-control and aggression,

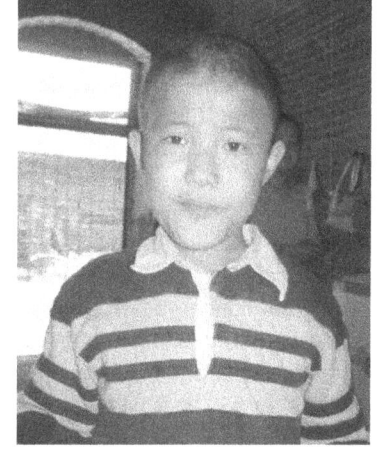

it is particularly dangerous in one specific group, namely children with a significant mental handicap. Unfortunately, this group often has even fewer rules and limits set for them than other children. This is because of the perception that 'the poor children' already have so much going against them that they deserve 'a bit of freedom'. This is a particularly great problem with children who are cared for by their parents, but occasionally it is also encountered with children in institutional care. Another reason sometimes seen is that a lot of people seem to think that a mental handicap means that the child is unable to learn anything.

This boy, autistic and mentally retarded, is usually very sweet, but if he is not taught clear limits, his occasional outburst will become dangerous to himself and his surroundings.

A teenage boy with a mental age of about three years old was in the habit of taking food from the plates of the children sitting beside him during meals. He also tended to get up halfway through the meal and walk around, grabbing handfuls of food from other plates, rather than finishing the food still left on his own plate. When I started to work at teaching him to eat from his own plate and not that of others, the staff told me not to bother: the boy was too stupid to learn. I went ahead anyway. At every meal I stood beside him and stopped him from putting his hands into plates other than his own, again, and again. When he tried to get up I made him sit down again and told him that he could eat from his own plate, not from that of others. If he really insisted on getting up, I reminded him that if he left his plate, the meal was over and he would not get any food until the next meal. Then I

> *would keep myself between him and other children's food until everyone finished eating, to prevent him from stealing food. Gradually, the message got through. After a month, someone still needed to stand beside him, to discourage him from grabbing, or getting up. But when that was the case, he would simply eat his own food and stay seated until he was full.*

In a child of two to three years old, running wild, destroying things and hurting people is mostly seen as cute. The hitting does not really hurt yet and the destruction only takes place on a small scale. From about four up to the age of about twelve, it becomes annoying. After that, it becomes dangerous.

A teenager with all the bulk and force of an adult, but a mental age of three years old or less has no concept of danger, value, or the fact that hitting, kicking or biting someone else hurts the other person the same way it would hurt her to be hit, kicked or bitten. At seven, it is still possible to pick a child up and drag her away from a dangerous place, or if she is about to destroy something valuable or important; to pick her up when she throws herself to the floor in a tantrum, because she does not want to go with you or to restrain her when she is really hurting you, or someone else.

Good luck trying to do that with a seventeen-year-old. If the seventeen-year-old has not learned to obey and accept certain limitations from an early age, she will be a real and great danger to herself and her surroundings. With no idea of her own strength and without having been taught how to control her aggression, she may accidentally gravely hurt someone or even beat him to death, without knowing what she is doing.

Of course, being a volunteer, you are not able to determine the way caregivers usually deal with the children. However, setting limits does not have to be an all-or-nothing venture. Children are very well aware of the individual people they are dealing with under the care of one person that they cannot get away with under the care of another person. In other words, you are able to set limits for children in their behaviour towards you and for the times when they are under your supervision. For example, if you consistently stop them from hitting you or other children when you are around, and refuse to give attention or play with them if they will not stop, they will pick up on it relatively quickly and behave differently under your supervision.

Breaking the Cycle of Negative Attention Seeking
In situations where there are relatively few adults looking after many children, attention for individual children can end up being

spread quite thin. It does not take the average child very long to find out that while positive attention is in very short supply, negative attention can always be had, if you play your cards right. Every time you break something, get yourself stuck, or hurt another child, a caregiver is sure to come over and yell at you. Of course, negative attention is not great, but a child's deep-seated need for attention is so great he feels that negative attention is a lot better than no attention at all.

Generally, this situation very quickly spirals into a **vicious cycle**. Bad behaviour and tantrums demand so much negative attention and cause such irritation that both the time available and the will to give positive attention to this particular child will disappear fast. The caregiver starts feeling bad about the child, and about herself, because she is constantly shouting at him. The child feels powerful on the one hand – because he can control his caregiver to a certain extent – and he has very low self-worth on the other hand, because he is constantly told he is bad.

Escaping this vicious cycle is entirely possible, but not at all easy. The caregiver needs to become very conscious of the situation that has developed and make a determined effort to change it. The way to change the situation is to demonstrate to the child that good behaviour is more rewarding than bad behaviour.

Giving positive attention has to be the first step, to prove that there is something better to be had than negative attention.

Step 1: Introduce positive attention and praise. This is not an easy thing to do, especially if the spiral has been whirling downward for some time already. You will need to actively search for something that you can praise the child for and reward him with a few moments of positive attention every time. To start with, what you are looking for are not exceptional accomplishments, but simply 'not-bad behaviour'. If he has been playing for five minutes without hitting anyone, breaking anything or screaming, you praise him. Tell him you think he is playing very well and that you like seeing him doing it. If he has spent a few minutes eating without throwing his drink all over the table or his food on the ground, praise him. If he does anything only remotely 'special' in a tiny way – handing a toy over to another child, holding out his arm or leg so that you can more easily dress him, anything at all – praise him. At the very beginning, if things are already rather out of control, you generally need to look very hard to find something to praise, and you need to constantly remind yourself to do it. However, if you do manage to praise him regularly and keep doing it for some time, it will pay off.

At the start, this is a scary thing to do. You do not want to interrupt the few moments during which the child is not causing trouble and draw attention to yourself. Because to start out with, this is almost guaranteed to set him off. He will use negative behaviour again, to try to keep your attention. Still, it is very important to praise him anyway. If he starts with negative behaviour again, gently – as friendly as you can – tell him that you liked it better when he was doing so well and move on to step 2.

Step 2: Ignore negative behaviour as much as possible. Unless it causes a danger to the child or others around him, ignore it completely. Even if that means having to put up with a lot of noise or some destruction. If there is a danger involved, keep the attention to an absolute minimum. Take the dangerous object away from him, while explaining to him why he cannot play with it. Or pick him up and put him down somewhere else, where he cannot continue to hurt another child or himself, and explain to him why. Other than that, ignore him, his crying, screaming and the whole situation. Pretend to be busy with another child or another chore – while obviously keeping an eye on the situation discreetly, to make sure the child does not get himself into danger again. If negative behaviour and tantrums

Make a point of making room for some playtime to help remove the need for negative attention seeking.

consistently do not bring the desired attention, while on the other hand it becomes clear that there *is* attention to be gained with positive behaviour, the child will realise this quite soon and start changing his tactics.

Step 3: Make time for happy playtime together every day, for several minutes at the very least. That is to say, give the child your complete and undivided attention, at a moment when he is well-behaved. This can consist of him sitting on your lap and you reading to him, playing with a toy on the floor or at the table together, singing or playing games together, or whatever works for the two of you. If the child becomes difficult during this playtime, explain to him that you would love to play with him, but not if he behaves like this. If he does not improve his behaviour, say you are sorry, but that if he does not want to play nice with you, you will go and do something else and walk away. In this case, if at all possible, you should try to initiate another playtime on the same day, when the child is well-behaved again, to show that there is no resentment.

Using this system, the problematic situation will not resolve itself from one moment to the next. As I have mentioned already, it is not an easy thing to do. But it does, in fact, work. For an outsider who is consistent, it usually takes little more than a day to break through the pattern. For the caregiver and child who have been in the vicious cycle together for some time already, it is likely to take at least a week, and it will only work if the caregiver is completely committed to making the change and is completely consistent in her approach to making this happen, because the two of them are stuck in a head-lock. To start with, the cycle of negative attention seeking is going to have to be broken individually by everyone involved in a particular child's care. Each person needs to show that they will not reward bad behaviour with attention and that they will make an effort to give positive attention.

I met a caregiver and a two-and-a-half year old stuck in such a headlock at one point. She was completely convinced that there was nothing that could be done, because it was simply a question of the little boy's nature, in her eyes. So much so, that she refused to change anything about her own approach to him or to believe that anything could possibly change. During the two weeks that she had been away and I had taken charge in her stead the boy had been no trouble at all, but even this fact was a coincidence, according to her. To me it was quite clear that once she returned, the boy was almost impossible to deal with whenever she was there, while he remained quite easy-going with me when she was out of sight.

While there is usually a rocky transition period, making sure enough positive attention is given will almost always reduce negative attention seeking behaviour. Just do not expect the difficult child to turn into a model child – this is too much to ask of anyone. And make sure that you continue to offer positive attention after the change has taken place. Because, even if the cycle has been broken, every child still needs attention, and when no positive attention is available, he will do what it takes to get any kind of attention whatsoever.

A group of volunteers visited a children's home every Sunday afternoon to do activities with the children. They complained that certain boys would not participate in the activities of the group they were assigned to. After a while the boys would go and wander around and try to join other groups. As a suggestion, I proposed an adapted version of the strategy explained above. I told them to tell the boys that

they could do an activity with the group they were assigned to, or if they chose not to, they would simply not have anything to do. The next step was not to give the boy any attention if he wandered off, but even more importantly that none of the volunteers were to give attention to any child who was not in their group. This way the boys soon found out that they could not find attention outside their assigned groups and were better off taking part in the activity.

A hoe is not a safe toy, but they do not know that.

The Purpose of Rules

How does one go about making sure that the limits become clear to the child and are obeyed?

Rules and authority should be kept as simple as possible. The following list breaks down what rules should be about:

- Keeping the child safe from serious physical harm: Children are often not aware of the risks of walking along the edge of a cliff, crossing a busy road, going near an open fire, or playing with sharp objects. So, activities that have a high likelihood of ending in serious physical harm are generally forbidden if there is no adult supervision. The reason for this is to prevent the child from seriously hurting himself. It is, however, important to note the word 'seriously'. Accidents will happen: children will fall, scrape themselves, get minor cuts and bruises; all of this is part of growing up, learning and living. If you set out to prevent all of these things, you essentially prevent the child from having a life, which is in fact in many ways harmful to the child's psychological and even motor skill development.
- Keeping the child from harming others: Especially young children do not yet grasp the concept that if they hit someone, they hurt that person, because the child who does the hitting does not feel the pain. They have even less of an understanding of the possibility of causing injuries. Somewhat older children

are aware that they can hurt someone else, but they often do not quite realise the full danger and seriousness of the injuries that they can inflict. So, they are given rules to stop them from being aggressive towards other people to prevent them from causing injury or pain.
- Keeping the child from causing destruction: Younger children are not yet aware that if they take something apart or break it, it may not always be possible to put it back together again or to replace it. So until they start to develop an awareness that stops them from destruction, they are given rules about not destroying things.
- Teaching the child socially and culturally appropriate behaviour: Every culture and social situation has its own rules as to what is appropriate to do and what is not. The knowledge of these rules is not present at birth. They need to be learned over the course of childhood. So, as children get older, they will be taught more and more rules about appropriate behaviour when dealing with elders, with family and strangers, with people from the opposite sex, and how to behave in various settings and occasions. As they learn these rules, they become what is seen as well-mannered people.
- Aiding the child's development: Rules such as having to tidy away toys, helping out with chores, and washing hands before eating, are all designed to teach children something about living and taking care of themselves and helping others. These rules benefit children's development and prepare them for their adult lives.

Not the Purpose of Rules

It is important to realise that if rules are imposed in excessive numbers, with excessive force, or for no valid reason, the chance of children actually following the rules becomes smaller. In most cases, their goal will shift from obeying rules to wanting to avoid getting caught breaking them. In this, they are likely to make no distinction between rules that are there to protect them and other rules, often because they are still unable to tell the difference between the two categories. Thereby, they possibly put themselves or others at serious risk.

That is why it is important to be aware of the following two categories of rules, which in no way help a child's development or well-being, even though they are widely used. Being consciously aware of the existence of these two categories may help you to avoid them.

- Rules for the sake for authority: These are the 'because I say so' rules. They are rules that do not advance the protection or development of the child, but only serve to inflate the ego of the enforcer. Randomly saying 'you cannot play with your favourite toy today', can be enforced and may make the enforcer feel powerful very briefly. However, if decrees such as this one are a regular occurrence, the child is likely to become very sceptical about the value of all the rules that are given by this person. Nor will he learn anything about justice and fairness this way. Inventing rules for no other reason than to assert authority is counterproductive. It generally only means that you end up sounding like a monster shouting and reprimanding almost non-stop. This will not make you more respected by the children., In fact, it will probably make you less respected. It is amazing how quickly and flawlessly children see through a mere authoritarian front and lose respect for the person hiding behind it.

- Rules to solely improve the caregiver's life: While there is nothing wrong with a rule like 'no screaming in the house' to protect the caregiver's ears and that of the other children, in some cases the pendulum swings too far to the other side and the majority of rules become not about keeping the child safe and advancing his development, but about making the adult's life more comfortable. A rule such as 'between meals you are to sit on the sofa and not make a sound' makes the caregiver's life a lot easier: there is no noise, the children do not need a great deal of supervising and no mess is made, nor do they become dirty. However, from the side of the children, they get a lack of exercise, fresh air, and opportunities for learning through experience, stimulation, language development, and social skills. In other words, this may be convenient for the caregiver, but it is very bad for the children's development. Plus, it invites bad behaviour, because small children are quite simply not capable of sitting still without anything to do for more than a minute or two.

Just like in a game, children are more likely to follow rules in life if they are clear, fair and consistent.

A group home consisted of babies, toddlers in the age up to two-and-a-half years old, and, due to circumstances, one five-year-old. This five-year-old was not allowed to play around the house with the toddlers, because the caregiver felt that he was too rowdy and that would mean she would have to keep a constant eye on all the children playing together – something I would consider advisable anyway when there is a group of toddlers running around. He was also not allowed to interact with the older boys from the other group home on the compound, because the caregiver felt that they would be a bad influence on him, which would only lead him into trouble. So, instead, the whole time he was not in school, he was only al-

lowed to play in the little park on his own – within the compound and within view of the house –mostly watching groups of younger and older children playing from a distance. Except for the times that he was eating his meals or sleeping, he was kept in complete isolation. This is not an acceptable situation. The five-year-old was not treated as a little boy, but as a nuisance to be kept out of the way.

Imposing and Enforcing Rules

The most important things are to be clear and consistent about what the rules are, to follow through on what you say, and to be fair. Explaining to a child why you are not allowing something or why you make him do something, will help him learn and develop. Once a child starts to understand the reasons behind the rules imposed on him, he is much more likely to obey them than when he has always simply been told 'because I say so' or 'because that's the way it is'. Explaining why something is not allowed while you reprimand a child, makes the rules clearer to the child. Rules and authority should be kept as simple as possible. There should be as few rules as possible, simply to keep the child safe and guide him towards socially acceptable behaviour. This approach will provide more than enough restrictions in a child's life.

The importance of consistency cannot possibly be overstated. Small children learn mostly from having the same thing repeated over and over again, in exactly the same way or with slight variation. Bit by bit, they begin to recognise how that particular situation works, and in the end they will have absorbed it. This goes for limits and rules as much as for anything else. Constantly changing the rules is very confusing and unsettling for children. It deprives them of their sense of stability and security. In the end, it does not really matter whether you let them drink/have/do something or not. What is important is not to say 'no' 5x first, and then give in. If you do this only once, it will inevitably lead to a period with lots of tantrums, because the child has just learned that a bit of perseverance may be rewarded. Plus, as explained earlier, while the child might be very pleased with having 'won' the one extra cookie, or whatever it is that he got, if it happens regularly, it will actually become very unsettling for him.

Following through means making sure something does or does not happen, according to what you have just told the child. If you say 'you cannot play with that', but then let it happen anyway, only shouting at the child for not listening much later, you show the child that you do not need to be taken seriously when you say things like that. Instead, if the child continues to play with it, you could give one more warning: 'I told you that you cannot play with that, if you do not put it down, I will take it off you.' Give the child a moment to do what you said, and if he does not do it, take the thing away from him. This shows him that you are serious when you tell him something.

A caregiver complained that three toddlers never listened to her. She would tell them to sit down to start their meal, and they would still be running around. Once they started to eat, they would get up again and run around some more. She felt that they were very badly behaved children. What I saw was that the children were told to sit down to eat and then ignored. After another ten minutes of playing, another request would be made for them to sit down. The same if they got up while they were eating: they were allowed to run around, come back for more food, and run around some more. They would get shouted at a little, but nothing else would happen. So the children did not have the impression that the shouting was all that serious, because nothing happened after it.

When I was in charge of these three children on the caregiver's day off, I told them to sit down to eat and got them to sit down straight away. If they got up, I would put them back behind their plate again, and again, and again. Towards the end of the meal I would warn them that if they got up from behind their plate, they would be done with the meal and the food would be taken away. Every time they wanted to get up I asked them if they were done eating and if not, to sit down again. The next week, when I covered the day off, the three toddlers would come almost immediately when I called them to dinner and made fewer attempts to get up, and the week after was even better. They knew I was going to follow through on what I said, so they saved themselves the energy of trying to go against it without hope of getting anything out of it. Meanwhile, with their caregiver the situation was still the same.

First 'offences' should always be met with a warning and an explanation as to why it is an offence. Toddlers, and in some cases older children too, do not have the insight or capacity to realise what consequences might be connected to their actions. They only see as far as 'hey, my finger fits into that hole' or 'that's a funny sound when I whack this toy on the floor, what would happen if I whacked it on that girl's head?' They do not understand and cannot foresee danger. They do not know that things that are broken become unusable and cannot always be fixed. Nor, for that matter, do they understand why it would be a bad thing if something is broken, or that there is money involved.

So while you might get a tremendous shock or scare with something a child does, it is not fair on the child to punish her when the child has not been made aware that what she did is wrong. Punishing her in a situation like that is nothing more than taking out your fright on someone much smaller than you. The first time, children should be warned very sternly not to do it again, and have it explained as plainly as possible why. Then, if they do it again, they can be reprimanded for doing something they have been told not to do – not for causing danger, because they still will not truly realise that.

Discipline Strategies

For babies, discipline comes into play around six months of age, when they start to reach out around them, to explore the world. At this age, babies do not yet have the ability or need to learn social rules, but they do need to be kept safe and to start to learn what behaviour is 'wrong' because it brings them into danger. Setting limits and discipline at this age simply consists of preventing the baby from doing something. The first tactic used here is usually to pick the baby up and put him down again somewhere else, out of reach of danger, or out of reach of the other child he was hurting. While moving him away, explain that he cannot do that particular thing and why this is so, even if he is at an age where he is not likely to fully understand. The repeated explanations will start the development of understanding.

Once a baby starts moving around by himself, this is no longer always effective. If the activity that he is prevented from continuing is interesting enough, he will do what he can to make his way back to where he was originally to continue what he was doing. At this stage, holding his hand – or both hands – away from where he wants to use it by gently, but firmly, grabbing his arm by the wrist, is usually eventually effective after it has been repeated several times. Hold the hand long enough – usually about a minute or so – that he does not think it is a funny game anymore and becomes annoyed at not having the use of his hand. Again, while holding the hand, explain what he is not allowed to do and why.

He needed to be removed repeatedly before he gave up.

This technique can be effectively used with children of all ages – basically until they become stronger than you – to counter them hitting or otherwise hurting other children or yourself. If you start using it at a young age, once the child becomes older, there is usually no need for it anymore, as just explaining that hitting is not allowed because it hurts someone and warning him not to do it when he starts becomes enough in most cases.

If grabbing hold of the baby's hand or moving him is not effective in stopping him from going back to where he is not supposed to go after two or three tries, then the most effective way is to block his way. Either put yourself between where the baby is and where you do not want him to go, or put something else in his way that he is unable to get under, over or around.

As a child moves out of the baby stage into toddlerhood, he becomes more inventive in ways to explore the world. He is able to get himself into more trouble. And he begins to have a greater understanding of the world around him and of social rules. So, step by step, it becomes not only necessary to keep him away from things that are dangerous, he also needs to start learning some of the social rules that are part of his culture. From this time onward, he can start learning more from what is explained to him and what he experiences himself.

'Punishments', or consequences, from this age onwards should ideally be as close as possible to natural consequences. This will help teach the child about the way the world works and why his behaviour is undesirable. There is no point or sense in punishing a child by depriving him of food or sending him to bed several hours earlier than normal. Nor is it effective to punish a toddler who has broken something in the morning by not allowing him to go on an outing in the afternoon. These kinds of things hold no connection. Neither in the natural order of things, nor in the mind of the child. When the two-year-old is crying over not being allowed to go out with the other children in the afternoon, he will have no memory of what happened that morning, and telling him again will not truly bring it back. To the child, this will seem like an unpredictable, random act, which seems to him more like favouritism than like discipline.

In the case of a child who won't stop throwing toys – across the room/ at other children/out the window/onto the roof – after being warned not to, a more effective and understandable way would be to let him play without toys for half an hour. Explain why this is so, and in the set time period calmly take away any toys from him, and any toys that he might attempt to get his hands on afterwards. Every time you take away the toys, calmly explain that no, he cannot play with toys right now. Because, if you throw toys, you are left with nothing. Also tell him that later on he will be allowed to play with toys again, and then he can show whether he is able to play without throwing them.

Do not rant on, piling on accusations. There is no need to raise your voice to the child, nor do you need to bring the subject up again yourself, unless he attempts to grab a toy before the time is up. Keep an eye on the clock and after the agreed time – do not let it go on longer than the period which you have stated to him – let him know that he can play with the toys again now, if he wants, but that he is not to throw them anymore. If he starts playing with the toys, without throwing, that is the end of the 'episode'. If he starts throwing toys again, whether it is straight away or later on, treat it as a new incident: still without raising your voice, give one warning and if it happens again, take the toys away again for half an hour.

If natural consequences are impossible or too dangerous to be experienced by a child – for example paying for the damages done to a car or letting him injure another child –, giving him a time-out is a good alternative. Time-out is a period during which the child is to sit on his own – in a safe place, preferably not his bed, because this can cause negative associations with being put in the bed – and does not receive any attention. When the child is put in this spot, it should be explained to him why he is there. For example, 'you are not allowed to hit Mary, if you hit someone, you have sit here until I come and get you, to learn that you cannot do that.' Only that, in a calm voice. If you continue to criticise him while he is sitting there, you are giving him attention. For almost all children, negative attention is still better than no attention at all, which would make the time-out more of a reward than a punishment.

Watch the clock: make the time-out too long and it becomes useless.

If the child starts screaming, crying and ranting, ignore him. If he gets up from the spot where you have told him to stay, simply put him back again, without saying anything to him, nor making eye contact. Put him back as many times as he gets up and leaves. The time-out period starts from the last time he has sat down: if he keeps getting up, the clock keeps resetting.

Time-out should last a reasonable time, according to age. One minute per year of their life is a good guideline. So two minutes for a two-year-old, and six minutes for a six-year-old. Leaving a young child in time-out for 15 minutes to half an hour will not accomplish anything and can even be counterproductive. After a few minutes, a toddler will have forgotten why he is where he is, and will only have a vague recollection that he is supposed to stay there. So it actually invites more 'bad' behaviour. The child will not remember what he is doing on the step or the stool, he will get bored because he is 'isolated', and he will start looking around for something to relieve the boredom, and… 'Hey, that looks interesting, I wonder what happens if I pull at it….' To us, two or three minutes do not seem like a very long time, but to a toddler, it is half an eternity.

A child put in time-out, away from the rest of the group and facing away, an adult nearby to make sure she stays where she is, without giving her attention.

Keep an eye on the clock to make sure that the child is not left in time-out longer than he is supposed to. When the time is up, go and get him. Before letting him go off to play, explain to him again why you put him in time-out. Tell him 'You can go and play now, but 'don't [....] again, all right?' With that, the issue has to be left behind you. There is no need to drag it up again.

With somewhat older children, you can teach them to tell you they are sorry for what they did and that they will not do it again, before they go off to play again. With toddlers, it is possible to teach them to say this, but it would be very naïve to think that they will have spent their time-out thinking about what they have done and come out regretting it. They simply do not understand enough about the situation to do that.

Do not hold a grudge. After a child has been disciplined, life goes on as if nothing happened – when you allow him to join the normal activities again, remind the child once more not to do whatever he was being punished for, and leave it at that. It is not always easy, but it is important to remember that your memory stretches back a lot further than theirs.

Physical Punishment

Making children understand that they are not allowed to hit other people is high on any caregiver's priority list. Interestingly enough, this is true even for caregivers who themselves use hitting, slapping or spanking children as a means of disciplining them. It is very important to realise that if someone uses hitting as a means of correcting children, they are teaching those children in the clearest possible way that hitting is an acceptable means to let someone know you are unhappy with their behaviour. 'Do as I say, not as I do', as mentioned before is an often heard quote and a command that most caregivers would like to see followed, but that is not the way it works. Ultimately, children learn by following examples, and if the caregiver hits, that must be the right thing to do.

There are several issues associated with physical punishment that a lot of people are not aware of:

- Using physical punishment is showing your weakness, rather than you power or strength. This is something not everyone realises. In human nature, violence is a last resort. When we are completely desperate and feel thoroughly powerless, what remains is to use violence to try to escape from the situation we are in. If this last resort, this tool of desperation, is the first thing someone uses when they discipline children, they are showing their weakness. They are making clear that it is all they

have; they apparently do not have any other ways to deal with the situation. Not really the position of power they might have thought they were displaying.
- It is quite simply not very effective. Inflicting pain will never establish respect in the person you hurt. It only raises fear. In a limited sense, fear can be a strong motivator, and it is likely to lead to obedience in your presence, if you are feared enough. What you need to ask yourself however, is, what is fear a motivator for? The answer is that it is not a motivator for doing the right thing or for pleasing you. It is only a motivator for making sure that you do not find out about anything you do not approve of.
- The following argument is often heard in defence of using physical punishment. 'A child should not be beaten in anger, but a slap given when the caregiver is calm is necessary to make the child understand what he can and cannot do'. I certainly agree that a child should not be beaten in anger, because this is very dangerous: frustration and anger can blind you and lead to much unintended damage. I have come across two children so far whose severe **Cerebral Palsy** was known to have been caused by beatings from their caregivers. On the other hand, I do not know many people who are able to hit a small child when they are *really* calm. This argument is mostly used by people who tend to hit children when they are only slightly less angry with them and are still in danger of losing control.

As a volunteer, it is important to understand that physical punishment takes place in almost all children's homes, whether it happens in your presence or not. You also need to understand that it is generally seen both as a cultural tradition and as 'the only way they will listen'. Trying to change people's minds about this as a young, foreign volunteer is most likely a waste of energy. It will either end in a bitter debate or in you being laughed out of the room as a fainthearted foreigner. So you are probably better off staying away from the subject and limiting yourself to not taking part in this kind of punishment.

"My worst experience during my time as a volunteer was the struggle I had with the physical violence that caretakers/teachers used against children. I found it very hard to take a position in these situations as an outsider. I didn't want to judge the staff, but the last thing I wanted was to see the children suffering."

Chapter 6: Temperature

Fever

Unlike what is commonly believed, a fever is not a problem caused by bacteria or viruses. Rather, it is a way for the body to fight bacteria or viruses. When the body's immune system comes across something that it cannot overcome easily, the body raises its temperature to help the fight against 'invaders'. All processes in the body slow down when temperature drops and speed up when temperature rises. So, with a higher body temperature, the immune system is more active in its fight against intruders.

Often a child has a fever for two or three days, maybe with a runny nose and a cough, and then he is all better again. This fever probably started because of a virus or a small infection. The child's body raised its temperature to a fever level and was able to fight off the virus or bacteria like this, without the help of medication.

The body raises its temperature by adjusting its **internal thermostat**. Normally, this is set at about 37°C. When the body creates a fever, it will use the same measures to raise its temperature as it normally uses in a cold environment. In fact, when the brain feels that a fever needs to be created, it will send a message to the body saying that it is feeling cold. This is why when you have a fever you think you are cold, even though your temperature is high. You brain tells you to feel this way, to make you create more heat. During a fever, blood flow to hands and feet decreases to prevent loss of heat, making them cold. If this is not enough to reach or stay at the desired temperature, the body will start shivering to generate the heat itself. When someone with a fever starts shivering, you can expect his fever to start rising very quickly.

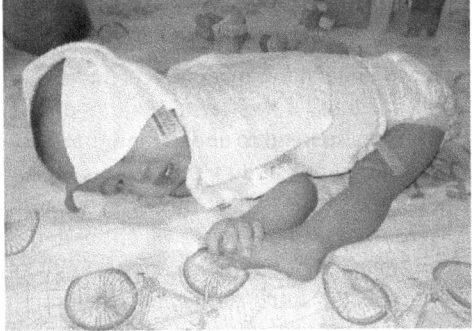

A baby with a fever, covered in wet cloths to cool him down.

Often, a child who has a fever will not be feeling well and may not want to eat anything. This is not usually a problem, as long as the child continues to drink enough fluids. Because of the increased body temperature, a child with a fever can get dehydrated more easily than a healthy child. So, make sure that the child gets plenty to drink. If he does not want to drink milk or water, see if you can find other things that he might be willing to drink.

The rise of the body temperature is useful in the fight against infections and diseases. This is why it is not helpful to **suppress** a temperature as soon as it is above normal. Suppressing a fever – especially a low grade one – will make it harder for the body to fight off infections and the child might be ill for longer because of this. When the immune system is having a lot of trouble fighting off an infection, fevers sometimes do need to be suppressed. This is because the body may raise its temperature to a level so high that it is dangerous. Keeping the body temperature down – suppressing the fever – can be done with certain kinds of medication called fever suppressants. They will be discussed in more detail in a later section of this chapter.

Interpreting Temperatures
All the temperatures given here are temperatures as measured by putting the thermometer in the child's armpit. If you take the child's temperature by putting the thermometer in her mouth or anus, the temperature you get will be about 0.5°C higher than the temperatures given here. All temperatures in this book are given on the Celsius scale, as °C. If you are more used to thinking about temperatures on the Fahrenheit scale, °F, you can find a table at the end of this book that tells you what temperature in Celsius corresponds to what temperature in Fahrenheit in the Appendix.

The effect of different temperature ranges on the well-being of a child:

Below 35°C
The child is too cold – this is called hypothermia – and she should be dressed in warmer clothes and covered with blankets. Hot water bottles (wrapped up in a cloth, never directly against the child's skin or clothes) should be placed under the blankets with the child to warm her up. Later on in this chapter, more information will be given about what to do in case of hypothermia.

With temperatures outside being over 25°C, this is not only excessive, it can be dangerous.

35-35.5°C
This temperature is a little lower than normal for most people, but no reason for serious concern. A temperature like this can easily be reached if a baby is not dressed or covered warmly enough. If a baby's temperature drops below 35.5°C she should be dressed more warmly, as well as being given a hat, and she should be covered with warm blankets.

35.5-37°C

This is a normal range for body temperature. We like to see the child like this. Most people have a normal body temperature between 36°C and 37°C. However, some people have a body temperature slightly lower or higher than that.

37-37.5°C

This temperature is a little higher than normal for most people, but no reason for serious concern. A temperature like this can also be reached if the child is dressed or covered too warmly. So putting on some lighter clothes or taking away a blanket may be enough to bring the temperature down to normal.

> It was the cold season; in this country that meant temperatures around 18°C outside. Afraid that the ten-month-old baby would get cold in the night, her caregiver dressed her in thick, warm clothes, a woollen jumper and over that a snowsuit that had been donated. The girl was put in bed and covered with a thick duvet. I found her dressed and covered like this in the morning. The little girl was hot and covered in sweat. When I said that she was dressed rather warmly and that she was sweating, I was told that the girl was just like that, she was always sweaty. I explained that the way she was dressed and covered, she was able to be outside safely at a temperature of -15°C. I then explained the dangers of overheating a baby.

37.5-38.5°C

This is a low grade fever indicating that the child's body is fighting an illness or infection. In this range, the fever is beneficial to getting better. Giving medication to suppress the fever will make it harder for the child's body to fight off the illness. The child's hands and feet are probably very cold. This does not mean that the child is actually cold. It means that the child's body is working to raise her central temperature by not letting heat escape through hands and feet, where heat is lost easily. A child with this temperature should not be wearing warm clothes, socks or a hat. Instead, she should be dressed in thin clothes, to try to stop her fever from becoming too high.

> A baby had had a fever during the night and was given Tylenol to prevent it from getting too high. After taking Tylenol, her temperature went back to normal for a few hours. Then in the morning, her hands and feet became very cold quite suddenly and she started shivering. Her caregiver felt bad, thinking the girl was very cold, and she put warmer clothes on her and covered her with a blanket. The little girl continued to shiver. It was time to take her temperature again –

something that was done once an hour until the child had been fever-free for at least 24h – and the caregiver was shocked to discover that the girl's temperature had shot up from 37.4°C to 39.2°C in just one hour, and she was still shivering. So, she was given a bath and more fever suppressants to stop her temperature from rising further and the caregivers were reminded that when she starts shivering, a baby who has a fever should be cooled down, not warmed up.

In adults, it can sometimes be effective to cover up warmly, with lots of blankets. Because in an adult, this will cause a lot of sweating and that helps cool the body down. In babies and small children, this does not work. They are generally much less able to sweat than adults are. Dressing and covering babies warmly only drives their temperature up, it will not help cool them down.

A boy with a fever was wrapped up in a thick blanket. When his temperature was taken, it turned out to be 40.8°C. The blanket was taken away and the boy was put on a mattress under the fan and kept wet until his temperature was below 38°C. In this process, his shivering did not start until he got down to 39.3°C, so that was most likely the temperature his body was aiming for. Everything over that was caused by being overheated because of the blanket.

38.5-40°C

A temperature up to 39°C is called a fever and above 39°C it is called a high fever. In case of a high fever, you can begin to bring the temperature down by giving a bath in warm water (not hot or cold) for a while. The child should not be wearing anything more than a nappy or underwear if her temperature is above 39°C. You can further help her cool down by putting wet (lukewarm, not cold) cloths on her head and chest.

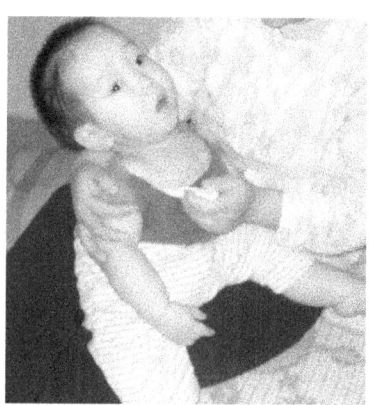

When the temperature is not normal, it should be checked regularly.

Since keeping a cloth on a baby's head can be quite a challenge, a wet hat may be more practical. When cooling down someone who has a fever with water, always use lukewarm water. Putting cold water on a fevered skin will only make the body work harder to raise its temperature. Definitely never use ice, ice water or a freezer element. Using any of these things can cause not just discomfort or pain, but also serious damage.

If the child's temperature reaches 38.6°C, you can give her fever suppressants to stop it from rising further. You will find more information about this in the next section. With a temperature above 39°C, a child usually looks very sick, may not want to eat, and lacks energy. Hands and feet can be very, very cold, and even appear a little purple. The child may be shivering. Again, this is not a sign that you should warm the child up. A child with a high fever needs help to cool down.

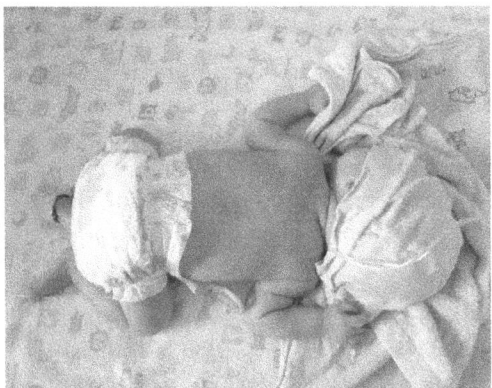

A combination of removing clothes, a wet hat and fever suppressants is often needed to keep a fever under control in babies.

At this temperature range, children who have had seizures in the past and children with cerebral palsy have a greater chance of febrile seizures, particularly if they are less than six years old. These children need to be monitored in case such a seizure happens.

When a child has a fever, her temperature should be checked once every hour, even if a fever suppressant has been given. This is because, while we hope that this medication will bring the fever down, there is no guarantee that it will work. Even if the temperature does go down, it might come back up much sooner than expected. Only if the fever stays down for more than ten hours after a suppressant was given can you say the fever may have broken. Be aware that a child is often fever free and active during the daytime, only to spike a high fever again during the night. So only after the child has been free of fever for 24 hours, without using fever suppressants, can you be pretty sure that she is really better.

Above 40°C

Temperatures above 40°C can be dangerous for the body. All young children, not just those generally at risk of seizures, are in danger of febrile seizures at this temperature. With a temperature above 40°C, every effort must be made to bring the temperature down, and these efforts should not be stopped until the temperature is below 40°C again. The temperature should be checked every half hour, as long as the temperature is above 40°C.

If a child's temperature reaches more than 40°C despite having already taken a suppressant, the most effective way to cool a child down is to keep her wet constantly. You can do this by putting her in a bath or on a towel on the floor and keeping every part of her body wet by pouring water over it without stopping until her temperature starts coming down. If there is a fan present, keeping the child under the fan is helpful.

In older children, a fever is not likely to rise quite as quickly or get quite as high as it does in a baby or a toddler. In older children this only happens with some very serious illnesses such as malaria or meningitis. While for a baby it is quite common for a fever to reach 40°C, if a child over four years old has a fever of more than 40°C, he should be taken to a doctor straight away, without waiting to see if the problem will go away on its own.

Fever Suppressants

Fever suppressants are medications that stop the body from creating a fever. They do not fix the problem causing the fever. They do not make the child better. They only bring the body's temperature down to – close to – normal level for a few hours. Usually, they work for six to eight hours. After that, the child's temperature will generally go up again. As mentioned before, because fevers have an important function in fighting disease, it is not a good idea to suppress them the moment they become a little higher than usual. Fevers should only be suppressed when they become so high that they can form a risk to the body in themselves.

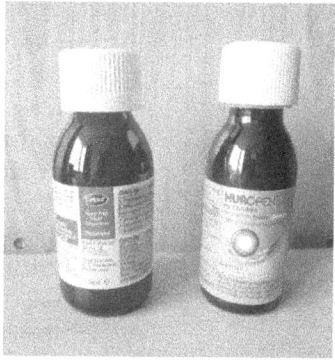

Example of fever suppressants that are often used.

The body's temperature rarely goes above 41°C unless there are problems with the temperature control of the body, which is located in the brain. However, febrile seizures – seizures that are caused by a fever – and other damage at the cell level in the body can begin to happen at 40°C. It takes fever suppressants some time to become effective, and a baby's temperature can rise very quickly. Therefore, it is wise to administer fever suppressants when the baby has a temperature above 38.6°C.

In children who have a history of seizures – either while they have a fever or while they do not – the chance of febrile seizures is increased (See Part 2, Chapter 5: 'Special Needs' for more information about what seizures are). These children should be given suppressants when they reach 1.5°C above their normal temperature, instead of waiting until they reach 38.6°C. This is both in order to prevent seizures caused by high temperatures, and to prevent seizures caused by a fast rise or fall of the temperature.

The two kinds of fever suppressant that are most easily available and most commonly used for babies and children are Paracetamol and Ibuprofen.

Paracetamol
Paracetamol is sold under various brand names such as Tylenol

or Calpol, it is also known as Acetaminophen. You can buy it over the counter, this means you can get it without needing a doctor's prescription in most places, and it comes as a tablet, a syrup or a suppository. The latter two are generally easier to give to a baby or toddler. Paracetamol works both as a painkiller and as a fever suppressant. This is the first line of medication for fevers. Babies under six months should only be given Paracetamol, not any other suppressants, unless a doctor says otherwise in a specific case. Older children need to be given Paracetamol first, and only something else if that is not effective.

Most forms of Paracetamol should be given no more often than once every four hours, and no more than five times in 24 hours. Make sure that you are giving the right dose for the age and weight of the child. Often the bottle or package has information about how much children of different age groups should be getting, but in a situation where children are much smaller or more malnourished than most children their age, it is not safe to follow this. When calculating the dose for a particular child, it is important to know what the child's weight is at that moment. You also need to remember that if you are giving a syrup, you will first have to look up how many mg (milligrams) of Paracetamol are dissolved in a certain number of ml (millilitres) of syrup – this will be written on the bottle – and then you need to calculate how many mls of syrup to give the child to make sure she will get the right amount of mgs of Paracetamol. Having a 2.5ml syringe is helpful to be able to draw out the right amount of syrup, though some bottles come with their own syringe or dosing spoon when you buy them.

Infant Paracetamol Dose

2.5 - 4 kg	40 mg
4 - 5 kg	60 mg
5 - 7.5 kg	80 mg
7.5 - 10 kg	120 mg
10 - 12 kg	160 mg
12 - 15 kg	200 mg
15 - 17 kg	240 mg

The bottle says that 'each 5ml of Calpol contains 120mg of Paracetamol', and the baby with the fever weighs 4.5kg. So 120mg in 5ml, needing 60mg: 120mg/2=60mg. To get that, you need 5ml/2=2.5ml. That means that the baby will need to be given 2.5ml of Calpol per dose, a maximum of 5 times a day.

Even if a child is old enough to be able to go and get a Paracetamol tablet from the medicine cabinet by himself, he should not be allowed to do so. Children do not fully understand the risks of taking medication, and when a child is allowed to go get his own Paracetamol once, he may go and get more pills when you do not know about it, because he thinks it will make him feel better. Medication should only be handed out by adults. With almost all medication, it is possible that a child will be poisoned if it is not used properly. And poisoning with Paracetamol by taking too much is particularly common. An overdose of Paracetamol can lead to serious liver damage and in some cases even to the liver shutting down completely. If the liver does not work anymore, the only hope of survival is a liver transplant.

Ibuprofen
Ibuprofen is sold under various brand names such as Motrin, Neurofen, Ibumex and Advil. It is part of a class of medication called nonsteroidal **anti-inflammatory** drugs (NSAIDs). It works as a painkiller, a fever suppressant and an anti-inflammatory agent. Ibuprofen has a stronger effect than Paracetamol, but it also has more side effects, such as problems with stomach and kidneys. Giving it immediately before or after eating helps prevent stomach pain or an upset stomach. If a child has problems with his kidneys or if he has stomach ulcers, you should never give him Ibuprofen. Ibuprofen should not be given to babies under six months old. Generally, Ibuprofen should only be given if Paracetamol is not effective, or if a doctor specifically tells you the child needs it.

You can give Ibuprofen once every six hours, and no more than four times in 24 hours. You need to calculate the right dose for the age and weight of the child. Often the bottle or package has information about how much children of different age groups should be getting, but in a situation where children are much smaller or more malnourished than most children their age, it is not safe to follow this. When calculating the dose for a particular child, it is important to know what the child's weight is at that moment. You also need to remember that if you are giving a syrup, you will first have to look up how many mg (milligrams) of Ibuprofen are dissolved in a certain number of ml (millilitres) of syrup – this will be written on the bottle – and then you need to calculate how many mls of syrup to give the child to make sure she will get the right amount of mgs of Ibuprofen. Having a 2.5ml syringe is helpful to be able to draw out the right amount of syrup, though some bottles come with their own syringe or dosing spoon when you buy them.

The bottle says that there is 100mg of Ibuprofen in 5ml of Motrin and the baby with the fever weighs 4.5kg. So 100mg in 5ml, needing 25mg: 100mg/4=25mg and 5ml/4=1.25ml. That means that the baby will need to be given 1.25ml of Motrin per dose, a maximum of 4 times a day.

Infant Ibuprofen Dose

4 - 5 kg	25 mg
5 - 7.5 kg	50 mg
7.5 - 10 kg	75 mg
10 - 12 kg	100 mg
12 - 15 kg	125 mg

Even if a child is old enough to be able to go and get an Ibuprofen tablet from the medicine cabinet by himself, he should not be allowed to do so. Children do not fully understand the risks of taking medication, and when a child is allowed to go get his own Ibuprofen once, he may go and get more pills when you do not know about it, because he thinks it will make him feel better. Medication should only be handed out by adults. With almost all medication, it is possible that a child will be poisoned if it is not used properly. Taking too much Ibuprofen can cause stomach ulcers and kidney problems. Ibuprofen in tablet form should always be taken together with food, to prevent stomach problems.

If a child's fever does not go down much after giving Paracetamol, and the child is more than six months old, you can give Ibuprofen four hours after giving Paracetamol to attempt to suppress the fever. If a child's temperature reaches 41°C after taking Paracetamol, you can give Ibuprofen as soon as one hour after giving Paracetamol. If the child is having a febrile seizure due to his fever still being high, despite taking Paracetamol, you can also give Ibuprofen as soon as one hour after giving Paracetamol.

Giving both suppressants this close together should only be done in extreme cases.

Make sure that in a 24-hour period, you do not give Paracetamol more than five times and you do not give Ibuprofen more than four times in total!

A little girl was very ill and, despite being given fever suppressants, her fever would shoot up again very quickly every time. Halfway through the night the supervisor contacted the medical care manager. She told her that they had already given the girl Tylenol five times and Motrin 4 times in the past 24 hours, and there were five hours left until she could be given more. But her temperature had reached 39.1°C again. What had happened was that every time the girl's temperature had reached 39°C, she had been given a fever suppressant, alternating between the two. Mostly, this had happened within three hours of taking one last. No attempts had been made to cool her down in any

other way or to extend the time between fever suppressants. So now, cooling her down with water was the only option left for the next five hours.

After giving Paracetamol or Ibuprofen, the child's temperature will not go down instantly. The medication needs at least half an hour to an hour to start working. So, check the child's temperature again about 30-45 minutes after giving the fever suppressant, to see if the temperature has started going down, or at least if it has stopped going up further.

Causes of Fevers

While it is necessary to keep a fever under control, it is important not to forget to try to find out the cause of the fever. Treating the cause of the fever will remove the need for the body to create the fever. In most cases, the body creates a fever in response to the presence of harmful bacteria or a virus. You should monitor a child for three to four days to see if she is able to win the fight by herself. If the child still has a fever after four days or if the fever is very high and

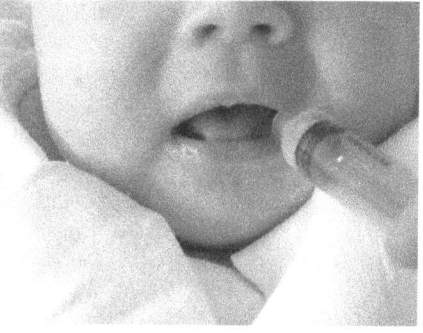

Usually, the most practical method of getting a baby to take the syrup is by squirting it into the back of a cheek.

very hard to get under control, something needs to be done to help the child's body fight the illness. At that point, the child should be taken to a doctor to have her checked out and to see if she should be given antibiotics. Giving antibiotics will not get rid of the fever immediately, but if the antibiotics are effective, you should see some improvement within 24-48 hours.

Sometimes, a fever is caused by something that is not very serious and that you cannot do anything about. Getting new teeth or having an asthma attack can cause a low grade fever, for example.

In rare cases, the brain will give messages to the body to create a fever when there is no reason to. This generally only happens in children with some form of brain damage, such as cerebral palsy or **hydrocephalus,** and even in these groups of children it does not happen very often. These kinds of fevers – neurological fevers – can get extremely high and can be very hard to suppress with medication. This is because it is not the normal body functions creating the fever, but the brain causing it on its own by working incorrectly. Anti-

Part 3: Basic Childcare and Child Psychology

Generally happy and healthy, but from time to time unexplained, hard-to-control fevers would strike.

biotics or other medications will not be effective in putting an end to a fever like this, since there is no infection to clear away. The only thing you can do for these fevers is to use fever suppressants and water to cool down the child, and wait until the brain stops creating the fever. Usually, these fevers last a few days and then stop. In some children, these fevers come back quite regularly.

A two-year-old boy with cerebral palsy had a very serious fever once every five to six weeks. Most of the time, nothing could be found wrong with him, and giving him antibiotics did nothing to lower or shorten the fever. His fever would often get as high as 40-41°C, and giving fever suppressants would rarely be effective. Often, especially at night, his temperature would still continue to go up after he had been given fever suppressants, and he would have to be placed on a towel naked and kept wet for more than an hour before the fever would start to go down slowly. After three to four days, the fever would disappear as suddenly as it had started.

When to Worry?

- If a baby less than three months old has a fever higher than 38°C.
- If the child has had a fever for more than four days.
- If the child is becoming dehydrated.
- If the child is very lethargic or weak.
- If the child recently had surgery.
- If the child's symptoms get a lot worse despite using Paracetamol or Ibuprofen.
- If a child over four years old has a fever above 40°C.

If you come across a situation like this, the child should be taken to a doctor – or a doctor should be called to come to see the child – as soon as possible.

Hypothermia

When the body temperature rises too high with a fever, it can cause damage to the brain and other body parts. On the other end of the temperature scale, you have hypothermia: a body temperature that is too low. This too can cause a dangerous, even life threaten-

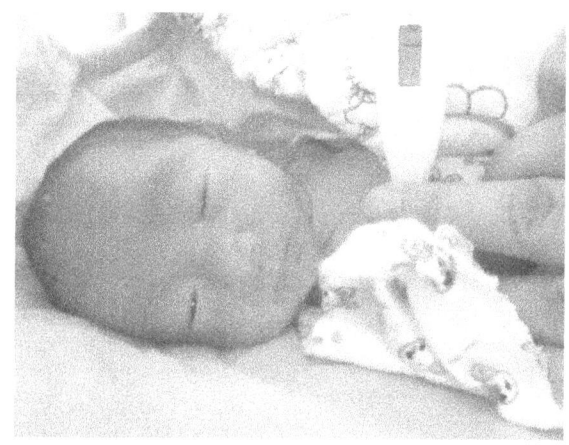

When an electronic thermometer does this, it cannot register the temperature, which means the baby's temperature is below 32°C.

ing situation. It is easy to underestimate how dangerous low body temperature can be in babies. Particularly small babies are at risk of hypothermia. Thankfully, if action is taken in time, it is amazing how effectively and simply it can be reversed, completely low-tech.

Hypothermia will cause all body systems to slow down. Heart rate and breathing will become very slow, which may cause the oxygen level in the blood to drop. The baby will become **drowsy** and may become too weak to drink. This leads to a vicious circle, because without the heat of warm milk and the calories gained from it, the baby is unable to heat himself up and gets weaker and colder. Premature and low-birthweight babies are at particular risk of hypothermia, as their bodies are not strong and mature enough yet to regulate their temperature properly. However, many full term newborns struggle to regulate their temperature in the first few months of life too. Surprisingly, you can even find babies with a body temperature of barely 32°C, while the air temperature around you is above 30°C.

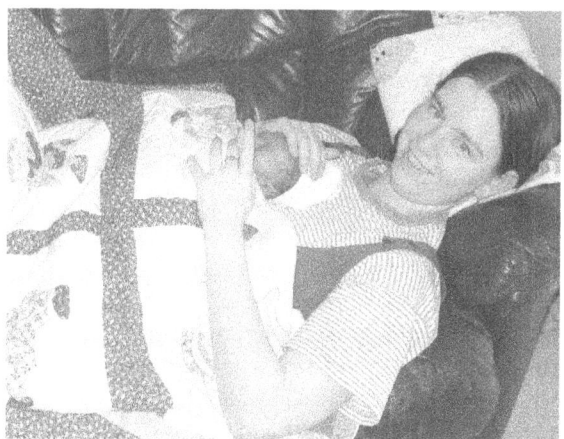

Warming up a hypothermic baby; the outside temperature was above 30°C, so I was very warm.

To prevent hypothermia, newborns need to be dressed warmly and be wrapped up – although at the same time care must be taken not to wrap a baby up too warmly, because overheating a small baby can also cause serious problems. Covering the head with a hat is especially recommended, since babies lose a lot of heat through their head. If a baby has trouble keeping his temperature above 36 °C, it is advisable to add hot water bottles inside his wrappings, though never directly against his skin, because this can cause serious burns.

If a baby with a temperature below 35°C is not warmed up quickly, his temperature is almost certain to continue going down – even with plenty of blankets – and he may only have a few more hours to live if nothing is done. Blankets are very effective in making sure heat does not escape. However, when a baby's temperature has gotten below 35°C, just preventing heat from getting out is not enough. He needs an external heat source to raise his temperature to normal level, because he does not have the energy to create this heat himself. So, in a case where the baby's temperature drops below 35°C, more drastic measures need to be taken. Fortunately, an extremely effective heat source is always available: body heat.

> On my first visit to a particular baby home, I introduced the method of heating up a baby with body heat by placing babies who were too cold skin to skin on my belly, underneath my clothes, and covering them with a pile of blankets and hot water bottles. Initially, this was seen as a very strange thing to do. After having seen the positive results, the caregivers were starting to see the advantage. When they had a hypothermic baby, they would ask me if I was going to warm it up. However, I was still the only one doing it, because caregivers found it rather embarrassing to do it themselves.
>
> Five years later, I visited the same children's home. There was a new children's home director now, who had not been there when I introduced the method, and most of the caregivers had also been replaced. One day, we received a premature baby whose temperature did not register on the digital thermometer, which means it was lower than 32°C. Before I could say or do anything, the children's home director said: 'Right, who is going to lie down to warm the baby up?' And several staff members volunteered. It had now become standard practice and was saving many babies' lives.

The quickest, most effective, low-tech, way of raising a baby's body temperature is to have an adult lie down and bare their stomach as far as they are comfortable. The baby is to be stripped down to his nappy and placed skin-to-skin on the adult's belly. It can be helpful to stick the baby's legs inside the adult's trousers or skirt in order to place his feet up against drawn up legs, for maximum contact and heat transfer.

The adult places one hand – provided it is warm – on the back or stomach of the baby (depending on whether he is lying facing up or down). Then both adult and baby are covered with as many clothes and blankets as are available, always making sure that the baby is still able to breathe unhindered. If the baby's head is exposed, cover it with a hat. If hot water bottles are available, add them in between the first covering layer of clothes/blankets and the layers on top of that. If the adult feels slightly overheated, all the better, as this means she will give off more heat to help the baby warm up.

Chapter 6: Temperature

The baby's temperature should be checked every half an hour to an hour, and will usually be back to normal in less than two hours. Once the baby's temperature is back to normal, the baby can be dressed and wrapped up warmly – with a water bottle if available – and fed. Keep checking the baby's temperature regularly over the following days, to make sure he is able to maintain a normal temperature without help.

This is all that is needed to save a hypothermic baby's life.

The children's home I was visiting was asked to pick up two small babies from another orphanage and take over their care. I went along in the van to pick up the babies. It was autumn and quite cold outside, so we had brought warm blankets and hot water bottles, to make sure the babies would not cool down too much on the way to the children's home. When the babies were handed to us, one of them was doing quite well. She was warm and just needed to be wrapped up in a blanket, to keep her that way. However, the other, smaller, baby felt extremely cold. We did not have a thermometer with us, but she was clearly severely hypothermic.

So, I lay down on the back seat of the van, took off my coat and jumper, stripped the baby and put her against my skin under my T-shirt. Then I covered both of us with the jumper, put the two hot water bottles against that, covered that with my coat and then put the blanket over everything. The two of us bounced back to the children's home like that, on the back seat of the van, throughout the 45 minute drive. When we arrived at the children's home, the little girl's temperature was 35.3°C. There is not much chance that she would have arrived at the children's home alive any other way.

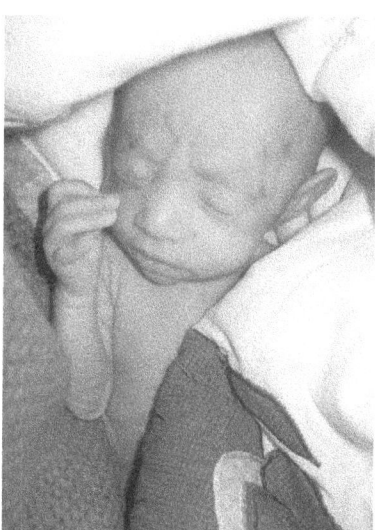

The baby as I took her out from under my clothes.

Older children are generally able to regulate their own body temperature and will only become hypothermic if they have been exposed to extreme cold. For example if they have been outside in freezing weather conditions without adequate clothing to protect them, or if they have been in very cold water for some time. In these cases, the child will need help to warm up too. Make sure the child is dried off, dressed in warm, dry clothes and wrapped in blankets with hot water

233

bottles underneath. Placing the child close to a fire or a radiator to help warm him up is useful, as is giving him something warm to drink or eat. If the shivering does not stop soon, lying the child down on a surface between two warm bodies – this does not need to be skin-to-skin – covered with blankets can help speed up the warming process. If the child is a little bit cold, a warm bath can be helpful to warm him up. However, if he is really hypothermic, warm water will feel like it is burning him, so it is better to warm him up before putting him in a warm bath.

Chapter 7: Dehydration and Malnutrition

Diarrhoea and Vomiting

Diarrhoea can be caused directly by damage done by bacteria, but more often it is something the body causes to get rid of bacteria or other harmful things as quickly as possible. When the body notices that there is something harmful in the bowels, it sends a message to the bowels that they need to let it through as quickly as possible. The bowels stop with the slow **digestion** of the food and only take out whatever they can as the food is rushed through to be moved out. Particularly in the large intestines, the process speeds up and they stop absorbing all of the water that is still mixed in with the undigested food remains. Instead, the water is pushed out of the body, together with the undigested food. This is why **stool** is softer and sometimes even watery, during diarrhoea. The more watery the stool, the more urgently the body feels that everything needs to be cleared out. Sometimes, diarrhoea can start because of an allergic reaction to food: the body makes a mistake and overreacts to something that is not really harmful at all.

Because the water is not reabsorbed in the large intestines, children can lose a lot of water in a short time when they have diarrhoea. This means they can easily get dehydrated. When small babies have watery diarrhoea – which is not the same as just soft poop –, they can become severely dehydrated within a few hours. This is a situation that can become dangerous very quickly and can even lead to death. Therefore, it is very important to be very vigilant and to take action quickly when any baby has watery stool.

Rotavirus had broken out in a children's home – a virus that causes fever, vomiting and watery diarrhoea. A four-month-old baby had 14 bowel movements in one day, and what came out was yellow water. A feeding tube had been placed and ORS was given regularly. Despite the attempts to rehydrate him, at the end of the first day of the diarrhoea, his eyes started to look sunken. He was given more ORS, but by morning he was very weak and drowsy. He had to be taken to hospital to receive IV rehydration to save his life. He was losing liquid so fast that it was not possible to keep up with it by any other method than giving IV fluids.

Apart from water, children also lose **electrolytes** and **minerals** when they have watery diarrhoea. These are small elements that are needed to keep the body working well. One of the minerals that is lost in large amounts with diarrhoea is zinc. So it is a good idea to give a child with diarrhoea zinc **supplements**, to replace the zinc in his body that has been lost through the watery stool. Giving zinc has been shown to make a bout of diarrhoea less severe and to help it pass more quickly. It also lowers the chance of another bout of diarrhoea in the next two to three months.

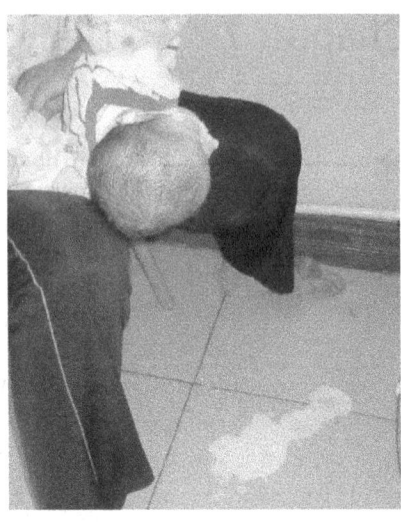

When the body notices something in the stomach that it thinks might do damage to the body, the brain gives the stomach a message that the food needs to be pushed out of the stomach and out of the body as quickly as possible. When this message is received, you will start gagging and vomiting. This is done to make sure that whatever the body thinks might damage it, spends as little time as possible inside, so that it does not get much chance to spread around and cause problems. So vomiting is not an illness. It is what our body does to protect itself.

When a baby vomits, holding him face down is the first priority, to prevent milk from flowing back and possibly ending up in the lungs, where it can cause choking or pneumonia.

Unfortunately, sometimes when a child is allergic to something, the body will react this way too. For example, it will react to the arrival of milk in the stomach the same way it should react to the arrival of bacteria. A milk allergy can be a reason for frequent vomiting.

Sometimes, vomiting is caused by a blockage of the digestive track. In other words, food that is unable to move down the digestive track as it should, comes back up and out. If the blockage is an inborn deformity, it is usually discovered in the first few days or weeks of life. A blockage that developed later on can start at any point of life. If vomiting is caused by a blockage, the child will vomit several times a day, every single day. The child will probably not poop, or hardly at all, and the problem will not go away on its own. If a blockage is the reason for vomiting, a doctor will need to look at the cause and surgery may be needed to resolve the problem. On rare occasions, a problem in the brain – for example high pressure inside the skull because of hydrocephalus – can cause the message to vomit to be sent to the stomach even when there is nothing bad in there. In older children, migraines can also be a cause of vomiting.

Hygiene practice like providing filtered drinking water can greatly reduce the problem of vomiting and diarrhoea.

About 50% of babies spit up some of their milk – a few mouthfuls at a time – during the first few months of their life. This is not really vomiting, and it does not put them at risk for dehydration. With time, as their digestive system matures, these babies will stop spitting up. Anti-diarrhoea or anti-vomiting medication should not be given to young children. These medications do not prevent dehydration, nor do they improve appetite, and some have dangerous, occasionally even fatal side-effects. Anti-diarrhoea and anti-vomiting medications may prolong the presence of bacteria in the poop, and using them is a waste of money. Instead, children over one year old could be given a drink of warm water and ginger to help them feel less nauseous and vomit less. Antibiotics should only be prescribed if the diarrhoea is bloody and the doctor has found that it is caused by bacteria that are sensitive to antibiotics. Randomly giving antibiotics can actually make the diarrhoea worse, because many antibiotics have diarrhoea as a side-effect.

To make vomiting and diarrhoea stop, you need to find out the cause behind it and see if there is anything you can do about it. It is also important to do what you can to prevent spreading the problem.

When rotavirus broke out, every effort was made to educate everyone on the importance of even stricter hygiene than usual, and rooms where there were no cases of rotavirus yet were strictly isolated. No one – even the medical staff – who had held a baby who had rotavirus that day could touch any baby who had not had it yet without gloves. If you had held a baby with rotavirus already that day, under no circumstances were you allowed to hold a baby who was not infected yet against your body. Thanks to these measures, in a children's home with 45 babies and toddlers, only 10 babies caught the virus in the first round. Two of them had to be admitted to hospital, but everyone survived.

When the first round was over, attempts were made to remind the caregivers that those ten babies would still be able to infect other babies for another ten days. However, hygiene standards slipped, and after three rotavirus-free days, the second round hit. The same measures were put in place and the second round only had five victims, who all survived. Now it had gotten through to people what the risks were, so we were spared a third round of rotavirus.

Dehydration
Dehydration means that the child does not have enough fluid in her body for it to work normally. Dehydration can be very serious. If it is not treated in time, babies die from it quite quickly.

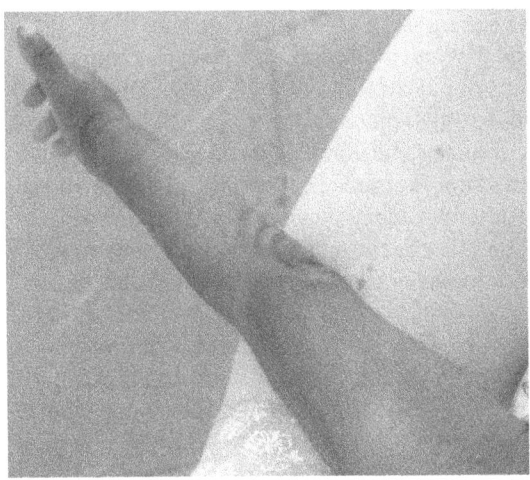

Loose, wrinkly skin on a small child is a sign of dehydration.

In older children, dehydration over a longer period of time can cause serious damage and eventually lead to death. Dehydration can get worse very quickly, so it is important to know how to recognise the first signs and to know how to prevent and treat it. In the early and middle stages, you may still be able to take care of dehydrated babies and children at home. If they reach the later (severe) stage, they will need to go to the hospital to receive **IV fluids** and possibly other medication to be able to survive. Few people realise how serious dehydration is and how rapidly it can progress in babies. If no action is undertaken, death may follow within not much more than twenty-four hours in babies. On the other hand, if action is taken at an early stage, it is usually not very difficult to reverse the process.

In the very first weeks of my starting to volunteer in a children's home for the first time, we received a newborn baby with serious diarrhoea. After a day or two, he did not drink very well anymore and he was very sleepy most of the time. I realised that he was getting dehydrated, but did not yet have the knowledge of how to deal with something like that. I had some ideas about what should be done, but I felt 'who am I to intervene, these people have been dealing with situations like these for years', so I stepped back and just observed. I did ask advice from people who might have relevant information about this kind of thing, but did not receive any answers in those first few days. The baby became weaker and weaker. It became almost impossible to get him to drink anymore. He was asleep all the time, but on the second day, even while he was asleep his eyes did not quite close, Then his lips started to become very red, and his breathing very fast. At that point, he was taken to hospital, where he died the next day of dehydration and acidosis.

If anyone with access to a clinic or hospital and enough funds to make use of their services suspects that a child, particularly a baby, might be dehydrated to any extent, I would advise them to take the child to a doctor straight away. This section is written for people involved in childcare in situations where hospitals or outside medical assistance are unavailable or can only be considered as a very last resort. It outlines how dehydration can be recognised, prevented and treated, and what causes it. As a volunteer, you will have to discuss with management what the options are in your situation and whether they will let you give advice, or take the lead, in handling a dehydration case.

Chapter 7: Dehydration and Malnutrition

Signs of Dehydration

When dehydration sets in, the child's skin and mouth will become very dry. The skin will lose its stretchiness, and if you pinch the skin up, it will take several seconds to smooth back into place. The child's eyes will appear sunken and she may not close her eyes fully anymore, even when asleep. She may stop blinking her eyes altogether.

A new baby was brought to the children's home I was visiting. I was in the office and received the senior of the two people; the other person had gone straight through to the baby room with the baby. The senior person told me that this was such a cute baby, because even when he was asleep, he did not close his eyes entirely. I had not yet seen the baby, but I already knew he was severely dehydrated.

At this stage, the baby is likely to become very lethargic and quite **floppy**. She may drink less well, because she lacks the strength to do so, creating a vicious cycle. If she cries, the cry is likely to be very weak, and basic reflexes may not be there anymore. She will by now have lost a significant percentage of her previous body weight through loss of fluids.

The main signs of dehydration are:

- *Fewer than four very wet nappies or trips to the toilet a day*
- *Dark urine*
- **Sunken fontanel** *(in a baby)*
- *Sunken eyes*
- *Crying without tears (in children over two months old)*
- *Dry mouth*
- *Very dry skin; when you pinch the skin, it does not go down straight away*
- *Does not close eyes completely when sleeping (severe dehydration)*
- *Very red lips and fast, shallow breathing (signs of acidosis – there is a section on acidosis, explaining the condition further, later on in this chapter –, caused by severe dehydration)*
- *Sudden, great weight loss – 10% of body weight or more within a day indicates serious dehydration*
- *Very high heart rate*
- *Low energy – sleeping all the time, floppy, too tired and too weak to drink*

Causes of Dehydration
- Not drinking enough: When a baby drinks less than 100ml/kg/day in fluids (that means milk, plus anything else he might

239

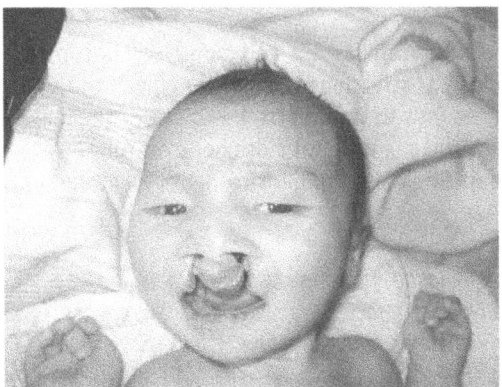 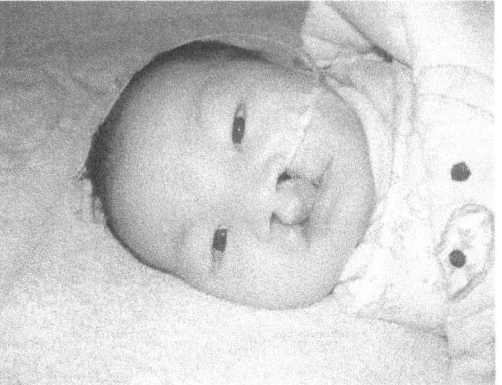

Dehydrated: dry mouth, wrinkly skin, sunken eyes and cheeks, weak cry, no urine, no tears, sunken fontanel, did not close his eyes.

The same baby four days later, rehydrated: looking chubbier and clear-eyed, with smooth skin.

drink), he is taking in less fluid than he is using up. This means that gradually, the amount of fluid in his body will decrease and he will become dehydrated. So it is very important to keep an eye on how much a baby drinks per day, and make changes if he is not drinking enough. If the baby sweats a lot, he might need to drink more than 100ml/kg/day to prevent dehydration. Older children need to drink at least a litre of fluids a day, more if they sweat a lot. Teenagers need at least 1.5 litres and more than 2 litres if they are sweating a lot.

- Diarrhoea: Because the water is not reabsorbed in the large intestines, children can lose a lot of water in a short time when they have diarrhoea, so they can easily get dehydrated. More information about this is given at the start of the chapter.
- Vomiting: When a child vomits most of the fluids that he took in, he is left with not enough fluids in his body. If a child vomits every time you give him something to drink and you are not able to stop the vomiting within a few hours, the child needs to be taken to hospital. In this case, it is not possible to treat him at home, because whatever you are trying to put into him will come out again. He will need to receive his fluids by IV. More information about vomiting is given at the start of the chapter.
- Not clear: Often there is a clear cause of dehydration, but occasionally you will notice dehydration in a child who is drinking well, who is not vomiting and who does not have diarrhoea. If possible, try to find out the cause of the dehydration. If you do not know the cause, you can treat dehydration, but it will keep coming back.
- Possible hidden causes of dehydration:
    o Difficult or fast breathing through an open mouth – this way a lot of moisture can be lost through the throat and lungs.
    o Internal bleeding – something to keep in mind, particularly

if the child has had surgery recently.
o Excessive sweating – in cases of a high fever, hot climate or overheated rooms.

Preventing Dehydration
Our most important aim is to prevent dehydration. Treat it when you find it, but making sure it does not happen is always best. Important ingredients of prevention:

- Hygiene: making sure that you wash your hands very often, that bottles are really clean and sterilised before you put milk in them and that the eating implements and toys that children put in their mouths are clean, are very important in preventing dehydration. This is because it reduces the bacteria that enter the child's digestive system, which in turn makes it less likely that the defence mechanisms of vomiting and diarrhoea will be activated. That way, the risk factors for dehydration are taken away. This also goes for making sure that milk **formula** is made with safe drinking water, and that both milk and food are stored in the fridge and not kept out of the fridge for more than an hour.
- Choice of milk for babies: giving normal cow's milk to babies under six months old will almost always cause very severe diarrhoea – and sometimes vomiting – and this will lead to dehydration. So, making sure that babies are fed using appropriate formula is already a step towards preventing dehydration.

If there is absolutely no way to get baby formula for the babies, cow's milk should be diluted: add 50ml of clean boiled water to every 100ml of cow's milk, then add 10gr of sugar to it.
Goat's milk should also be adapted and not given undiluted.

Some babies are allergic to regular baby formula and this will make them vomit and/or have diarrhoea. These babies can often be helped by using lactose free formula. If the vomiting/diarrhoea stops within a few days of the formula being changed, that can be an indication that the previous formula was, in fact, the problem. To confirm that the allergy was the reason behind the vomiting and diarrhoea, you can try to give the baby regular formula again, two weeks after all the problems stopped. If the problems come back, you know not to give the baby regular formula anymore. If the problems do not come back within the first week or so, it is safe to continue to give the baby regular formula.

- Encouraging drinking: if a child is losing a lot of fluids through diarrhoea or vomiting or if he is at risk of dehydration for another reason, he should be encouraged to drink as much as possible. To start with, you offer what he normally drinks, which is usually milk for a baby, and if he does not drink as much as usual, you offer him the milk more often to see if he can increase the total amount of what he takes in by having smaller amounts more frequently. If he is unwilling to drink milk, you can try to persuade him to drink other drinks that he might find tastier. However, fizzy drinks and fruit juice should be avoided when a child is becoming dehydrated.

- Early **ORS**: if a child has watery diarrhoea or vomits, start giving the child ORS – Oral Rehydration Solution, the next section will give more information about this – before you see any signs of dehydration, to prevent it from starting at all. An older child with moderate diarrhoea and vomiting can be encouraged to drink several sips of ORS for every **bowel movement** or round of vomiting, to prevent dehydration. Generally speaking, for a preventative dose of ORS, you give no more than 1/3 of the volume of a normal formula feed in ORS to a baby. This amount of ORS is given between two regular feeds. So if a baby is fed every three hours, he will be given ORS 1.5h after his last milk feed and 1.5h before his next milk feed.

So this means that if the baby is normally fed with formula every three hours and received his last bottle of 120ml of milk at 10.00 a.m., he will be given between 10 and 40ml of ORS – depending on how watery his stools are – at 11.30 a.m. and then a regular bottle of 120ml of milk again at 1.00 p.m.

When the diarrhoea or vomiting stops, the ORS can stop too. If the situation gets worse and prevention was not effective, the next section will give more information on how to handle things.

Whether or not the diarrhoea or vomiting has stopped yet, if the child starts to pee much more than usual, he should be given less ORS. Otherwise, problems relating to too much fluid in his body may start.

Using safe water to make milk; tap water is not safe to drink in all countries, even if it has been boiled.

Treating Dehydration

When a child has watery diarrhoea or is vomiting a lot, he is not only losing water. He is also losing minerals, which are important to keep the body's systems in balance. If you only give the child water to replace the fluids that he is losing, he could get seriously ill because of the minerals that he is lacking and how this affects his body. So,

Chapter 7: Dehydration and Malnutrition

Coconut juice is a natural ORS, and much tastier too.

instead of giving the child added water, aside from the milk and other liquids he still drinks as always, you need to give him Oral Rehydration Solution (ORS), which contains a mixture of exactly what needs to be replaced in the child's body.

It is possible to get ORS from most health posts or clinics and you can buy it at most pharmacies. What you get there is a powder that can be dissolved in (clean, boiled) drinking water, to make up exactly the right mixture. The packet will tell you how much water to use to dissolve one packet of powder. It is important to follow these instructions very closely.

I was asked to come along to see a child in guided foster care, who was ill. When I saw the child, I noticed straight away that she was dehydrated and I told the foster care coordinator that he needed to make sure that the child was given ORS. In the local language, ORS translates to 'sugar-salt-water'. I heard the foster care coordinator ask the foster mother if she had any sugar and salt in the house to give the child with water. I had to stop him and explain that it is very dangerous to give a child a random mixture of sugar and salt in water, that you can cause a lot of damage to the kidneys that way. I advised him to get premade packets of ORS for the foster family at the children's home that this foster care programme was connected to instead.

If it is not possible to get or buy ready-made ORS, it is possible to make your own mixture. If you do, it is extremely important that you use exactly the right amounts and do not add a little bit more of this, or that.

ORS from packets often has a strange colour; here it is used to continuously drip-feed it through a feeding tube of a weakened baby.

The recipe for homemade ORS is:

One litre of boiled, cooled water with half a level teaspoon of salt and 8 level teaspoons of sugar added. Before adding the sugar, taste the salty water to make sure that it is less salty than tears. To make it taste better and make it more nutritious, you can add half a cup of fresh fruit juice, coconut juice, or some mashed up ripe banana to the drink.

Homemade ORS may not taste very nice, particularly if no fruit has been added for taste, and children may resist drinking it. The ORS that is ready-made in packets usually has a flavour added to it, to make it taste nicer.

If you are in a country where coconut trees grow, fresh coconut juice is a natural ORS. It contains everything needed to replace what is lost by diarrhoea or vomiting. It is very important that the juice is fresh, however. So, do not open the coconut to take the juice out until it is actually going to be used.

As soon as a baby has more than one very loose bowel movement a day, add up to 1/3 of the regular amount of milk in ORS between every two normal milk feeds.

For example, if the baby drinks 90ml every three hours, you add no more than 30ml ORS between the two feeds. If the stool is only a little loose and the baby is doing very well, you could give:
- *12.00 p.m. 90ml milk*
- *1.30 p.m. 10ml ORS*
- *3.00 p.m. 90ml milk*

If the stool is very watery and the baby is already quite thin or weak, you might give:
- *12.00 p.m. 90ml milk*
- *1.30 p.m. 30ml ORS*
- *3.00 p.m. 90ml milk*

If stool is very watery and frequent, feed the baby every hour alternating milk and ORS. This is done calculating how much milk the baby should be getting per two hours, and giving the milk every other hour with half that amount in ORS added in between.

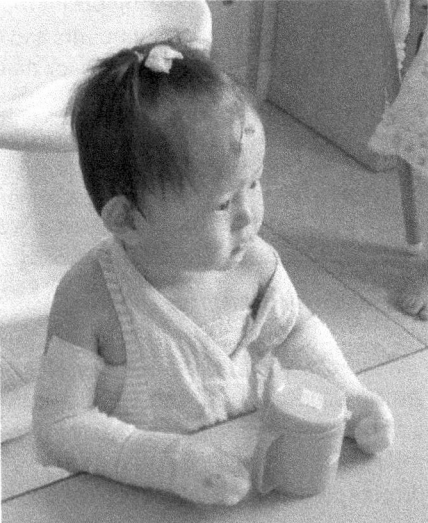

Older children also need to be encouraged to drink often to prevent dehydration and even more urgently to treat it.

For example, if the baby in the example above would need to be fed every hour alternating ORS and milk, it would be done like this:
- *12.00 p.m. 60ml milk*
- *1.00 p.m. 20ml ORS*
- *2.00 p.m. 60ml milk*
- *3.00 p.m. 20ml ORS*
- *4.00 p.m. 60ml milk*

The way this is calculated is: the baby needs 90ml of milk every 3 hours, so in 24 hours he drinks 90x8=720ml of milk. If you wish to feed him milk every two instead of every three hours, that means that the 720ml has to be divided over 12 feeds instead of over 8 feeds. 720/12=60ml. The ORS he was given 30ml every 3 hours, so in 24 hours that is 30x8=240ml, dividing 240ml over 12 feeds (one every 2 hours) gives 240/12=20ml per feed.

In a case of mild dehydration, when the baby is still able to drink well by herself, it is usually best to add ORS in between feeds, given by bottle. The amount of ORS depends on the size of the baby and the severity of the dehydration. The maximum amount of ORS to be given is 20ml/kg/hr. You will have to keep an eye on the baby's condition. As mentioned before, urine output is a good measuring tool. If the baby still looks dehydrated or does not pee very much despite receiving the amount of ORS she should be getting, the amount needs to be increased. If the baby starts peeing a lot, more than normal, the amount of ORS given to her should be lowered.

A three-month-old baby was dehydrated. She was weak, her fontanel was low and she did not close her eyes completely when she slept. She was still given her bottle with formula at the regular times, but she did not drink very much. She would suck hungrily for about three minutes and then she would be too tired to drink more. She would turn her head away and refuse to take the nipple in her mouth. The bottle was taken away. In this way, she became more and more dehydrated.

I fed this three-month-old dehydrated girl. I would let her drink as long as she was able to. Then I let her rest for five minutes, before putting the nipple in her mouth again. After having rested for five minutes and having done a burp, the little girl would suck well again for two to three minutes. In this way, she was able to finish most of the milk in the bottle in the course of one hour. It takes a lot of time and work to feed a dehydrated baby, but it can save her life.

If the baby is becoming too weak to drink by herself, a feeding tube (NG tube) needs to be placed. Through it, both formula and ORS can be given, in the same amounts as by bottle. Again, the amount of ORS needed has to be calculated depending on how severe the dehydration is and how big the baby is. If no one at the children's home is able to place and use a feeding tube, take the baby to a doctor or a hospital for treatment.

If an older child with severe diarrhoea and vomiting shows signs of dehydration, should be encouraged to drink one cup of ORS for every bowel movement or round of vomiting, in addition to what she usually drinks. If she is unable to drink this, or if you are unable to persuade her to do so, you will need to take her to hospital for treatment against dehydration. Although the process of dehydration progresses more slowly in older children than it does in babies, it is still a very dangerous medical problem. Even in older children, dehydration can eventually lead to death.

If dehydration is moderate to severe in a baby, it is a good idea to replace all the formula feeds with ORS for six hours to help the baby start to pee more. In case of moderate dehydration, this means that the amount of milk the baby would normally take is replaced by the same amount of ORS.

So, if the baby normally drinks 75ml of milk every 3 hours, she will now get 75ml or ORS every 3 hours, for a 6-8 hour period. After 6-8 hours of ORS only, you can do alternate feeds of milk and ORS for another 6 hours.
This means that when the baby usually gets 75ml of milk every three hours, she will now get 75ml of milk, three hours later she will get 75ml of ORS and three hours later she will get 75ml of milk again.

So:

9.00 a.m.	75ml of ORS
12.00 p.m.	75ml of ORS
3.00 p.m.	75ml of ORS
6.00 p.m.	75ml of milk
9.00 p.m.	75ml of ORS
12.00 a.m.	75ml of milk

After these last six hours, the baby will be getting normal milk feeds, with a smaller amount of ORS between two milk feeds.

In case of severe dehydration, the baby needs the maximum amount of ORS (20ml/kg/hr) according to his weight.

Chapter 7: Dehydration and Malnutrition

So if the baby normally drinks 75ml of milk every 3 hours, she will be about 4kg. That means that she will now get 20ml x 4kg=80ml of ORS every hour, for a 4 hour period. After 4 hours of ORS only, you can do feeds of regular amounts of milk with high amounts of ORS in between for another 6 hours.

9.00 a.m.	*80ml of ORS*
10.00 a.m.	*80ml of ORS*
11.00 a.m.	*80ml of ORS*
12.00 p.m.	*80ml of ORS*
1.00 p.m.	*75ml of milk*
2.30 p.m.	*80ml of ORS*
4.00 p.m.	*75ml of milk*
5.30 p.m	*80ml of ORS*
7.00 p.m.	*75ml of milk*

After these last six hours, if the baby looks like she has recovered from the dehydration, she will be getting normal milk feeds with a smaller amount of ORS between two milk feeds. If she still shows clear signs of dehydration, she will need to continue to get more ORS, or, if there is no real sign of improvement, she needs to be taken to hospital.

If a child starts vomiting during the rehydration process, you can try to give her less each time and giving her something to drink more often. Or you can put her on continuous feeding if you have the possibility to do so – this requires using a feeding tube and a pump or a drip. However, if she keeps vomiting, IV treatment is the only way to reverse the dehydration process, and the baby will need to go to hospital.

A two-year-old girl had a disorder that caused her to vomit a lot for about two or three days and then recover again and be fine for several weeks before she would start again. It was unclear what was causing this, but experience had shown that if you made sure she did not get badly dehydrated during these days, she would recover on her own. When one of these bouts of vomiting started, the new medical manager was very concerned about dehydration so she automatically applied the protocol for severe dehydration (which had the potential to develop, but had not developed yet): give 20ml/kg/hour of ORS through drip feeding by feeding tube. However, normally, this girl would get 105ml of milk every three hours, and now she was rehydrated with 160ml of ORS per hour. It was not surprising that she did not tolerate this large amount of liquid on an

already oversensitive stomach, and started vomiting even more. The situation was thought through again and the care plan was changed to giving 100ml of ORS per hour on slow drip feeding. This was tolerated, and she kept more of it inside. The girl started vomiting less on the second day and recovered well, as usual.

If the child starts to become more active, her fontanel – in case of a baby – feels fine again and she is peeing a lot, the ORS can stop. If she still has diarrhoea but has stopped vomiting, you can go down to a prevention dose of ORS between feeds.

Weighing Babies
Any baby with more than five watery bowel movements a day, or with a combination of watery bowel movements and vomiting, needs to be weighed every day. If his weight has decreased by 0.4kg or more, or by 10% of his body weight or more, the baby is severely dehydrated and needs to be taken to hospital immediately.

Acidosis
Acidosis is a problem of the blood. It means there is too much CO_2 in the blood, binding the **haemoglobin** that should be carrying oxygen. This means that there is less room for oxygen to be carried around the body. Having too much CO_2 in the blood lowers the blood's pH, so the blood becomes more acidic. This is a serious and even dangerous condition. Children can die of this condition, and babies are particularly sensitive to it. If the child does not get to hospital in an early stage for treatment, they may not be able to save his life in hospital either. When you think a child has acidosis, he needs to be taken to hospital as soon as possible. It is something you cannot treat at home.

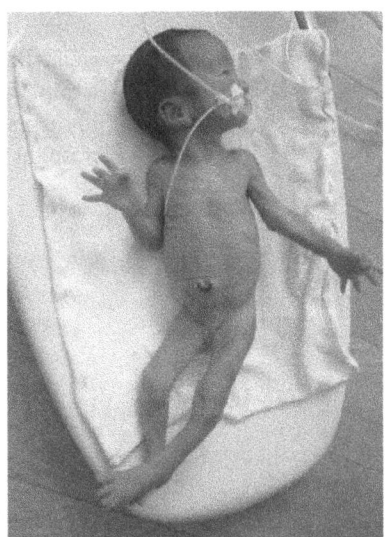

Signs of acidosis:
- Bright red mouth
- Fast breathing
- Shallow Breathing
- Pale/greyish skin colour

Common causes of acidosis:
- Severe dehydration
- Severe breathing difficulties

Her weight had dropped from 1.13kg to 1.08kg overnight; a loss that fast is always due to loss of fluids, so she was admitted to hospital shortly after being weighed.

Chapter 7: Dehydration and Malnutrition

 ——————— *Send to Hospital*

 *Even if you are able to provide the babies in your care with feeding tubes and continuous feeding, a dehydrated child still needs to be sent to hospital for IV fluids immediately, if he:*

- *Loses 0.4kg or more in a day*
- *Loses more than 10% of his body weight in a day*
- *Keeps vomiting almost everything that goes in for more than 6-8 hours*
- *Still looks dehydrated despite being on continuous feeding and maximum ORS (20ml/kg/hr)*
- *Shows signs of acidosis (red mouth, superficial fast breathing, greyish colour)*

 ——————— **Malnutrition**

Malnutrition is any kind of badly balanced nutrition. So it can mean eating too much, too little, or eating the wrong things. However, as it is discussed in this book, malnutrition only refers to the problem caused by getting too little food or not getting enough of the right foods. Children who are malnourished will get sick much more easily than children who get all the food they require. If a well-nourished and a malnourished child get the same illness, the malnourished child is almost certain to get much sicker from it, because her body does not have the strength and resources to fight the illness. Sometimes she may even lack the energy to cause a fever, which is needed to make white blood cells more active to help fight the disease. While the well-nourished child only gets a little ill, the malnourished child may die of the same illness. Malnutrition is recognised as the most common cause of immunodeficiency worldwide.

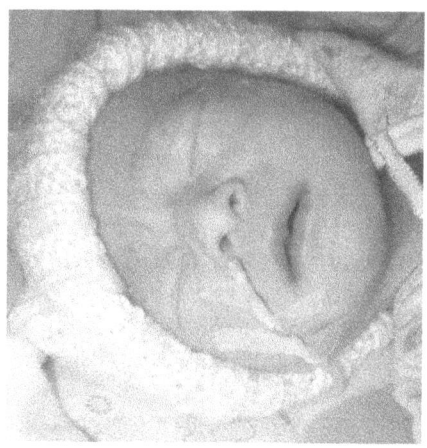

The cherry-red lips show that severe dehydration has progressed to acidosis.

When the body lacks a lot of the things it needs to stay healthy, there is little or no energy left for playing and developing. The child will usually just sit or lie somewhere because she is too weak to do anything else. This behaviour usually improves very quickly once the child receives enough of the right foods again. However, if the malnutrition is severe and lasts for a long time, it can permanently slow down a child's brain development.

 ——————— *What Children Need*

Malnutrition can mean 'not getting enough food overall' or 'not getting enough of a certain kind of food', which means that the body will lack something – a building block – that it needs to stay healthy. While it is possible for malnutrition to be caused by a simple inability to get enough food to give to the children – because of

These children don't get the little extras that children in families do get.

local shortages or because of lack of funds at the children's home –, in children's homes around the world, malnutrition is more often caused by incomplete knowledge of what children need in their diet to be well-nourished and to stay healthy and strong. Beliefs, tradition, religion, local cooking practices and local childrearing practices can lead to a poor diet, while the right foods are actually available locally.

A particular children's home provided its children with a strictly vegetarian diet, also excluding eggs, as was culturally appropriate. Although there was plenty of food available for everyone, several of the children under eight years old showed signs of malnutrition, particularly of a lack of proteins. It is perfectly possible to provide a healthy, balanced vegetarian diet, but in this place, that balance was not there.

The management did not understand how this could have happened. They showed me the menu of the month, which the kitchen supervisor had to submit every month for approval. I had to admit that the menu looked great, it was in fact nicely balanced nutritionally. However, I had been eating together with the children for a while by then and I could vouch for the fact that many of the items on the menu – particularly protein and iron sources – had never once made it onto my plate. The kitchen supervisor was called to the office and asked to explain this. He explained that sometimes, when he went to the market to buy food, something that he had intended to cook would not be available that day, or would be very expensive. In a case like this, he would buy something else instead and make that. That is perfectly logical and reasonable, except that when you cannot buy the cheese you had wanted to buy, you should not buy onions instead. You need another protein source. When something like that happens once in a very long while, there is no big problem. But it was clear that in this home, it happened more often than not.

Something else that needed to be addressed was the way food was served. Because there were many children, food would be put in a bucket and then scooped onto the plates where the children sat waiting for it. The problem was that often, a child would get a scoop from the top, giving mostly the water in which, for example, the pulses were cooked, with only a few pulses actually ending up on the plate. While the pulses are a good source of protein, the water in which they are cooked is not.

Even though the children in a children's home often get more or less the same kinds of things to eat as the children in families who live in the same area, the 'more or less' can make a bigger difference than you might think. Children in a family often receive the best or most nutritious parts of the food available, and extra bits from their mother's plate. From time to time, they receive a little extra treat from someone in their extended family. This does not happen with children in a children's home. This small difference between just being given what everyone else gets and getting a few little extras from time to time, can make the difference between being healthy and being malnourished.

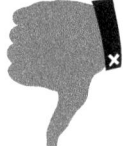

A three-month-old girl was HIV positive, dehydrated and malnourished. When I asked what she was given to eat I was told formula, which I was very glad to hear. However, later I found out that they would feed the girl porridge (made with fortified flour, water and sugar, no milk) first and then she would be offered milk. This was much cheaper, because after eating the porridge, the girl felt quite full and could not drink very much expensive milk, made from baby formula. However, the porridge did not have much in it that the baby's body was able to use for growing and gaining weight. So doing this was actually causing the girl to become malnourished and dehydrated. She needed more milk!

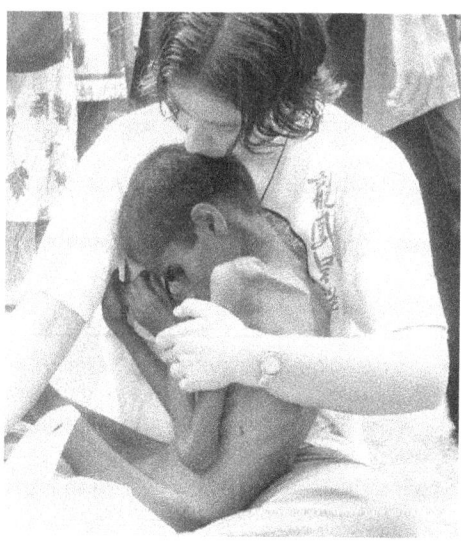

Outright starvation is hard to miss.

The foods children need to stay healthy, and how much they need per day for each age:

Food group	1-3 yrs	4-6 yrs	7-9 yrs	10-12 yrs girls	10-12 yrs boys	13-18 yrs girls	13-18 yrs boys
Cereal & Millets	120g	210g	270g	270g	330g	300g	420g
Chicken, Meat, Eggs or Pulses	30g	45g	60g	60g	60g	60g	60g
Milk	500ml	500ml	500ml	500ml	500ml	500ml	500ml
Roots & Tubers	50g	50g	100g	100g	100g	100g	100g
Green Leafy Vegetables	50g	50g	100g	100g	100g	100g	100g
Other Vegetables	50g	50g	100g	100g	100g	100g	100g
Fruits	100g	100g	100g	100g	100g	100g	100g
Sugars	25g	30g	30g	30g	35g	30g	35g
Fat/Oils (visible)	20g	25g	25g	25g	25g	25g	25g

Once a child gets to the point where her diet depends more on solid food than on milk – this should be starting around eight to nine months old –, it becomes especially important that she receives a well-balanced diet in order to continue to grow well and stay healthy. A well-balanced diet means that, aside from the cheaper energy foods such as rice, maize, cassava, millet, and so on, children need a variety of other foods in order to get everything they need. Protein – which is present in high amounts in meat, fish, eggs, dairy products, soy and pulses – is very important to help them build their muscles and strength. Particularly if the diet is vegetarian, it is easy to accidentally have too little protein and iron in the diet, which will lead to malnutrition.

Children who are HIV positive or suffer from other chronic illnesses or serious infections need about 30% more calories and protein in their diet than healthy children in order to keep up or regain their health. They use up these calories and proteins during the healing process of wounds and during the fight against illnesses.
To make sure that you will find out early if there is any problem with malnutrition, it is important to regularly weigh the children and keep records of their weight.

The most important indication of malnutrition:
Healthy, growing children do not lose weight, they gain weight steadily.

How to Recognise Malnutrition in Children
In some forms of malnutrition, like outright starvation, the effects are visible clearly. When you have a child who is only skin and bones, you can be pretty certain that she is malnourished. However, if a child is not getting everything she needs, it is preferable to be

Chapter 7: Dehydration and Malnutrition

able to recognise signs of malnutrition before you reach the skin and bones stage.

Signs of malnutrition:

- Lack of energy
- Loose skin folds
- Curly hair going straight
- Dark hair turning pale or red
- Hair becoming sparse and thin
- Buttocks wasting away, even when this is combined with a big bloated belly
- Swelling, puffiness of hands feet and face
- Changes to skin in colouring or 'flaky paint skin'
- Knock knees or bow legs
- Motor weakness
- Loss of some reflexes

INDICATIONS OF MALNUTRITION:

Mid-arm circumference of children aged one to five years old:

- \> 13.5cm is normal
- 12.5cm-13.5cm moderate malnutrition
- < 12.5cm severe malnutrition

If a child's weight is less than 70% of what would be expected for his age, this is considered an indication of high risk of morbidity and mortality.

Refeeding Starved Children

When a child has not had all of the nutrients he needs for a long time, it can cause big problems for his health. However, it can take a long time to discover something like this, because the effects usually only become visible after quite some time.

An eighteen-month-old girl weighed just over 4kg and was 63cm long – the weight of a healthy one-month-old and a the height of a healthy three-month-old. She was skin and bones. She was able to sit up unsupported, but that was the only thing she was able to do. She did not have the strength or energy to play or to do anything, really. She was too weak to ask for attention. Very occasionally, she would make a weak indication that she would like to drink water or eat something, but this was usually missed by the overworked caregiver, who had her hands full with all the other children she was responsible for and who were still able to scream for her attention.

The little girl shared the same, not very well-balanced diet that the other children got, and on top of that she was neglected. She got weaker all the time. By the time I met her, she was severely dehydrated and she had bronchitis. When the situation was pointed out to management, the girl was admitted to hospital where she was treated for dehydration and bronchitis. When she came out of hospital, a teenage girl from the same children's home was put in charge of her care and was effectively made her foster mother. The teenager did a wonderful job taking care of the little girl, making sure that she was given food and drink whenever she indicated that she wanted it and giving the little girl the attention and physical contact that had also been lacking in her life.

Despite still sharing the not quite balanced diet with the other children, the little girl was now getting the amount of food and drink that she needed and her psychological needs were met, allowing her body to produce growth hormone again and her immune system to build up strength. At twenty-two months of age, she started to look slightly chubby and she was crawling around, playing, laughing and standing without support. At twenty-four months she was walking without support.

When you find yourself with a child who has clearly been deprived of food for quite some time, it can be quite daunting. Usually, the child will be very weak, often she will be ill and she may have almost no strength left to eat. Although the aim is to feed her and make her gain weight quickly, **refeeding** a starving child is not about just stuffing as much as possible into her of whatever food or milk you have available. If the balance of nutrients and calories is not right, refeeding can lead to lack of growth or to rapid weight gain but with a lot of permanent damage caused by the well-intentioned refeeding. Again, as a volunteer you will have to discuss with management to see if they would like you to help them handle the care of a malnourished child.

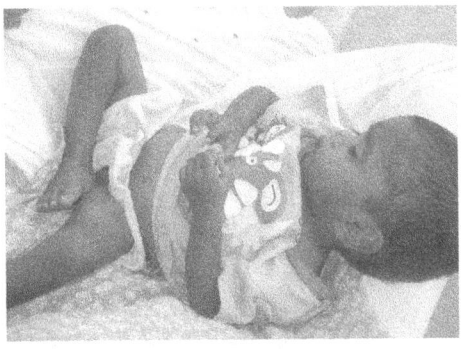

She has no energy to do anything but sleep; at eighteen months old she can only barely sit up by herself.

If a child has been severely hungry for only a week, it is all right to just start feeding her. If the child has had little or nothing to eat for more than five to seven days, you should start by giving no more than 50% of the normal energy requirement and then gradually increase this if there are no signs of refeeding problems, which will be explained below. If the child has been deprived for a month or longer, medical assistance will be needed to make sure that you have the best possible chance of success in refeeding. A doctor might be able to help you set up a refeeding plan that suits the situation of the child in your care. The result of refeeding is hard to predict:

it depends on how long the child was starved, how severe the starvation was, plus the influence of the general health and medical conditions of the child.

Some of the big issues that threaten a severely malnourished child, even once you start refeeding are:

- Dehydration: a severely malnourished child should not be rehydrated through IV unless she is unconscious, as this has been shown to cause problems
- Hypothermia
- Infections
- Electrolyte and micronutrient disorders: particularly iron is usually very low, but iron should not be given until after the first week of refeeding, because giving iron straight away had led to deaths in the past; severely malnourished children usually need to be given zinc, vitamin K, vitamin A, folic acid, iron (after a week and only orally), thiamin and multivitamin tablets, some of these for a week, some for months

Feeds should be built up to full feeds gradually, over the course of a week

When you receive a severely malnourished child into your care, you should take her to hospital first to be checked out. This is because in cases of severe malnutrition, just giving food is often not enough to make sure that the child survives. Most children with severe malnutrition will also be suffering from serious infections and they may be lacking very important micronutrients that need to be added separately from food for the child to become well again.

Refeeding a malnourished child is the second step, after visiting the hospital, for a severely malnourished child, and the first step for a mildly to moderately malnourished child. When you start refeeding a malnourished child, the aim is to provide the child with 150-200kcal, 3-4gr of protein and 100-165ml of fluid per kg of body weight per day. The total calculated amount is then divided into 6-8 feeds and can be given by mouth, or through a feeding tube if the child is unable to eat by herself and you have the ability to place feeding tubes and use them. During the daytime, feeds should be given every two hours. At night you can leave a gap, but of no more than five to six hours. In malnourished babies under six months, no gap should be left during the night. Babies should be fed at regular intervals day and night. Particularly if they are malnourished or weigh less than 5kg.

Problems with Refeeding
The hope is that once you start refeeding them, children will start gaining weight, become more and more healthy and thrive. But,

Part 3: Basic Childcare and Child Psychology

however well you do in refeeding a child, there is no guarantee that this will be the outcome.

Some children will have temporary problems such as struggling with many infections when refeeding starts because of a weakened immune system, making it harder to gain weight because calories are burned to fight off disease. Or they may get Nutrition Recovery Syndrome, which is a temporary problem where the child does not seem to be doing at all well. Her liver may become further enlarged, the belly may get swollen or gather liquids in it, her spleen may become enlarged, there may be swelling, and sometimes even some shaking. If this happens, the child should be monitored very closely, but refeeding should continue. Usually, this situation resolves itself after some time. If it does not, you need the help of a doctor.

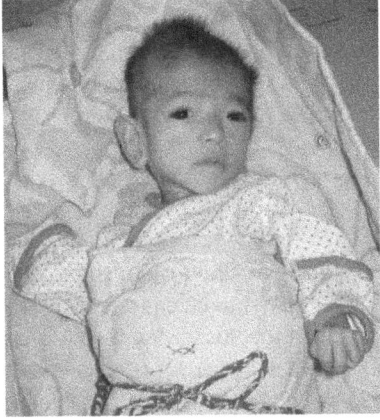

She arrived like this, seven months old, 2.5kg.

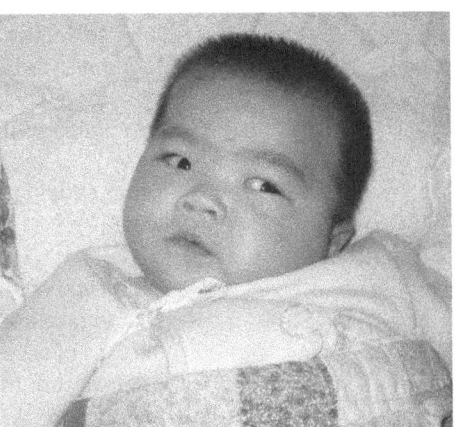

This is her a good three months later, all fat, with very little muscle.

A seven-month-old baby girl was brought into a baby home. She only weighed 2.5kg and was so dirty that it took several days of repeated washing to get her completely clean. It looked like she had been starved and neglected over a long period of time. When she was offered milk formula, she accepted it greedily. She drank really well. In the first few weeks she did have quite a lot of bowel problems; her body did not really seem used to processing food anymore. However, she steadily gained weight and everyone was optimistic about her progress.

After two or three months, it started to become apparent that there was something not quite right. The girl was gaining weight perfectly, but she was becoming really fat. She did not have the ability to even keep her head steady – except by resting her fat cheeks on her chubby shoulders – and did not seem to have any muscles to speak of. It was becoming clear that she had suffered brain damage *from her prolonged malnutrition, but it was more than that. It looked like her body did not quite know what it was supposed to do with food anymore and instead of building muscles, it turned all food into fat.*

It was a long and intensive process to help her start to build up and use some muscles again. About a year after she had arrived, with intensive physiotherapy, she had learned to roll over and sit up with support.

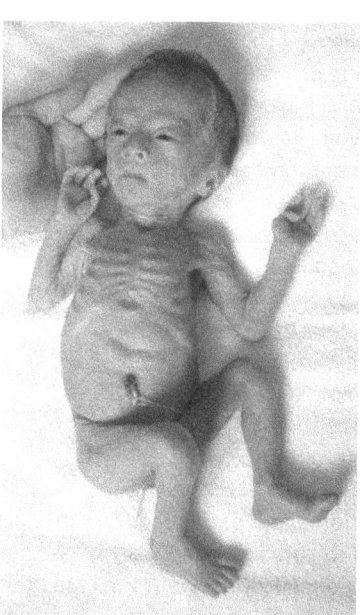

When confronted with this, you just do what you can.

In some cases, however, a child may get 'refeeding syndrome' (this can be a wide range of problems including serious infection or problems like the one described in the information box above). It is something that is not very well understood yet and the causes are not clear. What is clear, however, is that it can lead to very serious problems and even sudden death in children. Despite this risk, it is necessary to start refeeding malnourished children, because if you do not, they will get ill and most likely die in any case. Refeeding them gives them a chance at life.

Afterword

Despite having been brutally honest about the realities of volunteering in a children's home and the ways in which volunteering can potentially do more harm than good, as well as some of the heart-breaking situations that you may encounter, I hope I have not put you off. Regardless of some of the hardships that come with it, I think that volunteering in a children's home is one of the most rewarding things you can do. If I did not, I would not have spent much of the past nine years doing it, with no intention of stopping anytime soon.

If it's for you, then sitting there with a child, the whole world just disappears and being with the child is all that matters.

What I have tried to do is give you fair warning, so that you will be able to prepare yourself and make sure that your volunteering experience will be of maximum benefit to the children's home and particularly to the children. As well as some information to 'arm' yourself with, in case you are given the opportunity to make suggestions about the care of the children or the treatment of sick children. This will hopefully give you more of a chance to do something about some of the problems that you may encounter and to make a difference. I hope that with the information from this manual, you feel confident about going out there, to help out and enjoy yourself with the children.

My motto is: I cannot change the world, but I can change to the world for one child. And then another. And another... And my point is: so can you!

Finally, I want to leave you with some more quotes of people who have volunteered in children's homes in the past. These are their answers to what they enjoyed most and whether they would advise other people to go volunteer.

"Do it, throw yourself in heart and soul, and think what you can bring to be of service. What is going to make a difference? Just go with the flow."

"Performing a Bollywood dance alongside the other volunteers for the children, they all went crazy!"

"The group of volunteers as a whole became friends very easily and quickly"

"My most cherished memory of my volunteer experience was the moment that the students of 6th standard presented their Powerpoint presentation in English after a three days' workshop I conducted for them. It was incredible to see that all children, no matter how shy they were, were able to stand in front of their whole class and talk about their future dreams. That moment I realised how much they had grown in the last 3 months and felt so happy that they all have a whole future in front of them filled with ambitions and dreams."

Florence Koenderink, December 2015

Appendix

Conversion of Temperature from Celsius to Fahrenheit

°C	°F	°C	°F	°C	°F	°C	°F
30°C	86°F	36.2°C	97.2°F	38.4°C	101.1°F	40.6°C	105.1°F
31°C	87.8°F	36.4°C	97.5°F	38.6°C	101.5°F	40.8°C	105.4°F
32°C	89.6°F	36.6°C	97.9°F	38.8°C	101.8°F	41°C	105.8°F
33°C	91.4°F	36.8°C	98.2°F	39°C	102.2°F	41.2°C	106.2°F
34°C	93.2°F	37°C	98.6°F	39.2°C	102.6°F	41.4°C	106.5°F
35°C	95°F	37.2°C	99°F	39.4°C	102.9°F	41.6°C	106.9°F
35.2°C	95.4°F	37.4°C	99.3°F	39.6°C	103.3°F	41.8°C	107.2°F
35.4°C	95.7°F	37.6°C	99.7°F	39.8°C	103.6°F	42°C	107.6°F
35.6°C	96.1°F	37.8°C	100°F	40°C	104°F	42.2°C	108°F
35.8°C	96.4°F	38°C	100.4°F	40.2°C	104.3°F		
36°C	96.8°F	38.2°C	100.8°F	40.4°C	104.7°F		

Useful Resources

Ethical volunteering tips: http://learningservice.info/

Examples of useful travel guides:
Lonely Planet
Backpackers Guide
Insight Guide
Rough Guide

Word List

Ability	Something you are able to do	*Confidential*	Keeping information private, not passing it on to other people
Adequate	Good enough in quality or amount; meeting the most basic requirements	*Consequence*	The result of something that has happened or that has been done
Adopted	In this book a child: being taking into a new family permanently, as one of their own	*Consistently*	Reliably and the same way, every time
		Contagious	To do with illness: it spreads easily from one person to another
Antibiotics	Medication to put an end to infection caused by bacteria	*Cooperate*	Willing to work together with you
Antibodies	Cells in the blood that are specialised in fighting bacteria, viruses and fungi	*Decrease*	Make or become less
		Dehydration	A situation where the body has lost more liquids than it has taken in
Anti-Inflammatory	Reduces the reaction to infection in the body, reduces swelling and redness		
		Development	Progress from one stage to the next, often involves improvement, gaining of skills
Appropriate	That which is most likely to work in and be most suited to a particular situation	*Diet*	Kinds and amounts of food that a person eats
Attachment	In this book: A close bond or relationship with another person	*Digestion*	The processing of food that has been eaten by the body: food is broken down into very small parts and the body takes out of those what it needs to grow, heal and work well; what is not needed is removed from the body in the form of poop and urine
Attention Span	The length of time someone is able to concentrate on something		
Awareness	Understanding of the existence and meaning of something		
Bowel Movement	Pooping, pushing poop out of the body		
		Dorm	Sleeping area/room shared by several people
CD4	A particular kind of cell in the blood that is part of the immune system; these are the cells that get invaded by HIV when a person becomes infected	*Drowsy*	Not alert, sleepy, only partly conscious
		Electrolytes	Substances that are present in the body's fluids in very small amounts, but that are essential for the body to work as it should
Cerebral Palsy	A non-progressive paralysation of part of the brain that can lead to spasticity, mental retardation and seizure disorders among other things	*Experiment*	To try out how something works through trial and error
		Exploitation	Using someone to get a profit or a gain for yourself, without benefit to the person you are using
Chores	Small jobs in and around the house, often connected to housework		

External	On the outside, or from the outside
Faeces	Poop, excrement, the waste product of the body
Febrile	Caused by a fever
Floppy	Very weak, without any strength
Fontanel	The soft spot that babies have on top of their head
Formula	In this book: Milk sold in powder form that is made especially to be easily digestible for babies and to contain everything they need
Fostered	In this book a child: being taken into a family temporarily, to receive family care while more permanent solutions are explored or arranged
Fragile	Delicate, easily broken or disturbed
Haemoglobin	Particles in the blood that carry oxygen through the body
Hand sanitiser	A gel or liquid which you rub on your hands that will have killed most of the bacteria on your skin once it has dried
Hospice	An institution where people who are terminally ill receive care until the end of their life
Hydrocephalus	A condition in which spinal fluid gathers in the centre of the brain and is not absorbed; the build-up of these fluids causes the head to grow, and puts pressure on the brain
Hygiene	Actions or practices of cleanliness that lead to good health
Hypothermia	Very low body temperature, below 35°C
Immune System	The system that protects the body against illness and infection
Immuno-deficiency	The immune system not being able to work at full strength, because something is preventing it from working well
Impact	The result or effect of an action or situation
Improve	To make better or to get better
Increase	Making, or becoming, more
Initial	At the very start, first
Internal	On the inside or from the inside
Isolation	Separating someone from other people, not allowing any contact, or being or feeling separated from other people
IV fluids	Usually normal saline (salty) or a dextrose (sugary) solution, which is given directly into the blood through a needle and a tube to make sure someone stays hydrated or to rehydrate them
Lack	To not have a thing that is needed
Lethal	Leading to death
Malnutrition	Health problems caused by not eating enough of the foods that the body needs
Mental	To do with the brain and thinking
Micronutrients	Elements in food that are present in tiny amounts – despite the tiny amounts, not having them in the body can cause very serious problems
Minerals	Elements that the body needs in very small amounts to work properly, for example salt
Nappy	Diaper, pamper
Oral	To do with the mouth

Word List

ORS	Stands for 'Oral Rehydration Solution' – it is a solution that is mixed in just the right way, to replace both the fluids and the electrolytes that the body has lost when it became dehydrated		something wrong
Physical	To do with the body	Requirement	Something you have to have or do, as a condition for something
Physiological	To do with the body's function	Resources	What is needed or available for doing or making something; this often means money
Pitfall	A situation that can come as a big surprise and cause trouble or difficulties	Saliva	The water-like fluid produced in the mouth
Pneumonia	Lung infection	Seizure	Sudden tensing or relaxing of muscle groups, caused by a short-circuit in the brain; it can also involve unconsciousness
Possession	Something you own, that belongs to you	Skill	An ability to do something well
Praise	To show admiration or gratitude; to tell someone they did something well	Stage	A phase of development
		Sterilise	In this book: To make something free from all bacteria, viruses and fungi
Precaution	Action taken before something happens to prevent it, or to make sure the effect will not be too serious	Stigma	A strong negative opinion about someone with a certain background, job or medical problem
Prevent	To make sure something does not happen	Stool	Poop; or a seat without a backrest or armrests
Propriety	What is considered decent behaviour according to the rules of morality and social acceptability	Supplement	In this book: Vitamins and minerals given in addition to the normal diet
Protein	Body-building food necessary for proper growth and strength	Suppress	To push something down so that the effect cannot be seen anymore, without taking away the cause
Pulses	Vegetable food high in energy, protein and iron, such as beans, peas and lentils	Thermostat	Something that makes sure that the temperature stays stable at a certain level
Refeeding	Feeding a child who is malnourished, with the aim of having him gain weight and catch up on growth	Thrive	Grow and develop well
		Toddler	A child aged between one and four years old
Regulate	In this book: To control or make sure that a system of the body works as it should	Transfer	To pass something from one person to another or from one place to another
Reprimand	To tell someone they are doing		

Transgression	A mistake or an overstepping of limits that have been set	*Vomit*	Stomach contents that have come back out of the mouth or the action of having stomach contents coming back out of the mouth
Urine	Pee, piss, liquid waste from the body		
		Vulnerable	Easily hurt, without defence; this can relate both to physical harm and/or psychological harm
Vicious Cycle	A situation that continues getting worse; for example, a child is weak and does not eat well, then becomes weaker because it does not eat well and is able to eat even less, and so on	*Worthy*	To be worth something or to deserve something
Vocabulary	The total collection of words that a person knows		

References

Part 1

Friends-International (2013) *Children Are not Tourist Attractions* www.thinkchildsafe.org/thinkbeforevisiting/ (17/05/2015)

Nick Jones (2001) *The Rough Guide to Travel Health* Rough Guides, London

Florentine Kay (2008) *My Chinese Babies* Self-published

Florence Koenderink (2013) *Children Everywhere. How to Provide Good Institutional Care to Babies and Toddlers. Book 1: Essential Elements of Childcare in Institutions* Orphanage Projects, Scotland

Florence Koenderink (2015) *Orphanages for Money* http://www.orphanageprojects.org/orphanages-for-money/ (26/07/2015)

John Okell (2002) *Burmese by Ear or Essential Myanmar* Sussex Publications Limited, London www.soas.ac.uk/bbe/ (24/05/2015)

Bjarte Sanne (2008) *Understanding the Child. A mental needs manual for caretakers in children's homes 2nd Edition* http://www.myanmarorphanages.com/wp-content/uploads/2012/11/Understanding-the-child-English-2nd-edition.pdf (26/07/2015)

Stig Skaran, Lill Skaran (2013) Website: *Myanmar Orphanages. Information about faith-based 'orphanages' in Myanmar* http://www.myanmarorphanages.com/ (26/07/2015)

Unknown (2013) *Travel Vaccinations* NHS www.nhs.uk/conditions/Travel-immunisation/Pages/Introduction.aspx (24/05/2015)

Unknown Website: *Families Together. Helping children stay with their families.* http://www.famtogether.org/ (26/07/2015)

David Werner (1987) *Disabled Village Children.* http://www.dinf.ne.jp/doc/english/global/david/dwe002/dwe00201.html (20/12/2013)

Part 2

Kamalendu Chakrabarti (2005) *Pediatric Neurology* Jaypee Brothers Medical Publishers (P) Ltd, New Delhi

Magda Conway (2005) *HIV in Schools. Good practice guide to supporting children infected or affected by HIV.* National Children's Bureau, London http://www.ncb.org.uk/dotpdf/open%20access%20-%20phase%201%20only/hivforum_schoolsgpg.pdf (21/05/2011)

Alison Dunn (2005) *HIV/AIDS: What about very young children?* Working Paper 35 Bernard van Leer Foundation, The Hague, the Netherlands

Ruby Fayorsay, Elaine J. Abrams (2006 Draft) *Pediatric HIV/AIDS Care & Treatment* ICAP, WHO Columbia University Mailman School of Public Health, New York

Elizabeth Fischer (1999) *Psychological Issues in Pediatric HIV/AIDS Patients* Jacksonville Medicine, December 1999 http://www.dcmsonline.org/jax-medicine/1999journals/december99/psychological.htm (22/01/2011)

Susan Fox (2001) *Investing in Our Future. Psychosocial Support for Children Affected by HIV/AIDS.* UNAIDS Best Practice Collection. http://data.unaids.org/publications/IRC-pub02/JC606-InvFuture_en.pdf (21/05/2011)

International HIV/AIDS Alliance (2003) *Social Inclusion* Building Blocks: Africa-wide briefing notes, Brighton http://www.womenchildrenhiv.org/pdf/p09-of/of-05-05.pdf (22/05/2011)

International HIV/AIDS Alliance (2003) *Psychosocial Support* Building Blocks: Africa-wide briefing notes, Brighton http://www.womenchildrenhiv.org/pdf/p09-of/of-05-04.pdf (22/05/2011)

International Statistical Classification of Diseases and Health Related Problems. 10th Revision, version for 2007. By World Health Organisation. http://apps.who.int/classifications/apps/icd/icd10online/ (05/01/2014)

Florence Koenderink (2015) *Sick Children Everywhere. How to Provide Good Institutional Care. Book 2: Basic Medical Care for Children in Institutions* Orphanage Projects, Scotland

Kenneth W Lindsay, Ian Bone, Geraint Fuller (2010) *Neurology and Neurosurgery Illustrated (Fifth Edition)* Churchill Livingstone Elsevier, China

Tom Lissauer, Graham Clayden (2007) *Illustrated Textbook of Paediatrics* Mosby Elsevier, Spain

MMWR Morbidity and Mortality Weekly Report. Guidelines for the Prevention and Treatment of Opportunistic Infections Among HIV-Exposed and HIV-Infected Children. September 4, 2009/vol. 58/

no. RR-11. www.cdc.gov/mmwr (20/05/2011)

Save The Children UK (2003) *Care for Children Infected and Those Affected By HIV/AIDS. A handbook for community health workers.* Kampala, Uganda

Patricia O Shafer, Joseph I Sirven (2013) *Facts About Seizures and Epilepsy* Epilepsy Foundation and Epilepsy Therapy Project http://www.epilepsy.com/learn/epilepsy-101/facts-about-seizures-and-epilepsy

E. Richard Stiehm, Hans D Ochs, Jerry A Winkelstein (Ed.)(2004) *Immunologic Disorders in Babies and Children* Elsevier Health Sciences London

David Werner (1987) *Disabled Village Children.* http://www.dinf.ne.jp/doc/english/global/david/dwe002/dwe00201.html (20/12/2013)

WHO (2003) *Nutrient requirements for people living with HIV/AIDS. Report of a technical consultation.* Geneva, Switzerland

Part 3

Kevin Browne (2009) *The Risk of Harm to Young Children in Institutional Care.* The Save The Children Fund, London

Kendra Cherry *The Science of Love: Harry Harlow & The Nature of Affection* http://psychology.about.com/od/historyofpsychology/p/harlow_love.htm (26/05/2012)

Jason W. Custer MD, Rachel E. Rau MD (editors) *The Harriet Lane Handbook. A Manual for Pediatric House Officers* 2009 Elsevier Mosby, Philadelphia

KE Elizabeth (2010) *Nutrition and Child Development* Paras Medical Publisher, Hydrabad, India

Ruby Fayorsay, Elaine J. Abrams (2006 Draft) *Pediatric HIV/AIDS Care & Treatment* ICAP, WHO Columbia University Mailman School of Public Health, New York

Dr Ronald S. Federici *Help for the Hopeless Child: A Guide for Families* http://www.drfederici.com/ins_autism.htm (25/05/2011)

Arlene F. Harder (2002, revised 2009) *The Developmental Stages of Erik Erikson.* http://www.learningplaceonline.com/stages/organize/Erikson.htm (31/05/2011)

The Institute for Human Services for The Ohio Child Welfare Training Program (2007) *Developmental Milestones Chart* http://uppua.org/pdfs/CW%20II%20Handouts/Effects%20of%20Abuse%20and%20Neglect%20on%20Child%20Development/Development_Chart_for_Booklet.pdf (31/05/2011)

Marinus H. van IJzendoorn, Marian J. Bakermans-Kranenburg (2003) Attachment Disorders and Disorganised Attachment Similar and Different. *Attachment and Human Development Vol 5 No 3 (September 2003)* http://www.kidscomefirst.info/SimilarDifferent-Ijzendoorn-Kranenburg.pdf (30/10/2012)

Florence Koenderink (2013) *Children Everywhere. How to Provide Good Institutional Care to Babies and Toddlers. Book 1: Essential Elements of Childcare in Institutions* Orphanage Projects, Scotland

Florence Koenderink (2015) *Sick Children Everywhere. How to Provide Good Institutional Care. Book 2: Basic Medical Care for Children in Institutions* Orphanage Projects, Scotland

Terry M. Levy, Michael Orlans (2000), *Attachment Disorders as an Antecedent to Violence and Antisocial Patterns in Children.* http://www.hhs.csus.edu/sw/document/syllabus/fall%202008/sw224reader_gagerman.pdf (30/10/2012)

Kenneth W Lindsay, Ian Bone, Geraint Fuller (2010) *Neurology and Neurosurgery Illustrated (Fifth Edition)* Churchill Livingstone Elsevier, China

Tom Lissauer, Graham Clayden (2007) *Illustrated Textbook of Paediatrics* Mosby Elsevier, Spain

Jim Mann, A. Stewart Truswell (ed.) (2007) *Essentials of Human Nutrition.* Oxford University Press

Saul McLeod (2009) Attachment Theory. *Simply Psychology.* http://www.simplypsychology.org/attachment (07/11/2012)

Hisham M. Mehanna, Jamil Moledina, Jane Travis (2008) *Refeeding Syndrome: what it is and how to prevent and treat it* http://www.ncbi.nlm.nih.gov/pmc/articles/PMC2440847/ (29/08/2015)

NICE Guidelines (2009) *CG84 Diarrhoea and Vomiting in Children: Diarrhoea and Vomiting Caused by Gastroenteritis: Diagnosis, Assessment and Management in Children Younger than 5 Years* National Institute for Health and Care Excellence https://www.nice.org.uk/guidance/cg84/chapter/1-guidance (27/10/2014)

Maia Szalavitz, How Orphanages Kill Babies -- And Why No Child Under 5 Should Be In One. *Huffington Post, 23 April 2010.* http://www.huffingtonpost.com/maia-szalavitz/how-orphanages-kill-babie_b_549608.html (25/05/2011)

Unknown *Early Brain Development, What we know about brain development.* University of North Florida. http://www.unf.edu/dept/fie/PDF%20Folder/early.pdf (25/05/2011)

Unknown http://uppua.org/pdfs/CW%20II%20Handouts/Effects%20of%20Abuse%20and%20Neglect%20on%20Child%20Development/Development_Chart_for_Booklet.pdf Developed by: Institute of Human Services for the Ohio Welfare Training Program. 2007

Unknown http://w3.cns.org/university/pediatrics/Ch3Table2.pdf Congress of Neurological Surgeons University of Neurosurgery. 2009

David Werner (2010) *Where There Is No Doctor. A Village Health Care Handbook for Africa,* The Hesperian Foundation, Malaysia

WHO (2005) *Pocket Book of Hospital Care for Children. Guidelines for the Management of Common Illnesses with Limited Resources,* India

Janice Wood, Alberto August (2010) *Research Base 2009-10* Florida Institute of Education at the University of North Florida

Index

brain development 36, 185
child's dignity 76, 78, 117
commitment 31, 103, 104, 105, 131
danger 12, 25, 54, 106, 55, 125, 30, 133, 134, 135, 151, 152, 169, 170, 159, 172, 173, 143, 167, 152, 153, 173, 204, 170, 205, 206, 173, 208, 180, 211, 214, 215, 216, 204, 205, 217, 219, 221, 224, 231
   accident 49, 166
   burn 86, 134, 135, 172, 150, 173
   injury 152, 173, 211
discipline 179, 215, 216, 218
   correcting bad behaviour 186, 193, 218
   natural consequences 127
   physical punishment 206, 218, 219
   punishment 193, 217, 219
   time-out 111, 217, 218
harm children , 16, 21, 94, 36, 104, 102, 159, 106, 159, 176, 210, 210
health 29, 30, 36, 87, 108, 116, 158, 125, 145, 147, 149, 160, 161, 163, 164, 190, 193, 180, 187, 196
   bacteria 108, 49, 144, 160, 160, 163, 164, 220, 180, 229, 167
   immune system 47, 75, 109, 144, 145, 145, 147, 160, 179, 180, 220, 180, 220, 221
   parasites 163, 167
   vaccination 42, 45, 46
   virus 108, 144, 145, 145, 160, 229, 146, 220
hygiene 120, 89, 158, 160, 163, 164, 166, 147, 150, 167, 168, 175, 200
   bath 161, 164, 165, 166, 223, 224, 233
   brushing teeth 166
   hand washing 160, 161
   lice 21, 23, 75, 166, 194
   nappy 61, 161, 162, 163, 164, 223, 232
illness 47, 47, 144, 48, 75, 144, 144, 161, 180, 222, 229
   dehydration 158, 236, 237, 238, 239, 109, 240, 241, 244, 245, 246

dengue fever 42, 48
diarrhoea 234, 235, 236, 237, 87, 88, 239, 109, 240, 241
fever 45, 46, 47, 37, 47, 48, 151, 151, 220, 158, 221, 222, 223, 161, 224, 225, 226, 227, 228, 229, 230, 231, 151, 230
HIV 137, 109, 89, 144, 145, 146, 147, 148, 149, 148, 180, 148
malaria 19, 20, 42, 47, 48, 225
malnutrition 158, 226, 89, 227, 23, 75, 248, 249, 250, 251, 252, 253, 254
seizure 149, 150, 151, 152, 153, 154, 224, 225, 228
vomiting 234, 235, 236, 239, 240, 241, 243, 245, 246, 247, 248
mental retardation 137, 138, 139, 143
overwhelming 10, 20, 21, 68, 70, 71, 75, 77, 80, 88, 89, 90
pitfalls 11, 94, 120
primary caregiver 177, 178, 183, 189
psychological needs
   attachment , 21, 175, 98, 182, 183, 183
   attention 21, 21, 108, 90, 75, 24, 108, 107, 110, 119, 131, 137, 175, 176, 177, 160, 179, 180, 181, 143, 182, 183, 184, 185, 186, 148, 190, 191, 192, 193, 194, 184, 188, 206, 207, 208, 209, 195, 197, 217, 210
   confidence 184, 185, 186, 189, 194
   limits 20, 43, 55, 64, 87, 159, 173, 203, 204, 205, 206, 210, 213, 215
   physical contact 21, 55, 57, 68, 75, 142, 108, 175, 176, 160, 179, 180, 181, 184, 185, 186, 187, 189, 190, 194, 182, 198, 187, 198, 204, 198
   praise 75, 186, 188, 192, 195, 207, 208
   relationship 27, 53, 56, 76, 87, 101, 130, 159, 177, 181, 183

safety 16, 88, 95, 109, 154, 158, 169, 170, 175, 182, 184, 188, 190, 194
security 180, 182, 192, 213
stimulation 175, 186, 187, 188, 189, 190, 191, 212
responsibility 38, 97, 106, 116, 125, 172, 201, 204
role model 38, 56, 66, 110, 117
short term volunteering 16, 17
supervision 21, 118, 140, 142, 143, 173, 183, 206, 210
visa 18, 26, 27, 28, 29, 31, 38, 45, 130

www.ingramcontent.com/pod-product-compliance
Lightning Source LLC
Chambersburg PA
CBHW080358170426
43193CB00016B/2757